TWO PUZZLING BAPTISMS

First Corinthians 10:1-5 and 15:29. Studies in Their Judaic Background

Roger David Aus

Studies in Judaism

Hamilton Books
Lanham • Boulder • New York • Toronto • Plymouth, UK

Hamilton Books
4501 Forbes Boulevard
Suite 200
Lanham, Maryland 20706
Hamilton Books Acquisitions Department (301) 459-3366

Unit A, Whitacre Mews, 26-34 Stannary Street,
London SE11 4AB, United Kingdom

Printed in the United States of America
British Library Cataloging in Publication Information Available

Library of Congress Control Number: 2017940774
ISBN: 978-0-7618-6939-9 (paperback : alk. paper)
eISBN: 978-0-7618-6940-5

Dedicated

to

Peter von der Osten-Sacken

Professor emeritus of New Testament and Christian-Jewish Studies
at Berlin's Humboldt University,
former head of its Institut Kirche und Judentum,
generous friend and fair critic,

Recipient in 2005 of the Buber-Rosenzweig Medal of the
German Societies for Christian-Jewish Cooperation,

and

Recipient of Berlin's 2016 Moses Mendelssohn Prize
for the Furtherance of Religious Tolerance.

and to the memory of

Jacob Neusner

(b. July 28, 1932, d. October 8, 2016)

Foremost scholar of early Judaism in North America,
prolific writer and translator,
ecumenical editor of this series, "Studies in Judaism,"
who generously welcomed contributions to it from a Christian pastor.

"The gifts and the calling of God are irrevocable"
(Romans 11:29)

TABLE OF CONTENTS

Preface vii
Introduction xi

I. 1 Corinthians 10:1-5 and Judaic Tradition on Ezekiel 16 1
   Introduction 1
   1. Passage Through the Re(e)d Sea 11
   2. The (Pillar of) Cloud 16
      Appendix I. The Messiah as the Cloud Man 22
      Appendix II. The Name of the Messiah as "Lord" 23
   3. Manna 23
   4. Water from the Rock, Which Was Christ 26
   5. Three Examples of the Use of Ezek 16:9 in Judaic Midrash 41
      5.1 The Angels' Rewarding Abraham for his Hospitality in Genesis 18 ... 41
      5.2 God's Unusual Behavior Towards the Israelites in the Wilderness 44
      5.3 The Unusual Birth of Israelites Just Before the Exodus, and Their Recognizing God After Their Rescue from the Red Sea 45
   6. Idolatry in 1 Corinthians 10, Egypt in the Wilderness, and Ezekiel 16 with its Targum 53
      6.1 Idolatry in 1 Corinthians 10 53
      6.2 Israelite Idolatry in Egypt and the Wilderness in Judaic Tradition 55
      6.3 Idolatry in Ezekiel 16 57
      6.4 Targum Ezekiel 16, Including Idol Worship 58
   7. Being Baptized into Moses in the Cloud and the Sea 62
   8. Christ Considered as Pre-existent 67
   9. The Form of 1 Cor 10:1-5 69

II. Paul's Toleration in Corinth of Baptism on Behalf of the Dead (1 Cor 15:29), and Intercession for the Dead in Early Judaism 74
   Introduction 74
   1. Tobit 4:17 80
      1.1 Deut 26:14 80
      1.2 Ahiqar 81
      1.3 Sirach 7:33 and 30:18 82
      1.4 Letter of Jeremiah 27 82
      1.5 Mourning Customs for Bridegrooms and Brides Who Died Before Marriage 83
   2. 2 Macc 12:38-45 85
   3. The Testament of Abraham 90
   4. Korah 94
      4.1 Sirach 45:18-19 94
      4.2 Philo 95

4.3 Pseudo-Philo ... 96
4.4 Josephus ... 98
4.5 Jude ... 99
4.6 Rabbinic Sources ... 100
5. Deut 21:8 in Judaic Tradition ... 105
6. David and His Son Absalom ... 107
7. R. Meir and Elisha b. Abuya (Aḥer) ... 109
8. The Intercession of Children for Their Dead Fathers ... 111
8.1 *Eccl. Rab.* 4:1 § 1 ... 112
8.2 *B. Qidd.* 31b ... 113
8.3 *Eliyyahu Zuṭa* 17 ... 114
9. The Circumcision of Deceased Infant Boys ... 116
10. Summary and Conclusion ... 120

Sources and Reference Works ... 125
Author Index ... 133
Index of Sources Cited ... 136
About the Author ... 154

PREFACE

My gratitude is due to the following for critically reading one or both chapters in this volume: Hans-Jűrgen Becker, professor of New Testament and early Judaism at the University of Göttingen; Andreas Lindemann, professor emeritus of New Testament at the Kirchliche Hochschule of Wuppertal / Bethel; Dr. Niko Oswald, now retired from the Free University of Berlin's Institut fűr Judaistik; and Peter von der Osten-Sacken, professor emeritus of New Testament and former director of the Institut Kirche und Judentum at Berlin's Humboldt University. The contents of the first chapter were given in an abbreviated form as a lecture at the August 2016 meeting of the Society of New Testament Studies in Montreal, Canada. I am appreciative of the comments given on that occasion and afterwards. Charles Eypper of Berlin kindly proofread one essay, and the Rev. Dr. Thomas Day of Berlin also did so for both chapters, in addition making several helpful suggestions in regard to style and content. My son, Dr. Jonathan Aus, again generously took the time to format the text. The staff at the Theological Library of the Humboldt University has, as always, been very helpful.

I have attempted to interact with the most important commentaries and special studies related to First Corinthians 10:1-5 and 15:29 as they have been available to me in Berlin, without overburdening the footnotes. My emphasis, however, has been on letting the primary sources speak for themselves, therefore I quote them extensively. This is especially true for the rabbinic sources, to which many New Testament scholars intentionally or non-intentionally have little or no access in spite of the numerous translations into English by Jacob Neusner, his students, and others (see the *Introduction*).

While I usually employ the standard English translations, it is often the case that I modify them or make my own in order to better express the meaning of a particular passage. Thus "Soncino 6.147," for example, signifies that the passage cited is in fact found in the English edition of *Midrash Rabbah* at this point, but the rendering may be modified or completely my own. When Soncino English translations are quoted verbatim, I do not change the spelling of rabbinic names there. Otherwise I usually follow the form employed in Hermann Strack and Gűnter Stemberger's *Introduction to the Talmud and Midrash*. For those with no or only a minimal knowledge of Hebrew and Aramaic, I have included not only the original, but also an English transliteration, at times in simplified form, for example without expressing the dagesh. The letter ת is represented by *t*, ט by *ṭ*, ס by *s*, שׂ by *ś*, and שׁ by *sh*.

The section "Sources and Reference Works" at the end of the volume will aid the reader in ascertaining which edition of Judaic and other sources I have employed. This is especially helpful in regard to sources not usually found in a standard library. It also enables the reader to easily locate a particular passage in the original or in translation, and to form his or her own opinion regarding it. An index of the numerous sources quoted indicates the materials from which I have drawn, and the index of modern authors shows how I differ in part from the opinions of earlier and contemporary scholars. That's what makes research both interesting and worthwhile.

I would like to thank Professor Alan Avery-Peck for accepting this volume, my eighth, in the series "Studies in Judaism." It is a tribute to his ecumenical openness that he continues to welcome studies dealing with the earliest Jewish Christians from a Protestant pastor.

For those not steeped in rabbinic sources, the following list explaining many of the abbreviations and names employed in this volume should be helpful.

m.	Mishnah
t.	Tosefta
b.	Babylonian Talmud
y.	Yerushalmi or Jerusalem Talmud
bar.	Baraitha, a Tannaitic tradition not found in the Mishnah
ʾAvot R. Nat.	ʾAvot de Rabbi Nathan (versions A and B)
Mek. R. Ish.	Mekilta de Rabbi Ishmael, on Exodus
Mek. R. Shim. b. Yoḥ.	Mekilta de Rabbi Shimʿon b. Yoḥai, also on Exodus
Midr.	Midrash
Pesiq. R.	Pesiqta Rabbati
Pesiq. Rav Kah.	Pesiqta de Rav Kahana
Pirq. R. El.	Pirqe de Rabbi Eliezer
Rab.	*Rabbah*, the "large" rabbinic commentaries, e.g. *Gen. Rab.*
Sifre	Halakhic commentaries on Numbers and Deuteronomy
Tanḥ.	Tanḥuma

Tanḥ. B	Tanḥuma, ed. Buber
Tanna	An authority ranging from Hillel and Shammai to the early third century CE, the time of Judah the Prince
Amora	An authority ranging from after the Tannaim to ca. 500 CE[1]

Roger David Aus
December 2016
Berlin, Germany

[1] For the above, cf. also my volume *Essays in the Judaic Background of Mark 11:12-14, 20-21; 15:23; Luke 1:37; John 19:28-30; and Acts 11:28* (Studies in Judaism; Lanham, MD: University Press of America, 2015) xi-xiii.

INTRODUCTION

Mark 1:9 states that Jesus himself was baptized by John ("the Baptist") in the Jordan River. The earliest Christians basically took over this rite, which was a "baptism of repentance for the forgiveness of sins" (v. 4). They modified it in part by performing it "in the name of Christ,"[1] later to include the Father and the Holy Spirit (Matt 28:19). The Apostle Paul employs the noun "baptism" (βάπτισμα) only once (Rom 6:4),[2] and the verb "to baptize" (βαπτίζω) only once each time in Romans (6:3) and Galatians (3:27). Yet in First Corinthians he uses it ten times (1:13, 14, 15, 16 [2x], 17; 10:2; 12:13; and 15:29 [2x]). This shows how important this issue had become for the Corinthian Christians. Some maintained that through baptism "in the name of..." they belonged either to Paul, Apollos or Cephas (Peter - 1:12). The Apostle scolds them for such factional behavior, in part by noting that he himself had only baptized Crispus and Gaius, as well as the household of Stephanas (vv. 14 and 16). He admits to a memory lapse in regard to others (v. 16). He then buttresses his behavior by maintaining that "Christ did not send me to baptize but to proclaim the gospel" (v. 17).

---

[1] Cf. "in the name of Jesus Christ" in Acts 2:38 and 10:48, and "in the name of the Lord Jesus" in 8:16 and 19:5. In Gal 3:27 Paul abbreviates this to "into Christ," and in Rom 6:3 to "into Christ Jesus." Yet he was definitely aware of the fuller form, as shown in 1 Cor 1:13 and 15 - "in the name of." For a good general overview of baptism, see the art. "Taufe" in RGG[4] (2005) 8.50-92; the section on the New Testament is by Friedrich Avemarie (52-59). See also "Taufe" in *TRE* (2001) 32.659-741, with the section on Paul on pp. 666-70. Secondary literature on this topic is immense. Several significant recent studies are the following: Lars Hartman, "*Into the Lord Jesus.*" Baptism in the Early Church (Edinburgh: T & T Clark, 1997); Stanley Porter and Anthony Cross, eds., *Dimensions of Baptism.* Biblical and Theological Studies (JSNTSupp.Ser. 234; London: Sheffield Academic Press, 2002); Gerhard Barth, *Die Taufe in frűhchristlicher Zeit* (Neukirchen-Vluyn: Neukirchener, 2002[2]); Andreas Reichert, *Das Verständnis der Taufe im 1. Korintherbrief.* Eine exegetische, auslegungs- und wirkungsgeschichtliche Untersuchung (Aachen: Verlag Mainz, 2003); Everett Ferguson, *Baptism in the Early Church.* History, Theology, and Liturgy in the First Five Centuries (Grand Rapids, MI: Eerdmans, 2009); David Hellholm et al., eds., *Ablution, Initiation, and Baptism.* Late Antiquity, Early Judaism, and Early Christianity (BZNW 176, I-III; Berlin: de Gruyter, 2011); and Markus Őhler, ed., *Taufe* (Tűbingen: Mohr Siebeck, 2012).

[2] Cf. Eph 4:5 and Col 2:12 from the Pauline School. His own baptism by Ananias in Damascus is related in Acts 9:18 and 22:16.

Two of the ten occurrences of "to baptize" in First Corinthians have puzzled theologians and lay people for centuries. In 10:2 Paul boldly asserts that all the ancestors of the Jews and now also of the Christians "were baptized into Moses in the cloud and in the [Re(e)d] Sea." And in 15:29 he notes that some members of the Christian congregation in Corinth have themselves baptized (again) on behalf of the dead. How could he make such statements?

The above two enigmatic occurrences of "to baptize" in First Corinthians are analyzed respectively in Chapters One and Two of the following short volume. Both are elucidated primarily in light of early Jewish (Judaic) sources. While knowledge of Greco-Roman sources and rites often helps to understand Paul's letters better, in these two specific cases Paul's Jewish heritage proves to be most significant in appreciating their original meaning. For these reasons the two exegetical studies are well-suited to the series "Studies in Judaism."

While I consistently attempt to employ the earliest sources possible, reference is at times also made to rabbinic works, including the targums. Their final date of closure is often quite late. Unfortunately there is a widespread mindset, especially in North America, that the dating of such materials, including the attribution of a saying to a particular rabbi,[3] is so difficult that these cannot be seriously considered in dealing with NT texts. This is a cheap way to completely avoid consulting rabbinic sources. The problem of dating specific rabbinic materials will always remain. Yet early Palestinian expressions, motifs and topics / themes have at times survived not only in the earliest rabbinic works, those of the Tannaim, but also anonymously and in a modified form in later, Amoraic sources. Each case must be analyzed individually. Many specialists in the NT, if they cite rabbinic sources at all, rely exclusively on secondary works such as Paul Billerbeck's commentary (Str-B),[4] which

---

[3] On the issue of sayings attributed to specific authorities, cf. the discussion by Martin Jaffee, "Rabbinic Authorship as a Collective Enterprise," in *The Cambridge Companion to the Talmud and Rabbinic Literature,* ed. by him and Charlotte Fonrobert (Cambridge: Cambridge University Press, 2007) 17-37. See also the relevant essays in *The New Testament and Rabbinic Literature,* ed. Reimund Bieringer et al. (Suppl. JSJS 136; Leiden: Brill, 2010).

[4] As a Lutheran pastor myself, I may point to the pious Lutheran pastor Billerbeck's slightly anti-Jewish bent in regard to what he (and other Lutherans of the Law-Gospel dichotomy) falsely perceived as "Jewish works-righteousness." His collection of background materials can nevertheless still be helpful if used judiciously.

includes many Amoraic traditions. Yet they gladly cite the Church Fathers up to the fifth century CE who, with very few exceptions such as Origen, Jerome, and the Syrians Aphrahat and Ephraim, knew no Hebrew and had no access to rabbinic traditions. Strangely, they characterize the Amoraim from the same era as too late to be of relevance to the NT, even though these rabbis in part still stood in a tradition of biblical interpretation which was similar to that of the first Palestinian Jewish Christians. For these reasons I consider it legitimate also to cite rabbinic materials when they appear to be relevant, employing them judiciously, always aware of the major problem of dating them. A good example is the relevance of *Targum* Ezekiel 16 to 1 Cor 10:1-5, pointed out in Chapter I.

Other contemporary scholars also stress the relevance of rabbinic materials to NT research. Philip Alexander correctly issued a list of seven caveats the NT scholar of today should observe in dealing with rabbinic texts, yet he could also note: "only good can come from New Testament students studying Rabbinic literature...."[5] He also states that "Rabbinic models may be particularly relevant to elucidating how the early Christian groups elaborated and passed on their traditions."[6] Geza Vermes also maintains that "rabbinic literature, judiciously and sensitively handled, can throw valuable and sometimes unique light on the study of the Gospels."[7] He would certainly also have included other parts of the NT in his remark. In his essay "Rabbinic Literature in New Testament Interpretation," William Horbury quotes Vermes in this regard, adding a similar statement by David Flusser. He also notes that while the relevance to the NT of the Dead Sea Scrolls and Jewish sources in Greek is generally acknowledged today, one should also consider "not only the presence of early material in rabbinic sources, but also their extent and richness, and the light which they shed on Jewish texts of the Herodian and even the Hasmonean age - and the benefit of combining

---

[5] Cf. his "Rabbinic Judaism and the New Testament" in *ZNW* 74 (1983) 237-46, quotation p. 238.

[6] Cf. his "Orality in Pharisaic-Rabbinic Judaism at the Turn of the Eras" in *Jesus and the Oral Tradition*, ed. Henry Wansbrough (London and New York: T & T Clark International, 2004; original 1991) 159-84, quotation p. 184.

[7] Cf. his *The Religion of Jesus the Jew* (London: SCM Press, 1993) 7. On p. 8 he chides some Qumran enthusiasts for ignoring the rabbinic texts.

this with light from other sources."[8] Finally, Gudrun Holtz has recently cited a number of good reasons, including the model of "cultural codes," for students of the NT to take rabbinic sources much more seriously than they have in the past.[9]

The reader is invited to engage with all the sources, not only the rabbinic ones, employed in my argumentation in the following two chapters. Only by doing so can scholarly discourse proceed. And that should be welcomed, especially in regard to two passages in First Corinthians which have remained enigmatic for centuries.

---

[8] Cf. his *Herodian Judaism and New Testament Study* (WUNT 193; Tübingen: Mohr Siebeck, 2006) 221-35, quotations pp. 226 and 228. On pp. 224-25, agreeing with Vermes in this regard, he points out how rabbinic sources which Joseph Fitzmyer does not (want to) cite could strengthen specific arguments at Qumran. Horbury correctly emphasizes the continuity in Judaic sources in spite of the events of 70 (and I would add 132-35) CE (see p. 234).

[9] Cf. her "Rabbinische Literatur und Neues Testament. Alte Schwierigkeiten und neue Möglichkeiten" in *ZNW* 100 (2009)173-98. I had already noted some of the above statements in my *Essays in the Judaic Background of Mark 11:12-14, 20-21; 15:23; Luke 1:37; John 19:28-30; and Acts 11:28* (Studies in Judaism; Lanham, MD: University Press of America, 2015) xvi-xviii.

I. 1 CORINTHIANS 10:1-5 AND JUDAIC TRADITION ON EZEKIEL 16

Introduction

Verses 1-5 of 1 Corinthians 10 are a passage "fraught with several enormous difficulties," ostensibly showing "the oddity of Paul's ideas here."[1] How can Paul maintain in vv. 1-4 that "our ancestors" (lit., "fathers"), that is, also those of the Corinthian Christians, were all under the cloud, all passed through the Sea (v. 1), all were baptized into Moses in the cloud and in the Sea (v. 2), all ate the same spiritual food (v. 3), and all drank the same spiritual drink, for they drank from the spiritual rock that followed them, and the rock was Christ (v. 4)? This positive listing of God's very beneficent dealings with the Israelites at the exodus[2] and in the wilderness wanderings of forty years is then abruptly negated in the last verse of the unit, 5: "Nevertheless, God was not pleased with most of

---

[1] Cf. Alexander Wedderburn, *Baptism and Resurrection*. Studies in Pauline Theology against Its Greco-Roman Background (WUNT 44; Tűbingen: Mohr Siebeck, 1987) 241 and 244.

[2] Sylvia Keesmat maintains that Paul's "reference to the exodus narrative in 1 Cor. 10.1-13 is most evident," yet she only devotes a paragraph to vv. 1-5. Cf. her *Paul and His Story: (Re)Interpreting the Exodus Tradition* (JSNTSup 181; Sheffield: Sheffield Academic Press, 1999) 47 and 220. Interestingly, Paul omits an allusion to the gift of quail.

them, and they were struck down in the wilderness" (NRSV).[3] The chapter goes on to deal with idolatry, especially as related to the Lord's Supper.

Verse 4 with a rock accompanying the Israelites has been considered especially difficult. Already in 1888 Frédéric Godet spoke of it as a Jewish legend which was "a ridiculous fable."[4] This evaluation was basically shared by many others up until recent years.[5] Richard Hays, for example, in 1989 still spoke of Paul's "fanciful analogies" in vv. 1-4.[6]

In the following study, primarily of vv. 1-4, I cite not only relevant passages within the Bible, primarily the MT, but also *Pseudo-Philo*, Philo, Josephus, and rabbinic sources, if at all possible from the Tannaitic

---

[3] Bibliography on one or more of these verses is found in Matthew Thiessen, "'The Rock Was Christ': The Fluidity of Christ's Body in 1 Corinthians 10.4." in *JSNT* 36 (2013) 122-26; Dieter Zeller, *Der erste Brief an die Korinther* (Meyers; Göttingen: Vandenhoeck & Ruprecht, 2010) 325; Andreas Lindemann, *Der erste Korintherbrief* (HNT 9/1; Tübingen: Mohr Siebeck, 2000) 217; Helmut Merklein, *Der erste Brief an die Korinther, Kap. 5,1 - 11,1* (ÖTK 7,2; Gütersloh: Mohn; Würzburg: Echter-Verlag, 2000) 237-38; Anthony Thiselton, *The First Epistle to the Corinthians* (NIGTC; Grand Rapids, MI: Eerdmans, 2000) 720-21; and Wolfgang Schrage, *Der erste Brief an die Korinther. 2. Teilband. 1 Kor 6,12 - 11,16* (EKK; Zurich: Benziger, 1995) 380-81. A review of some twenty commentaries and the last thirty years of *New Testament Abstracts* regarding articles dealing with the pericope yields no interpretation similar to the major proposals I make here.

[4] Cf. his *Kommentar zu dem ersten Briefe an die Korinther* (Hannover: Meyer, 1888) 43. He calls it a "childish conceit."

[5] Cf. Philipp Bachmann, *Der erste Brief des Paulus an die Korinther* (Leipzig: Deichert, 1936[4]) 330: the Jewish saga is a "fable"; E. Earle Ellis, *Paul's Use of the Old Testament* (Grand Rapids, MI: Baker Book House, 1957 / 1981) 68: "the fable"; F. F. Bruce, *1 and 2 Corinthians* (NCB; London: Oliphants, 1971 / 1978) 91: "this material fancy"; and Peter Enns, "The 'Moveable Well' in 1 Cor 10:4 : An Extrabiblical Tradition in an Apostolic Text," in the *Bulletin for Biblical Research* 6 (1996) 28: "such an apparently fanciful and biblically unsupported notion."

[6] Cf. his *Echoes of Scripture in the Letters of Paul* (New Haven: Yale University Press, 1989) 91, Hays also speaks of "Paul's fanciful reading of Christ back into the exodus" (97). I appropriate his definition of an allusion and an echo: "allusion is used of obvious intertextual references, echo of subtler ones" (29). He maintains that except for the quotation of Exod 32:6 in 1 Cor 10:7, "the other wilderness episodes are evoked by Paul's summarizing allusions," which are "subtle gestures" (92).

or oldest period available to us.[7] In 1926 Paul Billerbeck had noted a number of the latter passages as relevant to 1 Cor 10:1-5.[8] Again and again, with few exceptions, the commentators and others only cite him without themselves dealing with the original sources.[9] For this reason I present a large number of them here, often with my own translation, and the reader can easily consult the original and / or an English translation, both of which I cite in the notes.

Before sketching the Israelites' wandering in the wilderness (1 Cor 10:5) as a wasteland, with hunger, thirst, snakes and scorpions, and scorching heat, several preliminary remarks concerning the structure and content of vv. 1-4 are appropriate, especially in regard to the repeated term "all."

All Our Fathers

1 Cor 10:1-4 is in Greek all one sentence, connected by the repeated καί, "and." In addition, πάντες, "all," is emphasized by its fivefold repetition.[10] Paul stresses that "all our ancestors (lit., fathers)" were present at the events described in vv. 1-4. In other words, he maintains that the Israelites, Hebrews, were also the "fathers / forefathers" not only

---

7 I believe that the attribution of a particular saying to a named rabbi during this period is often trustworthy. During the Amoraic era the task becomes more difficult. On the issue of sayings attributed to specific authorities, cf. again the discussion by Martin Jaffee, "Rabbinic Authorship as a Collective Enterprise" 17-37 and the relevant essays in *The New Testament and Rabbinic Literature*, ed. Reimund Bieringer et al. (see xii, n. 3).

8 Cf. Str-B 3.405-09. See already Louis Ginzberg, *The Legends of the Jews* 3.18-54, with the relevant notes.

9 Cf. for example Oskar Cullmann, art. πέτρα in *TDNT* 6.97; Merklein, *Der erste Brief an die Korinther* 246; Thiselton, *The First Epistle to the Corinthians* 727 (he is also very wary of employing rabbinic tradition at all, whose "issues of dating remain obscure and complex" - 728); Hans Conzelmann, *Der erste Brief an die Korinther* (Meyers; Göttingen: Vandenhoeck & Ruprecht, 1981²) 202, 204; and Christian Wolff, *Der erste Brief des Paulus an die Korinther*, Zweiter Teil, 7/II (THNT; Berlin: Evangelische Verlagsanstalt, 1982²) 40, 42. The very few writers who themselves deal with these sources, such as Bienaimé, will be cited at the appropriate places below.

10 Peter von der Osten-Sacken aptly characterizes this as "Das geradezu hämmernde *pantes*...." Cf. "'Geschrieben zu unserer Ermahnung...' Die Tora in 1 Korinther 10, 1-13," in his *Die Heiligkeit der Tora*. Studien zum Gesetz bei Paulus (Munich: Kaiser, 1989) 68.

of the Jewish-Christian members of the Corinthian congregation,[11] but also of the Gentile members, usually considered to form the much larger majority. This is only possible because Paul thought of the Christian church as the Israel of God (Gal 6:16; see Phil 3:3) with a new covenant (1 Cor 11:25; 2 Cor 3:6, with the "old" covenant in v. 14). Although he himself was an Israelite, a descendant of Abraham (Rom 11:1), Paul adamantly argues that now all those Gentiles who believe in Christ Jesus are also "the descendants of Abraham," based on the Scripture, "All the Gentiles shall be blessed in you" (Gal 3:7-8, with Gen 12:3 / 18:18 / 22:18). All who belong to Christ, whether Jew or Greek, are "Abraham's offspring, heirs according to the promise" (Gal 3:28-29; cf. Rom 4:16-17, with Gen 17:5).

Paul's message of non-Jews now having the possibility of becoming the children of Abraham, who was considered to be one of the three "fathers" (with Isaac and Jacob) of Israel in a narrower sense, was very appealing to Gentiles. This included God-fearers such as Titius Justus in Corinth (Acts 18:7), but also would-be proselytes, who were first required to be circumcised, immerse (and bring an offering, if possible in the Jerusalem Temple).[12] Paul vehemently rejected the necessity of circumcision for such non-Jews, for example in Gal 5:2-6.

I suggest that Paul derived the term "our fathers" (οἱ πατέρες ἡμῶν) in regard to the exodus event in 1 Cor 10:1 from early Judaic tradition on the celebration of Passover, commemorating the exodus from slavery in Egypt. Shortly before this he had stated in 5:7, "our paschal lamb, Christ, has been sacrificed."

In *m. Pesaḥ.* 10:5, Rabban Gamaliel states that a Jew must (during the celebration of the Passover / Seder meal) refer to three matters:

---

[11] Cf. 1 Cor 7:18; perhaps 9:20; 10:32-33; and 12:13; the Jew Aquila and his wife Priscilla in Acts 18:2; and Crispus, the president of the synagogue, with his entire household (v. 8; see 1 Cor 1:14, where in addition to Crispus, Gaius [also Rom 16:23] could also be a Jew, as well as Stephanas with his household - v. 16). If Paul stayed eighteen months in Corinth (Acts 18:11) with the God-fearer Titius Justus, who lived next to the synagogue (v. 7), he probably also converted this adherent of Judaism. In addition, if the president of the Corinthian synagogue was converted to the Christian faith with his entire household, it seems possible if not probable that other members of the congregation who supported him would have followed his example.

[12] Cf. the sources cited in the art. "Proselytes" in *EJ* (2007) 16.587-90.

> 1) *Passover* - because the Omnipresent passed over the houses of our forefathers [אֲבוֹתֵינוּ - *'abhōtēnu*] in Egypt.
> 2) *Unleavened bread* - because our forefathers [אֲבוֹתֵינוּ - *'abhōtēnu*] were redeemed in Egypt.
> 3) *Bitter herbs* - because the Egyptians embittered the lives of our forefathers [אֲבוֹתֵינוּ - *'abhōtēnu*] in Egypt.

The passage continues with a fourth mention of "our forefathers":

> In every generation a person is duty-bound to regard himself as if he personally had gone forth from Egypt, since it is said, "And you shall tell your son in that day saying, 'It is because of that which the Lord did for me when I came forth from Egypt'" (Exod 13:8). Therefore we are duty-bound to thank, praise, glorify, honor, exalt, extol and bless Him who did for our forefathers [אֲבוֹתֵינוּ - *'abhōtēnu*] and for us these miracles. He brought us forth from slavery to freedom, anguish to joy, mourning to festival, darkness to great light, subjugation to redemption, so we should say before Him, Hallelujah.

The Mishnah then asks in 10:6, "To what point does one say [the Hallel, psalms 113-118, at this section of the celebration]?" The House of Hillel says, "To ['Who turns the rock (צוּר [*ṣur*]) into a pool of water,] the flint into a spring of water" (Ps 114:8, the last verse of the psalm). This is concluded with (a formula of) Redemption. R. Tarfon, a Pharisee from a priestly family and a second generation Tanna,[13] then quotes it: "Who redeemed us and redeemed our forefathers [אֲבוֹתֵינוּ - *'abhōtēnu*] from Egypt."[14]

Rabban Gamaliel I, "the elder," was a first generation Tanna.[15] Acts 5:34 says he was a Pharisee in the Council / Sanhedrin, "a teacher of the law, respected by all the people," who then gave advice as to how to treat the apostles who had been arrested in Jerusalem (vv. 35-39). Acts 22:3 has Paul address a crowd there in "Hebrew" (i.e., Aramaic), when he was also arrested: "I am a Jew, born in Tarsus of Cilicia, but brought up in this city at the feet of Gamaliel, educated strictly according to our ancestral law, being zealous for God...." In Gal 1:14 Paul wrote: "I advanced in Judaism beyond many among my people of the same age, for I was far

---

[13] Cf. Strack and Stemberger, *Introduction to the Talmud and Midrash* 80, hereafter cited as *Introduction*.
[14] Cf. Albeck 2.178-79; Eng. Danby 150-51; Eng. Neusner, here, 250.
[15] Cf. *Introduction* 73.

more zealous for the traditions of my ancestors."[16] There is no reason to mistrust Luke's notice that Paul (as Saul) had earlier been a disciple of Rabban Gamaliel.[17]

This means that Paul probably learned from him the tradition of the necessity of mentioning three things (at the celebration of the Passover / Seder meal): Passover, unleavened bread, and bitter herbs. Each was interpreted by Rabban Gamaliel in relation to "our forefathers" (אֲבוֹתֵינוּ - *ʾabhōtēnu*). In addition, every Jew is obligated to regard himself as going forth from Egypt "because of that which the Lord did *for me* [לִי - *lî*] when *I* came out of Egypt" (Exod 13:8). Therefore all Jews are duty-bound to thank Him "who did for *our forefathers* and *for us* [לָנוּ - *lanu*] all these miracles." Finally, the benediction concluding the first part of the Hallel at this point includes "Who redeemed *us* and redeemed *our forefathers* from Egypt." This pictures all the Jews celebrating the annual Passover meal as imagining that they themselves were present hundreds of years ago at the time of the exodus. Paul says something very similar in 1 Cor 10:1-4 for those who now believe in Christ as their Lord:

---

[16] Cf. Phil 3:5-6, where he also states that he is a Pharisee. It should also be noted that Paul's nephew, his sister's son, was in Jerusalem and warned Paul of a plot against his life (Acts 23:16). Does this imply he or they also lived in Jerusalem? The church father Jerome noted in his work *De Viris Illustribus* 5 (ed. and trans. Claudia Barthold, 164-67), composed in Bethlehem in 392-93 CE, that Paul was from the tribe of Benjamin and the town of "Giscalis" in Judea. The latter is incorrect, for Giscala (Greek Γίσχαλα, Hebrew גּוּשׁ חָלָב - *gush ḥalabh*) was located in Galilee some 8 km or 5 mi northwest of Safed. It was the last town in Galilee to be taken in the Jewish - Roman War of 66-70 CE, a detail which may later have been added to the tradition regarding it as Paul's home town before his parents left with him for Tarsus in Cilicia. Yet this notice about the Romans more probably could instead refer to the Roman general Pompey's conquering Judea and Jerusalem in 63 BCE, at which time Paul's parents emigrated. On this garbled (Jewish-Christian?) tradition, see Barthold 275, and for the site the art. "Giscala..." by Michael Avi-Yonah and Shimon Gibson in *EJ* (2007) 7.617. Interestingly, they also note a local tradition that the graves of Shemaiah and Avtalyon, two important Sages from the pre-Tannaitic period, are found in rock tombs there.

[17] Cf. Str-B 2.763-64 on a disciple's sitting before his teacher, who also sat. Richard Bauckham makes a convincing case for Saul's having studied with Gamaliel I. See his art. "Gamaliel and Paul" in *Earliest Christianity within the Boundaries of Judaism. Essays in Honor of Bruce Chilton*, ed. Alan Avery-Peck, Craig Evans and Jacob Neusner (Leiden / Boston: Brill, 2016) 87-106.

they were all present then. This is his eschatological, typological interpretation of Scripture.

In *m. Pesaḥ.* 10:5-6 "our forefathers" (אֲבוֹתֵינוּ - *ʾabhōtēnu*) must first be mentioned three times, and then twice more. Each Jew should consider what the Lord did for *him*[18] when *he* came out of Egypt. This must have posed a major theological problem for Paul in his winning over God-fearers, proselytes and Gentiles to Christianity, for they were not allowed to say such sentences. The Mishnah at *Bikk.* 1:4 states, for example, that a proselyte is one who may bring first fruits (to the Jerusalem Temple), but may not recite "because he is not able to say, '[I have come into the land] which the Lord swore to *our fathers* [אֲבוֹתֵינוּ - *ʾabhōtēnu*] to give *us* [לָנוּ - *lanu*]' (Deut 26:3)." When he prays in private, he says, "God of the fathers of Israel." And when he prays in the synagogue, he says, "God of *your fathers*."[19]

Because Paul considered not only God-fearers and proselytes, but also Gentiles, to be descendants of Abraham[20] if they now believed in Christ, he strongly objected to the above practice. The imagery from the annual Passover celebration was no longer valid. For this reason he purposely stated in 1 Cor 10:1 in regard to the exodus event (which included the Passover of Exod 12:1-28, 43-50, followed by the exit in v. 51, and 13:2-10 with the important v. 8): "all *our* fathers." It was a slap in the face of any opponent who now maintained that God-fearers, proselytes and Gentiles

---

[18] For practical purposes I retain the original masculine form of the original, as elsewhere, well aware that the language is patriarchal and should be avoided in present-day translations, as in the NRSV.

[19] Cf. Albeck 1.312; Danby 94; Neusner 167, here. See also *Maʿaser Sheni* 5:13, where the proselyte cannot say Deut 26:15, "bless Your people Israel and the ground that You have given *us*, as You swore to *our fathers*" (Albeck 1.268; Danby 82; Neusner 147). In addition, a proselyte was excluded from participating in the "merit of the fathers" (זְכוּת אָבוֹת - *zekhut ʾabhōt*) in regard to the world to come. Instead, he had to rely exclusively on his own good deeds. See *Num. Rab.* Naso 8/9 on Num 5:10 (Mirkin 9.159; Soncino 5.232). This was another disadvantage to which Paul would have strongly objected.

[20] Interestingly, Judah (bar Ilai, a third generation Tanna active some one hundred years after Paul: *Introduction* 84,) in *y. Bikk.* 1:4, 64a (Eng. Neusner 10.139-40) in a baraitha (a Tannaitic tradition not found in the Mishnah) allows a proselyte to bring first fruits and to recite Deut 26:3. He too bases this on Abraham (Gen 17:5; cf. Rom 4:17). Two Amoraim agree with him. It must be emphasized, however, that this is after the destruction of the Temple and with possible knowledge of Paul's position.

who had come to believe in Christ were not now also the descendants of Abraham, true Israelites.[21]

The Wilderness

The positive examples of God's care of the Israelites which Paul cites in 1 Cor 10:1-4 took place "in the wilderness" (v. 5). The following five negative background materials from biblical and Judaic sources put the gracious, supportive, even miraculous deeds of God mentioned in vv. 1-4 into stark perspective.

1. *The Wilderness / Desert as "Wasteland"*

Deut 8:15 speaks of "the great and terrible wilderness, an arid wasteland." It is "a howling wilderness waste" (32:10).[22] Philo of Alexandria, roughly a contemporary of Jesus and the early Paul,[23] notes that it is "a long stretch of desert country" (*Mos.* 1.164), "a rough and pathless desert" (1.167),[24] which meant "painful journeying, desperate straits" (1.194). The earth there was "barren and unfruitful" (2.258).

---

[21] This certainly also partially accounted for major opposition to Paul on the part of the Jewish synagogue in Corinth. It not only had to choose a new president, Sosthenes (Acts 18:17). In light of his new, less demanding teaching, Paul most probably won over a number of God-fearers (not just Titius Justus) and proselytes, causing the synagogue leadership not only to be envious, but also to make Paul leave Corinth (18:12-17). The expression "our fathers" as related to the Israelites is also employed by Clement of Rome in his first letter to the Corinthians (60:4; cf. 4:8 and 31:2) from the end of the first century CE. Reference from Archibald Robertson and Alfred Plummer, *A Critical and Exegetical Commentary on the First Epistle of St Paul to the Corinthians* (ICC; Edinburgh: T. & T. Clark, 1914 / 1958^2) 199.

[22] Moses struck the rock at Mount "Horeb" (Sinai) in the wilderness of the Sinai Peninsula, and water flowed from it (Exod 17:6). The place name חֹרֵב (*ḥōrēbh*) derives from חָרֵב (*ḥarēbh*), to be waste, desolate (BDB 351-52). Larry Keitzer points this out in "1 Corinthians 10:4 and Philo's Flinty Rock" in *Communio Viatorum* 35 (1993) 110.

[23] Cf. F. Colson and G. Whitaker in the Loeb Classical Library edition of Philo, I. ix-x.

[24] Cf. "the trackless wilds" in 1.238, and "a long and pathless wilderness" in 2.247.

Josephus, an Aramaic-speaking native of Jerusalem and of priestly descent, completed his *Antiquities* in 93-94 CE.[25] He also states that "the country was absolute desert" (*Ant.* 3.1). It was "homeless and citiless" (3.314), making life "unpleasant and hard" (4.1). There "the fruits of earth failed" the Israelites (4.45), part of their "afflictions" then (4.239).[26]

2. *Hunger*

In the wilderness of Sin the Israelites complained that they could have died in Egypt, where "we sat by the fleshpots and ate our fill of bread." They think Moses and Aaron "have brought us out into this wilderness to kill this whole assembly with hunger" (Exod 16:3). Neh 9:15 also speaks of their hunger at this time. Philo mentions "the scourge of hunger," when the Israelites "were famished for lack of food" (*Mos.* 1.191). The "want of food" was "as great a misfortune as any that can befall mankind" (1.197).[27] A "continual famine" "beset them in their wanderings" (1.216), for food is "that primary and most necessary matter" (2.258). Josephus notes in *Ant.* 3.46 that the Israelites had contended in the wilderness with hunger.[28] *Exod. Rab.* Beshallaḥ 25/4 on Exod 16:4 states that the provisions the Israelites had brought along from Egypt lasted only thirty-one days.[29] After this their hunger began.

---

25 Cf. Thackeray's Introduction in the Loeb Classical Library edition of Josephus, IV. x, as well as *Ant.* 20.267. Josephus was fifty-six then, thus he was born ca. 37/38 CE.

26 Contrast Num 11:4-5 with the Israelites' eating meat, fish, cucumbers, melons, leeks, onions and garlic in Egypt. For the wilderness, see Num 20:5, which notes that in "this wretched place" no grain, figs, vines or pomegranates grow.

27 Cf. the comment by R. Joshua, a third generation Tanna (*Introduction* 83) in *Mek. R. Ish.* Vayassa 2 on Exod 16:3 (Lauterbach 2.101): "There is no death worse than death by hunger."

28 It is intentionally overlooked that the Israelites had "livestock in great numbers, both flocks and herds" (Exod 12:38). Cf. also Num 20:4 and 11, as well as 32:1. Philo, however, does mention the latter in *Mos.* 1.320, 331 and 333.

29 Cf. Mirkin 5.278; Soncino 3.304. See Exod 16:1 and Josephus, *Ant.* 2.316 on this time period.

3. *Thirst*

Neh 9:15 already mentions the Israelites' thirst in the wilderness. Philo notes that thirst "once more reduced them to despondency" (*Mos.* 1.181).[30] The Israelites thus thought "it is better to die at the hands of the enemy than by thirst" (1.183). During this period "famine and drought had alternatively attacked them" (1.215). Josephus relates that "the scarcity of water was extreme" (*Ant.* 3.1), causing the people to be "in extreme agony from thirst" (3.33).[31] In addition, their offer to pay for water was refused by the king of Idumea and by Sihon of the Amorites.[32]

4. *Snakes and Scorpions*

Deut 8:15 describes the wilderness as "an arid wasteland with poisonous snakes and scorpions."[33] According to 32:10 the Lord "found (Israel) in a desert land, in a howling wilderness waste." Verse 24 has Him threaten: "the teeth of beasts I will send against them, with venom of things crawling in the dust." Philo speaks in this regard of "reptiles that vent poison for the destruction of mankind, such as snakes and scorpions" (*Mos.* 1.192). The Tannaitic Tosefta notes in *Soṭah* 4:2 that the pillar of cloud which preceded the Israelites "would kill snakes and scorpions."[34] *Mek. R. Ish.* Beshallaḥ 1 on Exod 13:21[35] and *Sifre* Behaʿalothekha 83 on Num 10:34[36] maintain the same.

5. *Scorching Heat*

The extremely high temperatures of the Sinai Peninsula, especially in the summer, are well-known. Already in Wisd Sol 18:3 it is stated regarding the Israelites that God provided them not only with "a flaming pillar of fire" (at night, cf. Exod 13:22), but also during the day with "a harmless

---

30 Cf. 1.210.

31 It continues, describing the area as "an absolutely waterless region."

32 Cf. 4.76 (Edom in Num 20:19), and 4.86 (Num 21:23).

33 Cf. Num 21:6 for the Lord's sending poisonous snakes among the people, which Paul alludes to in 1 Cor 10:9.

34 Cf. Zuckermandel / Liebermann 298; Eng. Neusner 3.160.

35 Cf. Lauterbach 1.183.

36 Cf. Horovitz 79; Eng. Neusner 268.

sun for their glorious wandering."[37] According to *Targ. Ps.-Jon.* Num 14:14, an example of His care for them was that His "cloud was a covering over them so that they should not be hurt by heat...."[38] *Mek. R. Ish.* Beshallaḥ 3 on Exod 14:12 mentions the Israelites' fear that their corpses "will be exposed to the heat of the day."[39] Finally, "Hot wind and sun shall not strike them" (Isa 49:10) is cited in regard to the pillar of cloud and fire in Exod 13:21 in *Mekhilta de-Rabbi Shimon bar Yoḥai* Beshallaḥ ad loc.[40]

* * *

The above five negative characteristics of the forty-year wilderness wandering of the Israelites by way of contrast demonstrate the background of God's beneficent, supportive, even miraculous care of them noted by Paul in 1 Cor 10:1-4. Biblical and Judaic comment on the extraordinary passage through the Re(e)d Sea, the cloud, the food they ate, the beverage they drank, and the rock which accompanied them helps to understand why the Israelites should have been extremely grateful for these. Yet God was not pleased with most of them and struck them down in the wilderness (v. 5). After analyzing these four motifs in sections 1. - 4., I will cite three examples of the use of Ezek 16:9 in Judaic midrash (5.), discuss Israelite idolatry in Egypt and the wilderness and Ezekiel 16 with its targum (6.), and the motif of being baptized into Moses in the cloud and the Sea (7.). These are followed by remarks concerning Christ as pre-existent (8.), and in conclusion the form of 1 Cor 10:1-5 (9.).

1. *Passage Through the Re(e)d Sea*

In 1 Cor 10:1-2 Paul states that "our ancestors [lit., fathers] were all under the cloud, and all went through the Sea, 2) and all were baptized into Moses in the cloud and in the Sea." The "Sea" here is the Greek θαλάσση. The Apostle clearly alludes to the Israelites' "crossing / going through" (διέρχομαι διά) the Red Sea in Exodus 14, including the Song of Moses in

---

37 On the cloud's overshadowing the camp, see 19:7.
38 Cf. Clarke 174; Eng. Clarke 227.
39 Cf. Lauterbach 1.210.
40 Cf. Nelson 86.

15:1-19 and the Song of Miriam in vv. 20-21. It is sandwiched between the last words of chapter 14, which deal with the Lord's leading the Israelites in a pillar of cloud (v. 21), and the manna account of chapter 16 and water from the rock in 17:1-7. All of these topoi thus already occur close together in Scripture.

It is emphasized in Exod 14:16 that the Israelites will enter the Sea on "dry ground." Verse 21 emphasizes that the Lord then "turned the Sea into dry land; and the waters were divided." Verse 22 makes this specific: "The Israelites went into the Sea on dry ground, the waters forming a wall for them on their right and on their left." In contrast to the pursuing Egyptian army's being drowned in the Sea, which returned to its normal depth, "the Israelites walked on dry ground through the Sea, the waters forming a wall for them on their right and on their left" (v. 29, repeating v. 22). The Lord's "saving" Israel upon this occasion (v. 30) was a "great work" (v. 31) and became the constitutive redemptive narrative in Israel's history.

The Israelites' walking through the Red Sea upon "dry ground / land" here is emphasized by fourfold repetition. The motif is then repeated in 15:19. This alone makes it very improbable that Paul's mention of the Israelites' being baptized into Moses in the cloud and in "the Sea" (1 Cor 10:2) can refer to the waters of the Red Sea, not a drop of which made them wet, necessary for baptism. The motif of baptism through actual water must be sought elsewhere. In section 7. below I make a concrete proposal in this regard.

While the redemptive event of crossing through the Red Sea (the exodus) is understandably referred to countless times alone in the Bible, it is already found in a cluster with the other motifs listed by Paul in 1 Cor 10:1-4 in other passages of Scripture.

In Ezra's prayer, Neh 9:9-11 describes the Red Sea event as part of the Lord's "signs and wonders." "Our ancestors [lit., fathers]" (v. 10) "passed through the Sea on dry land" (v. 11). Then the pillar of cloud is mentioned in v. 12, bread from heaven in v. 15, and water from the rock (ibid.).[41]

Psalm 78 speaks of the "miracles" and "marvels" shown the Israelites in Egypt and at their departure from there (vv. 11-12). They passed through

[41] Cf. the pillar of cloud also in v. 19, as well as manna and water in v. 20.

the Sea, whose waters stood "like a heap" (v. 13). Then the cloud is mentioned in v. 14, and water from the rock in vv. 15-16.[42]

Psalm 105 speaks of the Lord's "bringing out" the Israelites from Egypt in v. 37, with a cloud in v. 39, and water from the rock in v. 41.[43]

Philo of Alexandria describes the Israelites' passage through the Red Sea in *Mos.* 1.170-80. It was a "great and marvelous work" (1.180). The middle part of the Sea "dried up and became a broad highway" (1.177). The Hebrews with their women and children "crossed on a dry road in the early dawn" (1.179). In addition to many haggadic details Philo notes the pillar of cloud, manna, and water from the rock.

Josephus describes the exodus scene at the Red Sea in *Ant.* 2.338-46. When the water receded, it left the soil bare, which was a clear manifestation of God, the Sea withdrawing from its own bed (2.338-39). It was miraculous salvation (2.339), miraculous deliverance (2.345) for the Israelites. In addition, Josephus adds numerous haggadic details to the narrative, certainly not all from him. Shortly after this the Jewish historian describes the manna of Exodus 16 and water from the rock in Exodus 17.[44]

Pseudo-Philo was originally written in Hebrew in Palestine, perhaps at the time of Jesus or sometime around 70 CE.[45] Chapter 10 describes the squabble of the tribes arranged in three groups as to how to proceed at the Red Sea. God enjoins Moses to lift up his rod and strike "the Sea, and it will be dried up. And when Moses did all this, God rebuked the Sea and the Sea was dried up" (10:5). This enabled Israel to "pass through the middle of the Sea on dry ground" (10:6).[46]

---

[42] Cf. water from the rock in v. 20, and manna, the grain of heaven, the bread of angels, in vv. 24-25.

[43] Wisd Sol 10:18 also describes the crossing of the Red Sea, and water from a rock in the nearby 11:4. Yet the pillar of cloud and manna are not mentioned here.

[44] He saves mention of the cloud until its connection with the tabernacle in 3.290 and 310.

[45] Cf. Daniel Harrington in *OTP* 2.298-99, including the likelihood of a dating about the time of Jesus, and George Nickelsburg, *Jewish Literature between the Bible and the Mishnah* 269, on around 70 CE.

[46] Cf. *SC* 229.116; Eng. *OTP* 2.317, where Exod 14:15-16 is paraphrased, then 14:22 / 29.

In *Exod Rab.* Beshallaḥ 22/3 on Exod 14:31, "Our Rabbis taught: He who recites the *Shema* ʿ[47] must mention [daily] the division of the Red Sea ... in the section beginning 'True and firm.'"[48] Deut 16:3 is cited in this regard: "that all the days of your life you may remember the day of your departure from Egypt."[49] This shows how deeply anchored the crossing of the Red Sea was in a Jew's daily prayers.

In *Mek. R. Ish.* Beshallaḥ 4 on Exod 14:15, R. Meir, a third generation Tanna,[50] has the Lord instruct Moses: "If for Adam the first man, who was but one individual, I made dry land - as it is said: 'And God said: Let the waters under the heaven be gathered,' etc. (Gen 1:9) - will I not for this assembly of holy people turn the Sea into dry land?"[51]

The first three of the ten miracles performed for Israel at the Red Sea, according to *Mek. R. Ish.* Beshallaḥ 5 on Exod 14:16, were the following: 1) "The Sea was broken through and made like a vault," as Hab 3:14 is interpreted. 2) "It was divided into two parts, as it is said: 'Stretch out your hand and divide it' (Exod 14:16). 3) Dry land was formed in it, as it is said: 'But the Israelites walked upon dry land in the midst of the Sea' (v. 29)."[52]

The term "vault" here is כִּפָּה (*kippah*), "arch."[53] In *ʾAvot R. Nat.* A 33, R. Eliezer (b. Hyrcanus, a second generation Tanna of the older group,)[54] made a similar statement, this time with the verb: "The deep arched [כפה - *kphh*] over them and under it Israel went across, so as not to be discomfited."[55] While acknowledging that the Israelites crossed the Red

---

[47] This consists of the Scriptures (Deut 6:4-9; 11:13-21; and Num 15:37-41) recited together in the daily morning and evening prayers. Cf. the art. "Shema, Reading of," by Louis Jacobs in *EJ* (2007) 18.454.

[48] S. Lehrman explains this in Soncino 3.277, n. 1. Jacobs (see preceding note) says this was the benediction after the recitation of the morning *Shema* ʿ.

[49] Cf. Mirkin 5.258.

[50] Cf. *Introduction* 84.

[51] Cf. Lauterbach 1.216.

[52] Cf. Lauterbach 1.223.

[53] Cf. Jastrow 635. It is especially used of the heavenly arch, the sky. Another meaning is skull-cap.

[54] Cf. *Introduction* 77.

[55] Cf. Schechter 98; Becker 240; Eng. Goldin 136. See other parallels in Lauterbach's footnote on lines 1-14 of *Mek. R. Ish.* 1.223. Another miracle which occurred at this time was that living (fresh) water for the Israelites to drink came forth from the salty Sea. See *ʾAvot R. Nat.* A 33 (Schechter 98; Becker 240; Eng. Goldin 136), and version B 38 (Schechter 100; Eng. Saldarini 227).

Sea on dry land / ground, commentators on First Corinthians such as Christian Wolff cite the above *Mekhilta* passage from Paul Billerbeck (Str-B) to make the comparison of the Israelites' being surrounded by the water of the Red Sea, and the water of baptism surrounding one.[56] This is thought to explain Paul's phrase in 1 Cor 10:2, "baptized into Moses in the cloud and in the Sea." Yet, as noted above, the motif of the Israelites' remaining completely dry during the entire crossing is emphasized again and again, not only in Scripture but also in Tannaitic sources, making this suggestion improbable.

Finally, I suggest that being baptized "in" (ἐν) the (Red) Sea is not meant spatially ("within") or instrumentally ("by") here. Rather, ἐν can also mean "during."[57] That is, the Israelites were baptized during / at the time of / or in regard to the entire exodus event, which according to Judaic tradition included the Israelite newborn infants' being "washed" by the Lord or an angel in the field and then abandoned there (Ezek 16:4 and 9). After the crossing of the Red Sea it was they as adults (or infants in another tradition) who proclaimed on the far side in regard to this earlier care, including being washed, "*This* is my God, and I will praise Him, my father's God, and I will exalt Him" (Exod 15:2). I shall elucidate the details of this proposal below in section 5.3.

---

[56] Cf. his *Der erste Brief des Paulus an die Korinther* 40. In addition, C. K. Barrett maintains in *A Commentary on the First Epistle to the Corinthians* (London: Black, 1968) 221 that "There is some evidence that Jews also regarded the passage through the Red Sea as a kind of baptism (analogous to proselyte baptism)." However, he can cite no sources for this assertion. Karl-Heinrich Ostermeyer, a student of Christian Wolff, also states: "Mit der Rettung Israels aus den Todeswassern, die Paulus ohne Bedenken als Taufe deklariert, beginnt das Leben der Getauften." See his *Taufe und Typos*: Elemente und Theologie der Taufapologien in 1. Korinther 10 und 1. Peter 3 (WUNT 2.118; Tűbingen: Mohr Siebeck, 2000) 141. Andreas Reichert in *Das Verständnis der Taufe im 1. Korintherbrief* 105 takes a similar position. In addition, he cites numerous Church Fathers on 1:1-13 on pp. 117-47. Everett Ferguson's view in *Baptism in the Early Church* 152 is comparable, as is that of Gerhard Barth in *Die Taufe* 76. Typically, he also cites Str-B here.

[57] Cf. BAGD 260, II. 3., especially Mark 15:7, "'during' the revolt." James Voelz, a specialist in Greek grammar, calls my attention to Gal 1:24 with ἐν ἐμοί as "in my case." For 1 Cor 10:2, this could mean that the Israelites were baptized in the case of / in the matter of / in regard to the Sea.

2. *The (Pillar of) Cloud*

In 1 Cor 10:1 the Apostle to the Gentiles states that "our ancestors [lit., fathers] were all under the cloud." In v. 2 he adds that "all were baptized into Moses in the cloud and in the Sea." Both instances of "cloud" here are the Greek νεφέλη.[58] The basic reference is to Exod 13:21-22 concerning the Israelites in the wilderness:

> The Lord went in front of them in *a pillar of cloud* [עַמּוּד עָנָן - *'ammud 'anan* ; LXX στῦλος νεφέλης] by day, to lead them along the way, and in a pillar of fire by night, to give them light, so that they might travel by day and by night. 22) Neither *the pillar of cloud* by day nor *the pillar of cloud* by night left its place in front of the people.[59]

It is noteworthy that in the second year of the Palestinian triennial lectionary system (the Babylonian was annual), on the third Sabbath of Nisan the reading from the Pentateuch began precisely with Exod 13:21 on the cloud. On the fourth Sabbath, Exod 15:21ff. was read, including bread from heaven / manna in 16:4-24. The next Sabbath is the first in Iyyar, with Exod 16:25ff., including water from the rock in 17:1-7. Three consecutive Sabbath readings in the larger period of Passover thus deal with the cloud, bread from heaven / manna, and water from the rock, all in the background of 1 Cor 10:1-4. In addition, the Pentateuchal reading for the second Sabbath of Nisan in the same year is Exod 13:1(-20), including directions for the festival of unleavened bread / Passover. Verse 8 there reads: "You shall tell your child on that day, 'It is because of what the Lord did *for me* when *I* came out of Egypt.'" The latter is relevant to "all *our* fathers" in 1 Cor 10:1, as pointed out above in the Introduction. Passover was celebrated at about this time (on the 14th) in the month of Nisan.[60]

---

[58] Elsewhere in Paul it is found only in the plural in 1 Thess 4:17.

[59] The LXX adds to the last phrase πάντος, "all" the people. Cf. Paul's emphasis on "all" the Israelites as being under the cloud in 1 Cor 10:1, and "all" of them as being baptized into Moses in the cloud in v. 2.

[60] Cf. the art. "Triennial Cycle" by Joseph Jacobs in *JE* (1905 / 1925) 12.254-57; "Triennial Cycle" in *EJ* (1971) 15.1387-88; and "Triennial Cycle" in *EJ* (2007) 20.140-43. The authors of the latter two articles believe the triennial cycle was not yet "definitely" established in the talmudic period. This is certainly true for some

The "pillar of cloud" occurs eleven more times in the MT. Within Ezra's prayer, Neh 9:12 is almost a paraphrase of Exod 13:21. The same is true for v. 19, an example of God in His great mercies not forsaking the Israelites in the wilderness. It should be noted that bread from heaven and water out of the rock are mentioned in v. 15, and manna and water in v. 20. The event of the dividing of the Red Sea is already noted in vv. 9 and 11. This again shows that the individual motifs found in 1 Cor 10:1-4 were already found together as a fixed cluster within the Hebrew Bible.

The latter is also true for Psalm 78. Among the miracles God showed the Israelites' "ancestors / fathers" (v. 12) were the division of the Sea (v. 13), His leading them by day in a cloud and by night with a fiery light (v. 14), and His splitting rocks[61] open in the wilderness, causing much water to flow (vv. 15-16). The rock from which water gushes out, and bread, are noted in v. 20.[62]

Psalm 105:38-42 demonstrates the same complex as described above. At the Israelites' departure from Egypt the Lord "spread a cloud for a covering, and fire to give light by night" (v. 39). He gave them "food from heaven [manna] in abundance" (v. 40). When He opened the rock, water gushed out, flowing through the desert like a river" (v. 41).[63]

The above three biblical passages, Nehemiah 9, Psalm 78, and Psalm 105, may have encouraged Paul to mention the same motifs together in 1 Cor 10:1-4. Other references to the (pillar of) cloud may also have influenced his thinking in this regard.

Num 14:14 has Moses tell the Lord about the Israelites: "Your cloud stands over them and You go in front of them, in a pillar of cloud by day and a pillar of fire by night." V. 15 mentions the possibility of the Lord's "killing" His people because of their rebellion. In v. 16 it is spoken of as His "slaughtering" them in the wilderness. The latter verb is the Hebrew שָׁחַט (*shaḥaṭ*), to slaughter.[64] The LXX employs the verb καταστρώννυμι

---

readings, but hardly for the festivals such as Passover and the Pentateuchal readings appropriate to them. They needed specific readings at an early time.

[61] The plural may refer to Exod 17:6 at Horeb, and Num 20:11 in the wilderness of Zin (v. 1).

[62] On the latter as manna, cf. vv. 24-25.

[63] God's thus remembering His covenant to Abraham in v. 42 may be related to the midrash on Genesis 18, analyzed in section 5.1 below.

[64] Cf. BDB 1006. See the threefold usage of the verb regarding this incident in *Cant. Rab.* 1:7 § 2 (Dunski 36; Soncino 9.63). A possible cross-connection to Ezekiel 16 is the occurrence of the same verb in v. 21.

at this point: to lay low.[65] In 1 Cor 10:5 Paul states that in spite of the beneficent acts found in vv. 1-4, God was not pleased with most of the Israelites, for "they were struck down" (κατεστρώθησαν) in the wilderness, employing the same verb.[66] Num 14:16 may have occurred to Paul at this point because of the mention of the catchword "cloud" in the neighboring verse (14).

Pseudo-Philo in the first century CE already paraphrases Exod 13:21-22 in 10:7, together with manna (bread from heaven), quail, and the well.[67]

Parts of rabbinic comment on the (pillar of) cloud may also have been known to the Apostle Paul. The Tannaitic *Sifre* Haʾazinu 313 on Deut 32:10, "He found him in a desert / wilderness land," states: "everything was prepared and supplied to them in the wilderness: a well arose for them, manna descended for them, quail were made available to them, the cloud of glory encompassed them." In addition, "He cared for him" means with two gifts: manna and water from the well.[68] This also attests the early Judaic cluster of the well, manna, and the cloud.

Mek. R. Ish. Beshallaḥ 1 on Exod 13:21, "And the Lord went before them by day," states: "You will have to say: There were seven clouds: 'And the Lord went before them by day in a pillar of cloud'; 'And Your cloud stands over them, and You go before them in a pillar of cloud' (Num 14:14); 'And when the cloud tarried upon the tabernacle' (9:19); 'And whenever the cloud was taken up.... But if the cloud was not taken up.... For the cloud of the Lord was upon the tabernacle' (Exod 40:36-38). Thus there were seven clouds, four on the front side of them, one above them, one beneath them, and one that advanced before them on the road, raising the depressions and lowering the elevations, as it is said: 'Every valley shall be lifted up, and every mountain and hill shall be made low; and the rugged shall be made level, and the rough places a plain' (Isa 40:4). It also killed the snakes and scorpions, and swept [the dust from] the road before them."[69]

---

65 Cf. LSJ 915, III., with 1 Cor 10:5.

66 Cf. BAGD 419. The divine passive is employed: "God" struck them down. The verb is found only here in the NT.

67 Cf. *SC* 229.118; Eng. *OTP* 2.317.

68 Cf. Finkelstein 355-56; Eng. Hammer 320.

69 Cf. Lauterbach 1.183. This is followed by the midrash on Genesis 18, to be analyzed in section 5.1 below. See also *Mek. R. Shim. b. Yoḥ.* on Exod 13:21 (Nelson 85), as well as *Tanḥ.* Beshallaḥ 3 on the same verse (Eshkol 280; Eng. Berman 413).

The Tannaitic *Sifre* Behaʿalotekhah 83 on Num 10:34 enumerates the seven clouds mentioned above. Then it comments on the verse's "And the cloud of the Lord was over them by day": "It was over the cripples and the blind, those inflicted with flux and with leprosy."[70] This implies that it especially protected them. Another comment on Exod 13:21 states that the Lord preceded the Israelites in the wilderness "as a quartermaster would."[71]

In *Exod. Rab.* Bo 19/6 on Exod 12:43 the Lord states: "In the past it was I and My court who walked before [the Israelites], for it says: Exod 13:21."[72] This suggests the Lord and the angels of service accompanied the Israelites in a pillar of cloud throughout the forty years of wilderness wandering. Passages such as Exod 14:19;[73] 23:20, 23; 32:34; and Num 20:16[74] emphasize the role of an angel in this regard. The Tannaitic *Mekhilta de-Rabbi Ishmael* interprets the angel of God of Exod 14:19 as the *Shekhinah,* or Divine Presence.[75] The latter also went before the Israelites in the pillar of cloud in the wilderness, as in Exod 13:21.[76] *Targ.* Ezek 16:12 has the Lord say regarding a single angel: "I placed the ark of My covenant among you, with My cloud of glory covering you, and an angel, sent before Me, leading the way ahead of you."[77] *Targum Pseudo-Jonathan* on Exod 13:21 states that "The glory of the Shekhinah of the

---

[70] Cf. Horovitz 79; Eng. Neusner 2.68.

[71] Cf. *Tanḥ.* Ki Thissa 35 on Exod 34:27 (Eshkol 430; Eng. Berman 622). *Num. Rab.* Bemidbar 1/2 on Num 1:1 notes that this cloud "advanced before them three days' journey" to prepare the way for them (Mirkin 9.11; Soncino 5.3; see in this regard Num 10:33-34).

[72] Cf. Mirkin 5.226; Soncino 3.237. For the heavenly court associated with "the Lord," see *Gen. Rab.* Vayera 51/2 on Gen 19:24 (Theodor and Albeck 533; Soncino 1.445), and *Exod. Rab.* Vaʾera 12/4 on Exod 9:23 (Mirkin 5.145; Soncino 3.146).

[73] Cf. *Mek. R. Shim. b. Yoḥ.* Baḥodesh 49 on Exod 19:4 (Nelson 217) for the interpretation of "the angel of God" of this verse as the angels of service.

[74] *Targum Pseudo-Jonathan* on this verse (Clarke 183; Eng. Clarke 245) has here "one of His ministering angels."

[75] Cf. Jastrow 1573 on שְׁכִינָה (*shekhînah*).

[76] Cf. Shirata 3 on Exod 15:2 (Lauterbach 2.27). See also *t. Soṭah* 4:2 on the *Shekhinah* as one of the seven glorious clouds, probably meant here as the one which went before them (Zuckermandel / Liebermann 298; Eng. Neusner 3.160). Josephus in *Ant.* 3.310 states that the cloud which rested above the tabernacle in the wilderness "signalized the Presence [ἐπιφάνεια] of God," certainly meant as the *Shekhinah.* On the cloud's function in making and breaking camp, see 3.290.

[77] Cf. Sperber 3.293; Eng. Levey 50.

Lord was leading before them by day in a pillar of cloud...."[78] Both *Targum Neofiti 1*[79] and the *Fragment Targum*, MS "P,"[80] have "the Memra" at this point. It is "the Word" of the Lord.[81] This circumlocution of the latter two targums could be quite early at this point, as indicated by Philo.

In *Mos.* 1.165 the Alexandrian philosopher may rely on tradition (φασι),[82] or he more probably has Exod 13:21 in mind when stating:

> We are told that there occurred a prodigy [τεράστιον], a mighty work of nature, the like of which none can remember to have seen in the past. 166) A cloud [νεφέλη] shaped like a tall pillar, the light of which in the daytime was as the sun and in the night as flame, went before the host, so that they should not stray in their journey, but follow in the steps of a guide [ἡγεμών][83] who could never err. Perhaps indeed there was enclosed within the cloud one of the lieutenants [ὕπαρχος][84] of the great King, an unseen angel, a forerunner [προηγητήρ][85] on whom the eyes of the body were not permitted to look.

Philo again refers to the "guiding cloud" of Exod 14:19-20 in 1.178, "a most extraordinary sign."[86]

Elsewhere Philo identifies this angel with the Logos. In *Questions and Answers on Exodus* 2.13 he comments on Exod 23:20-21, "Behold, I am sending My angel before your face..., for My name is upon him." He maintains in this regard that "of necessity the Logos was appointed as judge and mediator, who is called 'angel.'"[87] In addition, in *Agr.* 51 Philo comments with the aid of the same scriptural passage on the many parts of the universe: "This hallowed flock He leads in accordance with right

---

78 Cf. Clarke 82; Eng. Maher 198.

79 Cf. Díez-Macho 2.87; Eng. McNamara 57, who translates "the Word."

80 Cf. Klein 1.74; Eng. 2.40.

81 Cf. Jastrow 775 on מֵימַר (*mēmar*), 2), as well as the same in Sokoloff, *A Dictionary of Jewish Palestinian Aramaic of the Byzantine Period* 305, 2.

82 Cf. φημί in LSJ 1926 at II. 1. : they say, it is said. See 2 Cor 10:10. Elsewhere it can refer to a particular passage in Scripture, as in 1 Cor 6:16.

83 Cf. LSJ 763, I. : guide. II. leader, commander, chief.

84 Cf. LSJ 1853: subordinate commander, lieutenant.

85 Cf. LSJ 1480: one who goes before to show the way, guide.

86 In 2.254 Philo also notes that within the cloud (of Exod 14:19-20) there was "the vision of the Godhead, flashing rays of fire."

87 Cf. Ralph Marcus in *Philo Supplement II, Questions and Answers on Exodus*, 48. See the Lord and His court in notes 72-73 above.

and law, setting over it 'His true Word and firstborn son [τὸν ὄρθον αὐτοῦ λόγον καὶ πρωτόγονον υἱόν], who shall take upon him its government like some lieutenant [ὕπαρχος] of a great king. For it is written somewhere: 'Behold, I AM, I send My angel before your face to guard you in the way' (Exod 23:20)." Finally, in *Mig.* 174 Philo states regarding Abraham's being escorted by angels in Gen 18:16 that he has the "Divine Word / Logos" (λόγος θεῖος) as his guide (ἡγεμών). This is because of the oracle of Exod 23:20-21.

While the Apostle Paul does not designate Jesus Christ as the Word (ὁ λόγος), as the author of the Fourth Gospel does in 1:1, he does call him "the Son of God" several times.[88] In addition, God's Son is the firstborn (πρωτότοκος) among many brethren (Rom 8:29). From the Pauline School, Col 1:15 calls Christ "the firstborn of all creation," and in contrast in v. 18 "the firstborn from the dead."

The Hellenistic Jewish Christian Paul maintained regarding himself: "I advanced in Judaism beyond many among my people of the same age, for I was far more zealous for the traditions of my ancestors" (Gal 1:14).[89] It is thus entirely possible that he may have known of a strand of Hellenistic Judaism, as exemplified by Philo, in which he who led the Israelites in a pillar of cloud in the wilderness in Exod 13:21 was the Lord's special agent, His Memra or Word / Logos, who is His firstborn son. If so, while he does not mention it in connection with the cloud in 1 Cor 10:1-2, it may have encouraged him to state in v. 4 that Christ was the rock which accompanied the Israelites in the wilderness (for forty years). This is because for Paul himself, Jesus Christ is God's Son, His firstborn.

Finally, Paul not only notes that "our ancestors" (lit., "fathers") were all "under the cloud" (1 Cor 10:1). He adds in v. 2 that they were all baptized into Moses "in [ἐν] the cloud." The latter is not pictured as a dark rain cloud,[90] which produced a heavy shower of rain to provide the water

---

[88] Cf. Rom 1:4; 2 Cor 1:19; Gal 2:20; and from the School of Paul Eph 4:13. References to His "Son" are much more frequent. See Rom 1:3, 9; 8:3, 29, 32; 1 Cor 1:9; Gal 1:16; 4:4, 6.

[89] Cf. Acts 22:3. While a haggadic dramatization by Luke, the speech is most probably correct at this point.

[90] Cf. already Heinrich Meyer in 1849. See his *Erster Brief an die Korinther* (Meyers 5; Göttingen: Vandenhoeck & Ruprecht, 1849²) 201. See also Zeller in *Der erste Brief an die Korinther* 327: a cloud lets out moisture, so it is appropriate for

necessary for baptism. Rather, it is simply designated "the cloud." I propose that "in" (ἐν) here should be understood in the same sense as suggested in section 1. above for "in" the Sea. The Israelites were baptized "during," "while,"[91] or "at the time" the cloud accompanied them. This it did in Exod 13:21-22 just before the crossing of the Red Sea, as well as afterwards (14:19), and according to Judaic tradition for the entire forty years of the wilderness wandering. The latter also assumes the cloud was already present when Israelite women went out to the field to bear their children. These were "washed" and anointed there by the Lord or an angel. They then disappeared and later reappeared on the far shore of the Red Sea, exclaiming Exod 15:2. I shall comment more extensively on the connection between being "washed" and Paul's term "to be baptized" in section 7. below.

Appendix I. *The Messiah as the Cloud Man*

Exod 13:21 says that the Lord led the Israelites in the wilderness by day in a pillar of "cloud" (עָנָן; *ʿanan*). "Cloud man" became a messianic designation in some Judaic texts. It is based on the personal name "Anani" (עֲנָנִי ; *ʿananî*) of 1 Chron 3:24. The *Targum* reads at this point: "and Anani - he is the King Messiah who will be revealed."[92] *Tanḥ*. B Toledoth 20 on Gen 27:28 cites this verse and asks: "Who is Anani? This is the Messiah, as stated: 'I saw one coming like a son of man with the *clouds* of heaven' (Dan 7:13)." Here the plural "clouds" (עֲנָנֵי ; *ʿananē*) is read as the singular noun, עֲנָנִי , *ʿananî*. Other related verses are then also interpreted messianically.[93] A parallel tradition is found in *Tanḥ*. Toledoth 14.[94]

This tradition of the King Messiah as the "Cloud Man" related to the Son of Man of Dan 7:13 cannot be dated. However, if it is early, it too may have influenced Paul to think of "the Messiah," הַמָּשִׁיחַ (*hammashîaḥ*),

---

baptism and corresponds to the Holy Spirit, which comes down upon the person baptized.

[91] Cf. again BAGD 260, II. 3. on ἐν.

[92] Cf. Déaut / Robert 18; Eng. McIver 57.

[93] Cf. Buber 140; Eng. Townsend 167, with n. 84.

[94] Cf. Eshkol 118; Eng. Berman 182. Paul Billerbeck had noted these passages in Str-B 1.67.

ὁ χριστός, as somehow related to the (pillar of) "cloud" of Exod 13:21, the main scriptural background to the "cloud" of 1 Cor 10:1-2. Paul then goes on to designate the rock of v. 4 as "the Christ," ὁ Χριστός.

Appendix II. *The Name of the Messiah as "Lord"*

Exod 13:21 says that "the Lord" (יהוה [*yhwh*])[95] led the Israelites in the wilderness by day in a pillar of cloud. One designation of the Messiah in Judaic sources is "the Lord." In *Lam. Rab.* 1:16 § 51, R. Abba b. Kahana, a third generation Palestinian Amora,[96] responded to the question, What is the name of King Messiah? "'His name is the Lord' [ה' שמו - *h ´ shmw*], as it is stated: 'The Lord is our righteousness' (Jer 23:6)."[97] He may have repeated this from his teacher, R. Yoḥanan.[98] This tradition with Jer 23:6 is also found in *Midr. Pss.* 21/2 on Ps 21:2[99] and *Midr. Prov.* 19.[100]

Again, this tradition cannot now be given an early date. However, if it is much older than the present sources in which it is now found, it too may have influenced Paul in thinking of the Messiah as associated with Exod 13:21, and thus with the cloud of the same verse. More, unfortunately, cannot be said.

3. *Manna*

Paul states regarding the Israelites in the wilderness that "they all ate the same spiritual 'food' [βρῶμα]" (1 Cor 10:3). This is a clear allusion to the manna, the "bread from heaven" of Exod 16:4, described in the same chapter. It should be recalled that this episode is preceded by the pillar of cloud in 13:21-22 together with 14:19-20, and the crossing of the Red Sea in the latter chapter, followed by Moses' and Miriam's victory songs in

---

95 The LXX does not have κύριος, but ὁ θεός here.

96 Cf. *Introduction* 100.

97 Cf. Vilna 36; Soncino 7.135-36. For righteousness as an attribute of the Messiah, see Isa 11:4-5 as understood in Judaic (and later Christian) tradition.

98 Cf. *b. B. Bathra* 75b (Soncino 303), where the Messiah is one of three called by the name of the Holy One, blessed be He.

99 Cf. Buber 178; Eng. Braude 1.293.

100 Cf. Visotzky 141; Eng. Visotzky 90, where he forgot "the Lord is" before "our righteousness." On these passages, see Str-B 1.66, where his reference to *Pesiqta Rabbati* is wrong.

chapter 15. The manna narrative is found directly after this, and the rock episode in the adjacent chapter 17, showing that the cloud, the Sea, manna and the rock were already closely connected in the same book of Scripture, as in 1 Cor 10:1-4. This is why the same complex, including manna, is also found elsewhere in the Bible: Nehemiah 9 (bread from heaven in v. 15, manna in v. 20; the division of the Sea in v. 11; a pillar of cloud in v. 12; water from the rock in v. 15); Psalm 78 (bread in v. 20; manna, the grain of heaven, the bread of angels, in vv. 24-25; the division of the Sea in v. 13; a cloud in v. 14; water from the rock[s] in vv. 15-16, 20); and Psalm 105 (v. 40 - food from heaven in abundance; a cloud in v. 39; water from the rock in v. 41).

While Philo can describe the gift of manna in *Mos.* 1.200-208, he typically allegorizes it as the word of God in *Leg. All.* 3.162-76. The first-century CE, Palestinian *Pseudo-Philo,* originally written in Hebrew (see n. 45 above), in 10:7 quotes Exod 16:4, mentions the well of water following the Israelites, and then quotes Exod 13:21 with the pillar of cloud.[101] According to 20:8, God had given the manna for the sake of Moses, and it ceased at the taking of the Land (Josh 5:12).[102] Josephus in *Ant.* 3.30 labels it "food" (βρῶμα, as in 1 Cor 10:3) which was divine and marvelous.[103] The only occurrence of manna in the Mishnah is in *ʾAvot* 5:6, where it is enumerated together with the mouth of the well as one of the ten things created on the eve of the first Sabbath at twilight.[104]

Tannaitic comment on the manna elaborated on it in an haggadic manner. "Every day it shone like gold; on the Sabbath more so."[105] It was sixty cubits high when it descended.[106] "If one liked it baked, it would become baked for him; if one liked it cooked, it would become cooked for him."[107] "The manna would turn for the Israelites into anything they might desire, but with their eyes they saw only manna."[108] It was never

---

[101] Cf. *SC* 229.116, 118, and *OPT* 2.317.

[102] Cf. *SC* 229.170; *OTP* 2.329.

[103] The haggadic addition in 3.26 should be noted.

[104] Cf. Albeck 4.376; Danby 456; and Neusner 686. This tradition is also found in *Mek. R. Ish.* Vayassa 6 on Exod 16:32 (Lauterbach 2.124).

[105] Cf. *Mek. R. Ish.* Vayassa 3 on Exod 16:5 (Lauterbach 2.104).

[106] Ibid., Vayassa 4 on Exod 16:14 (Lauterbach 2.113).

[107] Ibid., Vayassa 5 on Exod 16:23 (Lauterbach 2.118).

[108] Cf. *Sifre* Behaʿalothekhah 87 on Num 11:5-6 (Horovitz 87; Eng. Neusner 2.86). See also Wisd Sol 16:21, where the bread (food of angels, v. 20) "was changed to suit everyone's liking."

excreted, but was absorbed in the limbs, for it was the bread of angels.[109] Finally, during the forty-year wilderness wandering, women never needed any spices (as perfume), "but simply adorned themselves with the manna." This is based on Deut 2:7, "you lacked nothing."[110]

The above sketch, from the biblical account to the Tannaitic period, shows how well-known and popular manna was in Judaic thought. This helps to explain why the Apostle Paul, a converted Jew, mentioned it in 1 Cor 10:3 in connection with the cloud, the (Red) Sea, and the water of the rock.

It also aids in understanding the term "spiritual" (the adj. πνευματικός) Paul employs for the "food" (βρῶμα) the Israelites ate in the wilderness (v. 4) - manna. The "bread" (ἄρτος) which Christians break in the celebration of the Eucharist means sharing in the body of Christ (10:16; "one bread" twice in v. 17).[111] Earthly bread becomes something special in the Lord's Supper because it stands for the body of Christ, "the Lord" (v. 21).[112] Elsewhere in correspondence with the Corinthians Paul can say, "The Lord is 'the Spirit' (τὸ πνεῦμα)" (2 Cor 3:17, and 18).[113] To this extent the earthly bread of the Eucharist becomes the bread of the Spirit, "spiritual" bread or food.

Paul says in 1 Cor 10:4 that corresponding to contemporary usage in the Eucharist, the Israelites in the wilderness already had "spiritual" food (manna). Scriptural and other passages describe manna in contrast to earthly food as "heavenly." Exod 16:4 labels it "bread from heaven," as do Ps 105:40 and Neh 9:15. Ps 78:24 calls it the "grain of heaven" (LXX 77:24 "bread of heaven") and "the bread of angels" (v. 25; see also Wisd Sol 16:20). And Josephus labels manna not only miraculous, but also "divine" (θεῖον) food (*Ant.* 3.30). Such epithets may also have encouraged Paul to designate the food the Israelites ate in the wilderness as "spiritual." It was of supernatural origin.

---

[109] Ibid., 88 on Num 11:6 (Horovitz 87; Eng. Neusner 2.87).

[110] Ibid., 89 on Num 11:8 (Horovitz 88; Eng. Neusner 2.90).

[111] The Lord's Supper and baptism are mentioned in this chapter together for the first time.

[112] In Did 10:3 ordinary food and drink are also contrasted to "'spiritual' food and drink," certainly meant here as the Eucharist.

[113] Cf. also 1 Cor 15:45, where Christ as the last Adam "became a life-giving spirit." See also section 8. below, where the spirit of God in Gen 1:2 is labeled the spirit of the Messiah.

The same type of reasoning applies to "the spiritual drink" (τὸ ... πνευματικὸν ... πόμα) in 1 Cor 10:4, drunk from the "spiritual" rock, Christ. The earthly (red) wine employed in the Eucharist signified the "blood of Christ" (v. 16)[114] when drunk from "the cup of the Lord" (v. 21). As noted above, Paul can also say the Lord is the Spirit. Thus at the Eucharist the earthly wine can also be thought of as representing something "spiritual," the blood of Christ the Lord, the Spirit.[115]

4. *Water from the Rock, Which Was Christ*

In 1 Cor 10:4 Paul states that the Israelites in the wilderness "all drank the same spiritual drink, for they were accustomed to drink[116] from the spiritual rock accompanying[117] [them], the rock being Christ." By the "drink" here, water is meant. The Greek noun for "rock" is πέτρα. Later Jews asked themselves where the Israelites in the wilderness / desert found enough water for well over 600,000 people.[118] They found the answer already in their own Scriptures.

---

[114] Cf. the remarks of Ambrose (d. 397 CE) in regard to 1 Cor 10:3 in "The Mysteries" 8.48 : "For them water flowed from the rock. For you blood flows from Christ. Water satisfied them for the hour. Blood satisfies you for eternity." See *1-2 Corinthians*, ed. Bray (Ancient Christian Commentary on Scripture, New Testament VII) 90. In John 6:48-49 Jesus states that "I am the bread of life. Your fathers ate manna in the wilderness and died." In v. 55 he adds: "my flesh is 'true' [ἀληθής] food and my blood is 'true' drink," clearly alluding to the Eucharist. The use of "spiritual" and "true" appear to be analogous here.

[115] The passage 1 Cor 12:13 is difficult to interpret: "we were all made to drink of one Spirit." Can it be connected to 6:11, "But you were washed ... in the Spirit of our God," as many commentators maintain? If so, "spiritual" drinking could also be associated with baptism, as it is in 10:3-4.

[116] This is the meaning of the imperfect tense of the verb, in contrast to the preceding aorist. It is analogous to (repeatedly) "drinking the cup of the Lord" in the Eucharist in v. 21.

[117] Cf. Peter Arzt-Grabner et al., *1 Korinther* (Papyrologische Kommentare zum Neuen Testament, 2; Göttingen: Vandenhoeck & Ruprecht, 2006) 364-65 for examples in the papyri of ἀκολουθέω as "to follow" in the sense of "to accompany." See also BAGD 31, 2: accompany, go along with. The rock thus should not necessarily be thought of as behind the Israelites.

[118] Cf. Exod 12:37 with "about 600,000 men on foot, besides children," as well as a "mixed crowd" in v. 38. Num 1:46 has 603,550 men "from twenty years old and

Except for the minor incident of bitter water made sweet at Marah (Exod 15:22-26), the main narrative describing a miraculous access to water in the wilderness is found just after the manna account of chapter 16. In 17:3 the Israelites complained to Moses that by bringing them out of Egypt, he was killing them, their children, and their livestock. They were almost ready to stone him (v. 4). Therefore the Lord instructs him to now employ the same staff by which he had struck the Nile (7:14-24). Then He states in v. 6: "I will be standing there in front of you on the rock [צוּר - *ṣur* ; LXX πέτρα] at Horeb. Strike the rock [צוּר - *ṣur* ;[119] LXX πέτρα], and water will come out, so that the people may drink." The MT says Moses then did so "in the sight of the elders of Israel." However, the LXX already in the third century BCE[120] generalized this to "before [all] the Israelites."

Judaic comment on Exod 17:6 is of relevance to Christ as the rock in 1 Cor 10:4. The LXX also shows early interpretation of the beginning of this verse. It reads: "I here have taken My stand, before you [Moses] came, upon the rock [πέτρα] at Horeb."[121] The Tannaitic *Mek. R. Ish.* Vayassa 7 on this verse states: "In every place you find the mark of a man's feet, there I am before you [sing.]."[122] The term "mark" here is רָשׁוּם (*rashum*), "mark, trace."[123] David Nelson translates the similar tradition with the same noun in *Mekhilta de-Rabbi Shimon bar Yoḥai* ad loc. as follows: "He said to him [Moses], Anywhere you see human footprints - in accordance with what is said in Scripture, 'there was the semblance of a human form' (Ezek 1:26) - there I am standing before you."[124] *Targum Pseudo-Jonathan* on Exod 17:6 also has here "the track of a foot on the rock at Horeb."[125] *Tanḥ.* Beshallaḥ 22 on this verse reads: "The Holy One, blessed be He, said to him: Wherever you find the imprint of a man's foot, there I stand

---

upward," as well as the Levites (v. 47); see also 26:51. Philo describes this number in *Mos.* 1.147. See also Josephus, *Ant.* 2.317.

[119] Cf. BDB 849: rock, cliff.

[120] Cf. Otto Eissfeldt, *The Old Testament. An Introduction* (Oxford: Basil Blackwell, 1966) 604-05, 702.

[121] Cf. the English translation of NETS (*A New English Translation of the Septuagint*) 63, as well as the apparatus of Rahlf's edition of the Greek text.

[122] Cf. Lauterbach 2.133.

[123] Cf. Jastrow 1499, referring to רֹשֶׁם (*rōshem*) in 1464. It could also be translated by "sign."

[124] Cf. Nelson 183.

[125] Cf. Clarke 87; Eng. Maher 210.

before you. 'And you shall smite within the rock.' It does not say 'upon the rock' [עַל־הַצּוּר - *'al haṣur*], but 'within the rock' [בַּצּוּר - *bhaṣur*]. And there shall come water out of it so that the people may drink."[126] This very unusual rendering emphasizes one aspect of the Lord as physically present here with the mark of his foot / feet.

The foregoing is probably related to the rock here as signifying the well. *Exod. Rab.* Beshallaḥ 25/4 on Exod 16:4 relates that when the Israelites' provisions brought along from Egypt were used up after thirty-one days, they murmured, hungry for bread and water. Instead of complaining, they should have implored God's compassion. "Thus Scripture states: 'I said, Behold Me, behold Me to a nation that did not call on My name' (Isa 65:1). Why does it say 'Behold Me [הִנֵּנִי - *hinnēnî*]' twice? This is because of 'Behold Me' at the well, for it says, 'Behold [הנני - *hnny*], I will stand before you upon the rock in Horeb' (Exod 17:6)."[127] It is important to note that the well and the rock of Exod 17:6 are equated here, even if this individual tradition cannot be dated.[128]

Finally, *Targum Neofiti 1* reads here: "Behold, My Memra shall stand in readiness on the rock at Horeb...."[129] This circumlocution of the name "the Lord" is similar to Philo's Logos / Word. Both lent themselves to the possibility of considering a separate, special aspect of the Lord's being to also be present here, for Paul or Jewish Christians before him Christ, as in 1 Cor 10:4, "and the rock was Christ."

A biblical narrative parallel to Exod 17:1-7 is found in Num 20:2-13. There the Israelites complain to Moses that "this wretched place" is not one for "grain, or figs, or vines, or pomegranates; and there is no water to drink" (v. 5). Again, the Lord tells Moses to take the same staff, and before the (entire) congregation together with Aaron to "command the rock [סֶלַע - *sela'* ;[130] LXX πέτρα] before their eyes to yield its water. Thus you [sing.] shall provide drink for the congregation and their livestock" (v. 8). Verse 11 relates how Moses carried this out. He "lifted up his hand and struck the rock [סֶלַע - *sela'* ; LXX πέτρα] with his staff;

---

126 Cf. Eshkol 301; Eng. Berman 441.

127 Cf. Mirkin 5.278; Soncino 3.304. The Soncino translator, S. Lehrman, renders: "Behold, it was I at the well."

128 Against e.g. E. Earle Ellis, who falsely states regarding the well: "it is nowhere called a rock" (*Paul's Use of the Old Testament* 68).

129 Cf. Díez-Macho 2.113; Eng. McNamara 74.

130 Cf. BDB 700: crag, cliff, synonymous with צוּר (*ṣur*).

water came out abundantly, and the congregation and their livestock drank."

In the very next chapter, the Israelites again complain to Moses that they have neither food nor water, only "this miserable food" (manna, 21:5). Therefore the Lord sent poisonous serpents which bit them, causing many to die (v. 6). Paul alludes to this incident in 1 Cor 10:9 when he says: "We must not put Christ to the test, as some of them did, and were destroyed by serpents."[131]

The same chapter 21 in Numbers describes how the Israelites continued on to the site Beer (בְּאֵר [*be ʾēr*];[132] LXX τὸ φρέαρ[133]), which was "the well of which the Lord said to Moses, 'Gather [all] the people together, and I will give them water' (v. 16)."

17) "Then Israel sang this song:

> 'Spring up, O well [בְּאֵר - *be ʾēr*, LXX τὸ φρέαρ]! Sing to it! - 18) the well [בְּאֵר - *be ʾēr*, LXX φρέαρ] that the leaders sank, that the nobles of the people dug, with the scepter, with the staff.'"

Verses 18-20[134] then describe the further route of the Israelites in the wilderness, at the end by mentioning the top of Mt. Pisgah. It was opposite or east of Jericho and was the site where Moses died (Deut 34:1). For this reason a major Judaic tradition relates that the well ceased

---

[131] The antidote of a bronze serpent (Num 21:9) is in turn alluded to as the Son of Man's being lifted up (on the Cross) in John 3:14-15.

[132] Cf. BDB 91, 1: well.

[133] Cf. LSJ 1954: well. It can also mean a spring.

[134] It is incomprehensible to me how Germain Bienaimé can maintain the entire Judaic well / water tradition developed from the "very ancient" targums of a single verse, Num 21:19. Perhaps this is due to the influence of his doctoral advisor, Roger Le Déaut, an expert in the targums. See Bienaimé's *Moïse et le don de l'eau dans la tradition juive ancienne: targum et midrash* (AnBib 98; Rome: Biblical Institute Press, 1984) 177 (including *Pseudo-Philo* 11:15!) and 277, n. 15. Usually the targums develop earlier traditions further. Nor does Bienaimé apply other haggadic sources to 1 Cor 10:4 (276). However, his remark concerning "the aggadic tendency to telescope traditions on the gift of water," that is, to combine disparate passages, is very apt (46, n. 139).

functioning at this time.[135] It is thought to have accompanied the Israelites for the entire forty years in the wilderness.[136]

Another definitely pre-70 CE interpretation of the well is found in the Damascus Document (CD-A) of Qumran at 6:2-11.[137] "Men of knowledge from Aaron" and "wise men from Israel," certainly meant as the leaders of the Qumran sect, dug the well, for which Num 21:18 is cited. In 6:4 it is then maintained that "The well is the Torah." Those who dug it are "the converts of Israel, who left the land of Judah[138] and lived in the land of Damascus..." (v. 5). The staff of Num 21:18 is "the interpreter of the Torah" (v. 7), probably the Teacher of Righteousness. The members of the community will adhere to the scepter's staves (regulations) "throughout the [present] whole age of wickedness" ..."until there arises [v. 10] he who teaches righteousness at the end of days" (v. 11).

"He who teaches 'righteousness' [צדק - *ṣdq*]" here cannot be the Qumranites' spiritual leader, the Teacher of Righteousness, for he had already appeared. This figure is still future, he will arise "at the end of days." He is thus most probably the Messiah of Judaic tradition on Isa 11:1-5, described as judging with "righteousness" (v. 4), which righteousness is the belt around his waist (v. 5). A major support for this suggestion is 4Q Patriarchal Blessings (4Q252) 5:3-4 on Gen 49:10. It reads: "Until the Messiah of Righteousness [משיח הצדק - *mshyḥ hṣdq*] comes, the branch of David."[139]

The above Damascus Document passage shows that one section of pre-70 CE Judaism, the Qumran sect, also reinterpreted the well of Num 21:18, in other branches of Judaism considered to be the well that followed the Israelites in the wilderness for forty years. For them it was

---

[135] Cf. e.g. *Pseudo-Philo* 20:8 (*SC* 229.170; *OTP* 2.329) and the Tannaitic *Seder 'Olam* 10 (Guggenheimer 102-03).

[136] Cf. *Num. Rab.* Ḥuqqat 19/25 on Num 21:17 (Mirkin 10.238, with parallels in n. 1; Soncino 6.773).

[137] The settlement was destroyed by the Romans sometime at the end of the Jewish-Roman War of 66-70. For the Hebrew text and an English translation, cf. Martínez and Tigchelaar, *The Dead Sea Scrolls Study Edition* 1.559. Joseph Fitzmyer says 6:2b - 7:9 deals with "The Community of the New Covenant." See his *A Guide to the Dead Sea Scrolls and Related Literature* 189. The "new covenant" is mentioned in 6:19.

[138] Jerusalem with its Temple, rejected by the Qumranites, is meant here. Cf. 6:11-12, "But all those who have been brought into the covenant shall not enter the Temple to kindle the altar in vain."

[139] Cf. Martínez and Tigchelaar 1.504-05.

the Torah - as defined by their Teacher of Righteousness. Yet this for them in the age of wickedness, the last days, was only preliminary. Its fulfillment will be found in the Messiah of Righteousness, who will arise at the end of days. Paul too believed "the end(s) of the ages" had arrived (1 Cor 10:11; 1:7-8; 7:26, 29-31). Yet for him the Messiah, the Christ, had already appeared. Indeed, he was also the rock / the well which accompanied the Israelites in the wilderness (10:4).

One tradition relates the "singing" of Num 21:17 to Miriam's "singing" in Exod 15:21 after passing through the Red Sea. Therefore the well was often labeled Miriam's well.[140] A variant of this tradition maintains that it continued on from Pisgah to Lake Tiberias, where it can still be sighted at times in the middle of the water.[141]

Already in the Bible the two rock narratives of Exod 17:1-7 and Num 20:2-13 appear to have later been combined. In Nehemiah 9 the pillar of cloud is mentioned in v. 12. Verse 15 continues: "For their hunger You gave them bread from heaven, and for their thirst You brought water for them out of the rock [סֶלַע - *sela* ‘; πέτρα in 2 Esdras 19:15]." After again mentioning the pillar of cloud in v. 19, Ezra says of the Lord in v. 20: "You did not withhold Your manna from their mouths, and gave them water for their thirst." Isa 48:21 has the Lord say: "They did not thirst when He led them through the deserts; He made water flow for them from the rock [צוּר - *ṣur;* LXX πέτρα]; He split open the rock [צוּר - *ṣur;* LXX πέτρα], and the water gushed out." Psalm 78 remarks on the Lord's dividing the Sea in v. 13, and His leading the Israelites with a cloud in v. 14. Verses 15-16 continue: "He split rocks open in the wilderness, and gave them drink abundantly, as from the deep. 16) He made streams come out of the rock [סֶלַע - *sela* ‘; LXX πέτρα], and caused waters to flow down like rivers." In v. 20 the Israelites are represented as asking: "Even though He struck the rock [צוּר - *ṣur;* LXX πέτρα] so that water gushed out, and torrents overflowed, can He also give bread...?" Finally, Psalm 105 mentions a cloud and food from heaven in vv. 39-40. Verse 41

---

[140] Cf. for example *Num. Rab.* Bemidbar 1/2 on Num 1:1 (Mirkin 9.11; Soncino 5.3-4).

[141] Cf. e.g. *Lev. Rab.* Aḥare Moth 22/4 on Lev 17:3 (Mirkin 8.37; Soncino 4.283). There the second generation Tanna R. Yoḥanan b. Nuri (*Introduction* 80) says the rabbis maintain it is "directly opposite the middle gate of the ancient synagogue of Tiberias." Parallels are found in n. 1 of Mirkin.

continues: "He opened the rock [צוּר - *ṣur;* LXX πέτρα], and water gushed out; it flowed through the desert like a river."[142]

In the above biblical accounts the rock can thus be labeled either צוּר (*ṣur*) or סֶלַע (*sela* ʿ); they are synonyms. The LXX always translates them by πέτρα, as in 1 Cor 10:4. Secondly, it is always the Lord who splits / makes water come out of the rock.[143] Since "the Lord" in these passages is always ὁ κύριος in the LXX, this may have been a bridge for Hellenistic Jewish Christians to associate "the Lord" as Christ with the rock. Indeed, Exod 17:6 boldly states that "the Lord" was standing upon the rock (with Moses).

In *Mos.* 1.210, Philo describes the situation of Exod 17:1-7 and Num 20:2-13 with the words: "a serious scarcity of water again occurred." At this point Moses "smote the steep rock [τὴν ἀκρότομον πέτραν] with [his staff]." It then provided an "abundance of drink 'for a longer time' [πρὸς πλείω χρόνον] for all these thousands." While he also mentions the well narrative of Num 21:16-18 in 1.255-56, the notice "for a longer time" in 1.211 probably is an echo of the rock / well haggadah of early Judaism.

The passages *Leg. All.* 2.86 and *Det.* 115 in Philo have been regularly cited by commentators on 1 Cor 10:4. They are connected to Wisdom of Solomon 11. There v. 4 states: "When [the Israelites] were thirsty, they called upon you [wisdom], and water was given them out of flinty rock, and from hard stone a remedy for their thirst."[144] In *Leg. All.* 2.86 Philo flatly states of the thirst of the Israelites' soul: "For the flinty rock is the wisdom of God, which He marked off highest and chiefest from His powers, and from which He satisfies the thirsty souls that love God."[145]

---

[142] Such imagery is later used to describe the water of the well. Cf. also Ps 114:8.

[143] Moses may be in the foreground, but emphasis is placed on the divine activity.

[144] This was "abundant water" given by wisdom to them "unexpectedly" (v. 7) in rebuke for the action of Exod 1:22. Cf. already Johannes Weiss, *Der erste Korintherbrief* (Meyers; Göttingen: Vandenhoeck & Ruprecht, 1910⁹ / 1970) 251. In the section "La Perigrination des Hebreux a Travers le Desert et le Christ Rocher (1 Co 10,1-5)" in his *Christologie Paulinienne et Tradition Biblique* (Paris: Desclée De Brouver, 1973) 11-22, André Feuillet emphasizes these Philo passages as well as Wisd 11:4 (pp. 17-18). He rejects any relevance of the water in rabbinic sources which followed the Hebrews in the wilderness (20), which he only knows from others in translated form (72-73, n. 14).

[145] Andrew Minto in "1 Corinthians 10:1-13 : Paul's Interpretation of Exodus and Desert Wandering Narratives and the Divine Pedagogy" in *Fides Quaerens Intellectum* 2 (2003) 199 overconfidently states: "The claim 'the rock was the

He then mentions manna, and that "the Word of God" (ὁ θεοῦ λόγος) is second to God. In *Det.* 115 Philo interprets the term "rock" (πέτρα) of LXX Deut 32:13 to mean "the solid and indestructible wisdom of God, which feeds and nurses and rears to sturdiness all who yearn after imperishable sustenance."

The Alexandrian philosopher as usual allegorizes in these passages. Yet they do show how the "rock" of the scriptural texts analyzed above could be thought of in Hellenistic Judaism as being very closely associated with God, indeed, as the wisdom which represented Him. However, this does not clearly explain how Paul could state that Christ was the rock of 1 Cor 10:4. Josephus and Palestinian Judaic comment on the rock / well motif lead one further in this regard.

After describing God's gift of manna for forty years in *Ant.* 3.26-32, Josephus in 33-38 relates the contents of Exod 17:1-7. The Israelites were "in extreme agony from thirst," "now being in an absolutely waterless region" (33). When Moses beseeched God to give them something to drink, He promised "that He would provide a spring / well [πηγή][146] with abundance of water where they did not look for it. He then bade him strike with his staff the rock [πέτρα] which stood there before their eyes, and from it accept a plenteous draught of what they needed" (35). Moses then informed the people that "a river was to flow for them out of the rock [πέτρα]" (36). At this time Moses "struck it with his staff, whereupon it opened, and there gushed out a copious stream of extremely clear water" (37). The latter was a marvel, being "sweet and pleasant" (38). All of these are haggadic details known to this native of Jerusalem and do not appear to derive from his own pen. Of priestly lineage, Josephus adds at this point another interesting detail: "A writing deposited in the [Jerusalem] Temple attests that God foretold to Moses that water would spring forth from the rock [πέτρα]." H. St. John Thackeray in a note on this passage surmises this is a part of a "collection of chants made for the use of the temple singers, and that the allusion here is to the little song to the well in Num xxi.16ff."[147] He is probably

---

Christ' makes a clear literary allusion to personified Wisdom...." Unfortunately he does not consider *Pseudo-Philo* and early rabbinic materials.

146 Cf. n. 133 on the other Greek term φρέαρ as meaning both well and "spring." Josephus probably has the Aramaic בְּאֵרָא (*be ʾēra ʾ*) in mind: well, spring (Jastrow 136).

147 Cf. his n. "a" in the LCL edition, 4.336-37, referring to his book on Josephus. The Jewish historian intentionally omits a description of this well in 4.86.

right, which would attest the close connection of Exod 17:1-7 and the well narrative of Num 21:16-18 *before* the destruction of the Temple in 70 CE.

Other Palestinian Judaic comment supplements the above. Originally written in Hebrew in Palestine in the first century CE, *Pseudo-Philo* mentions "a well of water" which the Lord made to follow the Israelites in the wilderness. It is found between bread from heaven (Exod 16:4) and a pillar of cloud (Exod 13:21) in 10:7. In 11:15 "it followed them in the wilderness for forty years and went up the mountain with them and went down into the plains."[148] According to *m. ʾAvot* 5:6, along with manna the mouth of the well was one of the ten things created on the eve of the first Sabbath at twilight.[149] Quoting Num 21:18 and 20, *t. Soṭah* 4:2 states that the Lord graciously gave the Israelites "a well in the wilderness, which gushed through the whole camp of Israel" and "went over the whole south and watered the entire desert."[150] According to *t. Sukk.* 3:11 the well camped with the Israelites "opposite the door of the Tent of Meeting." When the water bubbled forth and ascended, it went up "like a pillar on high," and each of the twelve princes drew water for his tribe and his family. In its mighty streams people sat in small boats and visited one another, as Ps 78:20 and 105:41 are interpreted. All the desirable things of the world were derived from it, as indicated in Deut 2:7, "you lacked nothing."[151] *Num. Rab.* Ḥuqqat 19/25 on Num 21:17 notes on the basis of Ps 23:2 that the well "caused numerous varieties of grass and trees to spring forth."[152] Num 20:5 is interpreted to mean that the well also produced various kinds of herbs and vegetables, in addition

---

[148] Cf. *SC* 229.118 and 124, and *OTP* 2.317 and 319, respectively. The Latin terms for "following" probably translate ἀκολουθέω, which as indicated above can simply mean "to accompany." The Hebrew would have been "to go with." The well, which God gave His people on account of Miriam, was then taken away at the death of Moses (20:8 in *SC* 229.170; *OTP* 2.329).

[149] Cf. Albeck 4.376; Danby 456; Neusner 686. It is the only occurrence of "the" well in the Mishnah.

[150] Cf. Zuckermandel / Liebermann 298; Eng. Neusner 3.160.

[151] Cf. 3:11-13 in Zuckermandel / Liebermann 197; Eng. Neusner 2.220-21.

[152] Cf. Mirkin 10.238; Soncino 6.776. On a woman's traveling by boat from the house of her father to that of her husband, see also *Midr. Pss.* 5/1, dealing with Num 21:19 (Buber 50; Braude 1.81). It also interprets Ps 105:41, together with Isa 33:21.

to wine for drink-offerings.[153] Finally, the well even provided fat fish for the Israelites in the middle of the wilderness.[154]

One aspect of the rock / water narrative may also have partially influenced Paul's five-fold emphasis on the term "all" in 1 Cor 10:1-4. Num 20:10 says that before Moses struck the rock and water came out of it abundantly, "Moses and Aaron gathered the [whole] assembly together before the rock" and addressed them. *Num. Rab.* Ḥuqqat 19/9 on this verse states: "This teaches that 'each and every one' [כָּל אֶחָד וְאֶחָד - *kol 'eḥad we 'eḥad*] viewed himself as standing before the rock [סֶלַע - *sela ʿ*]. In the same strain it says, 'And assemble the whole [כָּל - *kol*] congregation at the entrance of the tent of meeting' (Lev 8:3). And also when they crossed the Jordan, all [כָּל - *kol*] Israel entered into the space between the two staves of the ark.... In the present instance also all [כָּל - *kol*] Israel stood there and saw all [כָּל - *kol*] the miracles in connection with the rock [סֶלַע - *sela ʿ*]."[155] Here within only a few sentences there is a five-fold emphasis on "all." Well over 600,000 Israelites could not possibly have stood together before the one rock of Num 20:10, from which water then came out abundantly, yet haggadic exaggeration describes it so. Although Paul means "all" the over 600,000 Israelites were under the cloud, etc., in 1 Cor 10:1-4, his five-fold emphasis on "all" is also haggadic exaggeration. It is found nowhere in the relevant scriptural texts.

Another aspect of the rock / water narrative may be relevant to Paul's statement that all the Israelites were baptized into Moses in the cloud and in the Sea (1 Cor 10:2). This is because the well was thought retrospectively, that is, from the very outset, to have accompanied the Israelites for forty years in the wilderness. In *Mek. R. Ish.* Beshallaḥ 5 on Exod 14:19 with the angel of God and the pillar of cloud, R. Judah (b. Ilai, a third generation Tanna,)[156] illustrated this biblical verse by means of the parable of a man walking on the road with his son before him, and the father protecting him from various dangers. So it was with God and Ephraim (the Israelites) in the wilderness. God spread a cloud over him (Ps 105:39), gave him bread from heaven (Exod 16:4), and gave him water

---

153 This is in addition to trees. Cf. *Cant. Rab.* 4:12 § 3 (Dunski 123; Soncino 9.223).

154 Cf. the Tannaitic *Sifre* Beha ʿalotekha 95 on Num 11:22 (Horovitz 95; Eng. Neusner 2.105).

155 Cf. Mirkin 10.228; Soncino 6.758.

156 Cf. *Introduction* 84.

to drink, as it is said: "'He brought streams also out of the rock' (Ps 78:16). And 'streams' here can only mean living waters [מים חיים - *mym ḥyym*], as it is said: 'A fountain of gardens, a well of living waters [מַיִם חַיִּים - *mayim ḥayyîm*], and flowing streams,' etc. (Cant 4:15). And it also says: 'Drink water out of your own cistern, and running waters out of your own well' (Prov 5:15)."[157]

The following account is noteworthy in regard to such "living waters" and baptism / immersion. In *b. Shab.* 35a, R. Ḥiyya (the Elder), a fifth generation Tanna who taught in Tiberias,[158] first comments on the location of Miriam's well in the Sea (of Tiberias). His nephew and pupil Rab[159] then maintained: "A moveable well is clean [טָהוֹר - *ṭahōr*],[160] and that is Miriam's well."[161] The Soncino translator, I. Epstein, remarks at this point: "Its water cannot become unclean and it is fit for ritual purification (*ṭebillah*)."[162]

It should be noted on the basis of the above passages that the rock / well in the wilderness produced streams of "living waters." These were necessary for a proselyte's ritual immersion (often falsely labeled "baptism").[163] Although this connection could seem far-fetched to

---

[157] Cf. Lauterbach 1.224-25. A parallel is found in *Mek. R. Shim. b. Yoḥ.* Beshallaḥ on the same verse (Nelson 104), with R. Judah and "They told a parable. What does the matter resemble?" For the well as accompanying the Israelites for all the forty years in the wilderness, see also the early *Pseudo-Philo* 11:15 (n. 148) and the sources cited in n. 136.

[158] Cf. *Introduction* 90.

[159] He was a first generation Babylonian Amora who also studied under Rabbi in Palestine (*Introduction* 93).

[160] Cf. Jastrow 520: clean, pure; not subject to levitical uncleanness.

[161] Cf. Soncino 164.

[162] Cf. p. 164, n. 5. On טָבַל (*ṭabhal*) as to immerse, to bathe for purification, see Jastrow 517, 2). The noun טְבִילָה (*ṭebhîlah*) is thus immersion, purification (516-17). The well of Miriam in the middle of Lake Tiberias was also thought to cure people of maladies. A man is cured of his blindness when he bathes there in *Num. Rab.* Koraḥ 18/22 on Num 16:25 (Mirkin 10.214; Soncino 6.742). Another bathes there and is cured of his boils in *Lev. Rab.* Aḥare Moth 22/4 on Lev 17:3 (Mirkin 8.37; Soncino 4.282, with a parallel in *Eccl. Rab.* 5:8-9 § 5 in Soncino 8.143-44).

[163] Cf. the art. "Proselytes" in *EJ* (2007) 16.587-90 for the general theme, and *m. Miq.* 1:8 for "living waters" and 5:5 for "flowing waters" (Albeck 6.343 and 354; Danby 733 and 738; Neusner 1060 and 1067) in regard to the immersion pool. See also *Sib. Or.* 4.165 (*OTP* 1.388, and n. "e2"): "wash your whole bodies in perennial

modern ears, it may have been a minor influence upon the Jew Paul's thought that all the Israelites were "baptized" into Moses in the cloud and the Sea (1 Cor 10:2), for they all drank from the same spiritual drink (v. 4). This water came from the rock / well of Judaic tradition, and it was "living water" suitable for proselyte immersion and Christian baptism.[164]

---

rivers." Reference from Albrecht Oepke, art. βάπτω etc. in *TDNT* 1.535. See also Did 7:1 for Christian baptism with "living / running water" (ὕδωρ ζῶν). It is presupposed, for example, in Acts 16:13 and 15.

[164] R. Joshua (b. Ḥananyah), a second generation Tanna of the older group (*Introduction* 77), maintains in *b. Yebam.* 46a (Soncino 303) that a proselyte to Judaism does not have to be circumcised; he is only required to undergo a ritual ablution (immersion). He also claims that "in the case of the forefathers ritual ablution was performed." He bases this on Exod 24:8, where Moses sprinkles the blood of oxen on the people, calling it "the blood of the covenant." The Talmud adds at this point: "and we have a tradition that there must be no sprinkling without ritual ablution" (46b in Soncino 304). In the parallel passage in *b. Ker.* 9a (Soncino 67), circumcision is indicated by Ezek 16:6, and the sprinkling of the blood is also noted from Exod 24:5. It adds: "and there can be no sprinkling without immersion" (regarding proselytes before the loss of the Temple in 70 CE). Joachim Jeremias in "Der Ursprung der Johannestaufe" in *ZNW* 28 (1929) 312-20 deals with these passages in connection with 1 Cor 10:2 (317-18). He maintains on the basis of Num 15:14 that proselyte "baptism" (immersion) presupposes "a rabbinic theologumenon which by chance has not been preserved elsewhere" (318). Paul as a Hillelite ostensibly learned this from Gamaliel (319). Jeremias' proposal unfortunately remains quite theoretical. The following appears to be of greater relevance concerning this topic.

In Exod 19:10 the Lord tells Moses regarding the Israelites before the Mount Sinai event: "consecrate / sanctify them today and tomorrow. Have them wash their clothes." The verb "to wash" here is כָּבַס (*kabhas*), frequently synonymous with רחץ - *rḥṣ* (BDB 460). *Mek. R. Ish.* Bahodesh 3 on "and sanctify them" states: "He summoned them, and they washed their garments 'and purified themselves' (והטהרו - *whṭhrw*)" (Lauterbach 2.216). Rabbi (Judah the Prince, a fourth generation Tanna: *Introduction* 89,) then comments that this did not just mean the requirement of immersion (טבילה - *ṭbhylh*). *Eliyyahu Rabbah* (15) 16 (Friedmann 72; Braude and Kapstein 202) also deals with the above Exodus verse at the time Israel was in the wilderness. It says the Sages taught: "'And sanctify them' means [immerse them] in the ritual bath [בטבילה - *bṭbhylh*]." Exod 19:10 was considered to be a possible biblical basis for proselyte immersion in the discussion noted above in *b. Yebam.* 46b (Soncino 304). Yet it can hardly be alluded to by Paul in 1 Cor 10:2 because the cloud and the Sea are then mentioned there. John Lightfoot had called attention (only) to Exod 19:10 in this regard in his *Horae Hebraicae et Talmudicae,* published between 1658 and 1674 in

The major background to the water involved in the process of baptizing in 1 Cor 10:2, however, derives from Judaic tradition on Ezek 16:9 (see section 7. below).

The well could also be associated with the Messiah, although in the future. Eccl 1:9 reads, "What has been is what will be, and what has been is what will be done; there is nothing new under the sun." Judaic sources often state that as the first redeemer (Moses) was, so shall the latter Redeemer (the Messiah) be.[165] In *Eccl. Rab.* 1:9 § 1, R. Isaac (II Nappaḥa, a prolific haggadist and third generation Palestinian Amora,)[166] said: "As the first redeemer was, so shall the latter Redeemer be." Just as Moses set his wife and sons on a donkey (Exod 4:20), so the latter Redeemer will employ a donkey (Zech 9:9). Just as Moses caused manna to descend (Exod 16:4), so the latter Redeemer will do, as Ps 72:16 is interpreted. "As the former redeemer made a well to rise, so will the latter Redeemer bring up water," based on Joel 4:18.[167]

This is an Amoraic tradition dealing with the future activity of the Messiah in regard to manna and the well. It cannot be shown that in an earlier form it may have been known to the Apostle Paul. Nevertheless, it indicates how he himself may have associated the Messiah not only with manna, but also with the well. For him Christ, the Messiah, was the rock / well, not only of the end time in which he now found himself, but already at the time of the exodus and the wilderness wandering.[168]

Finally, an early allusion to Christ as the rock of 1 Cor 10:4[169] is found in Justin Martyr, who was born in Flavia Neapolis in Samaria and was martyred within the reign of Marcus Aurelius (d. before 180 CE).[170] He

---

Latin, in English in 1859. See now *A Commentary on the New Testament from the Talmud and Hebraica. Matthew - 1 Corinthians* (Peabody, MA: Hendrickson, 1989) 4.223.

165 Cf. the examples cited in Str-B 1.68-70, including this one.

166 Cf. *Introduction* 98; he was a student of R. Yoḥanan and was active both in Tiberias and Caesarea.

167 Cf. Vilna, Eccl. 4b; Soncino 8.33.

168 At least since Heinrich Meyer's 1849 *Erster Brief an die Korinther* 203, it has been falsely maintained that *Targ.* Isa 16:1 expressed the protective presence of the Messiah in the wilderness. Yet there the Messiah "prevailed over him who was *like* a wilderness" (Stenning, *The Targum of Isaiah* 52-53).

169 Is Jesus possibly also meant as the rock in the difficult passage John 7:38, where "rivers of living water will flow from his belly / heart"? See Wolff, *Der erste Brief des Paulus an die Korinther* 2.42.

170 Cf. L. Barnard, *Justin Martyr* (Cambridge: Cambridge University Press, 1967) 5.

writes in the "Dialogue with Trypho" 114: "And our hearts are circumcised from evil, so that we are happy to die for the name of the good Rock [πέτρα], which causes living water [ζῶν ὕδωρ] to burst forth for the hearts of those who by him have loved the Father of all, and which gives those who are willing to drink of the waters of life."[171] This is one of the rare allusions to 1 Cor 10:4 in the early church.

The Shape of the Rock / Well

A number of Judaic sources describe the shape of the rock / well. The Tannaitic *t. Sukk.* 3:11 states that the well "resembled a rock [סֶלַע - *sela* ʿ], the size of a large round vessel, surging and gurgling upward."[172] The "large round vessel" here is כְּבָרָה (*kebharah*).[173] *Num. Rab.* Bemidbar 1/2 on Num 1:1 asks how the well was constructed. "It was a rock [סֶלַע - *sela* ʿ] the shape of a large round vessel, and whenever they journeyed it rolled along and came with them."[174] The term "a large round vessel" here is כְּוֶורֶת (*kewewret*).[175] If one ascends Mount Carmel and gazes (eastward), one observes something "like 'a large round vessel' [כְּבָרָה - *kebharah*] in the Sea (of Tiberias). It is Miriam's Well."[176] A different comparison is found in *Num. Rab.* Ḥuqqat 19/26 on Num 21:20 regarding the well, which then entered the Sea of Tiberias. From the

---

[171] Cf. *Iustini Martyris, Dialogus cum Tryphone*, ed. Miroslav Marcovich 267, and the English of *The Ante-Nicene Fathers* 1.256.

[172] Cf. Zuckermandel / Liebermann 196; as well as Lieberman, *The Tosefta. The Order of Mo ʿed* 268; Eng. Neusner 2.220, who misleadingly translates "was a rock...."

[173] Cf. Jastrow 609. A second possible meaning is "*a basket* used as a *sieve*," inappropriate here. It has led some translators to falsely translate with "sieve."

[174] Cf. Mirkin 9.12; Soncino 5.5 falsely has "It was rock-shaped like a bee-hive." A parallel is found in *Tanḥ.* B Bemidbar 2 on the same verse (Buber 3, which omits the term "large round vessel"; see his n. 21; Eng. Townsend 3).

[175] Cf. Jastrow 617, 1). Only with the addition of דְּבוֹרִים (*debhōrîm*: Jastrow 276 on דְּבוֹרָה [*debhōrah*]) could it mean bee-hive.

[176] Cf. *b. Shab.* 35a (Soncino 164 falsely has "a kind of sieve"). *Lev. Rab.* Aḥare Moth 22/3 on Lev 17:3 (Mirkin 8.37; Soncino 4.283) has this as seen from the top of Mount Yeshimon (Num 21:20) and adds that it is a "small" round vessel.

desert, Yeshimōn, one sees in the middle of the Sea something as large as an "oven."[177]

In the above Judaic sources the well is again identified with the rock, as in the haggadic tradition on Exod 17:6 related above. Its shape is basically described as that of a large round vessel. This made it easier, for example, for those listening to a synagogue sermon or a lecture in the study house to imagine what the rabbi / teacher was talking about. It also aids modern readers of 1 Cor 10:4 to imagine what the "rock" there may have looked like.

An actual depiction of the wilderness well is found as a wall painting in the Dura Europos synagogue, finished shortly before the building's destruction in 256 CE. It lies on the Euphrates River in eastern Syria. It shows Moses striking the rock / well with the staff in his right hand, with twelve streams of water flowing off to the tents of the twelve Israelite tribes, six to the right and six to the left, with a tribal leader before each tent.[178]

* * *

Sections 1.-4. above described the motifs of the passage through the Red Sea, the (pillar of) cloud, manna, and water from the rock / well as found in biblical and Judaic tradition in relation to their relevance to 1 Cor 10:1-4. Before making the concrete proposal of the "washing" of Ezek 16:9 as the background of the Israelites' being "baptized" into Moses in the cloud and the Sea in 1 Cor 10:2 in section 7., I shall now prepare this suggestion be demonstrating how Ezek 16:9 was used for "washing" in three different midrashim (5.1-3), the last being most relevant to 1 Cor

---

[177] Cf. Mirkin 10.241; Soncino 6.777. See Jastrow 1680 on תַּנּוּר (*tannur*) as "oven." *Tanḥ.* B Ḥuqqat 50 on Num 21:18 has it as "about the size of the mouth of an oven" (Buber 128; Eng. Townsend 198). A parallel is found in *Tanḥ.* Ḥuqqat 21 (Eshkol 781). This may have been influenced by the tradition found in *m. ʾAvot* 5:6 regarding the "mouth" of the well as one of the ten things created on the eve of the first Sabbath at twilight. See n. 149.

[178] Cf. the reproduction in Erwin Goodenough, *Jewish Symbols in the Greco-Roman Period*, Abridged Edition, ed. Jacob Neusner 279. It is number 47, now found in the Yale University Art Gallery's Dura-Europos Collection. On it, see pp. 254-56. Goodenough labels it "the Well of the Wilderness" and maintains the twelve tribes represent the zodiac, which I consider doubtful here. The painting is also reproduced in Bienaimé, *Moïse et le don de l'eau* after p. 208, and is described on pp. 207-09. Its contents recall *t. Sukk.* 3:11 cited above.

10:2. In regard to the idolatry of 1 Corinthians 10, I then point out the Israelites' idolatry in Egypt and the wilderness in Judaic tradition, including an analysis of this motif both in Ezekiel 16 and its Targum (6. 1-4).

5. *Three Examples of the Use of Ezek 16:9 in Judaic Midrash*

5.1 *The Angels' Rewarding Abraham for his Hospitality in Genesis 18*

Gen 18:1-15 relates that the Lord appeared to Abraham "as he sat at the entrance of his tent in the heat of the day" (v. 1) in the form of three men (angels)[179] - v. 2. The reward for his positive behavior towards them is described in a very appealing midrash, which relates how his children, the Israelites, were later thereby benefited in the wilderness. These benefits include the motifs mentioned by Paul in 1 Cor 10:1-4.

In *m. Soṭah* 1:7 the principle is enunciated: "With what measure [מִדָּה - *middah*][180] a man metes, it shall be measured to him again."[181] Negative examples of the adulteress, Samson and Absalom are then cited in 1:8, and positive examples of Miriam, Joseph and Moses in 1:9. The Tannaitic Tosefta at *Soṭah* 4:1 notes that "the measure of goodness is five hundred times greater than the measure of retribution," and it then cites the case of Abraham in Genesis 18 for this. Because Abraham said, "Let a little water be brought" (18:4), God graciously gave his children a well producing water in the wilderness (Num 21:8). Because Abraham said "And rest yourselves under the tree" (Gen 18:4), God gave his children seven clouds in the wilderness, including the pillar of cloud which went before them (Exod 13:21). Because Abraham said "While I fetch a morsel of bread that you may refresh yourselves" (Gen 18:5), God gave his children manna in the wilderness (Num 11:8). Because it is said of

---

179 In *b. Yoma* 37a (Soncino 172), the three angels are Michael in the middle, Gabriel to his right, and Raphael to his left. See also *Derek ʾEreṣ Rabbah* 4:2 (*The Minor Tractates of the Talmud* 546), and *b. B. Meṣ.* 86a (Soncino 500).

180 Cf. Jastrow 732.

181 Cf. Albeck 3.235; Eng. Danby here, 294; Neusner 449.

Abraham, "And Abraham ran to the herd and took a calf, tender and good" (Gen 18:7), God rained down quail "from the Sea," for which Num 11:31 with quails "from the [Red] Sea" is quoted.[182] It is noteworthy that all of these are related to the time of the wilderness wandering.

Here five of the motifs (without the quail) Paul employs in 1 Cor 10:1-5 are mentioned together: the Sea, the cloud, water from the well / rock (spiritual drink), manna (spiritual food), and the wilderness. Other versions of this early midrash include the above as well as Ezek 16:9 as a proof text.

Gen. Rab. Vayyera 48/10 is a variant of the above midrash on Gen 18:1-15. It has Abraham's statement "Let now a little water be fetched" (v. 4) rewarded in the wilderness by the water of the well of Num 21:17. As a reward for Abraham's saying "And I will fetch a morsel of bread" (Gen 18:5), God promises to repay his children in the wilderness with bread from heaven (Exod 16:4). Quail "from the [Red] Sea" with Num 11:31 is also found here. As a reward for Abraham's "standing" [עֹמֵד - *ōmed*] by the angels under the tree while they ate in Gen 18:8, God repaid his children in the wilderness with Exod 13:21, "The Lord went in front of them in a pillar [עַמּוּד - *ʿammud*] of cloud by day."

Important for the motif of being baptized (with water at the Sea in 1 Cor 10:2, to be commented on in section 7. below,) is another way God repaid Abraham for his very hospitable behavior. He says to the Patriarch: "You said, '[Let a little water be brought,] and wash your feet' (Gen 18:4). I swear to you that I will repay your children. 'Then I washed you in water' (Ezek 16:9) refers to the wilderness."[183] This verse from Ezekiel is also cited for the same reason in the parallel traditions of *Exod. Rab.* Beshallaḥ 25/5 on Exod 16:4, "bread from heaven" / manna;[184] *Num. Rab.* Naso 14/2 on Num 7:48, which refers this to the time "when they went out of Egypt";[185] and *Eccl. Rab.* 11:1 § 1.[186]

---

[182] Cf. Zuckermandel / Liebermann 298-99; Eng. Neusner 3.160-61.

[183] Cf. Theodor and Albeck 487-88; Soncino 1.411-12. They cite parallel traditions in their note on line one of p. 487.

[184] Cf. Mirkin 5.278; Soncino 3.305, where "His children" should be "his [Abraham's] children."

[185] Cf. Mirkin 10.91; Soncino 6.569.

[186] Cf. Vilna 56; Soncino 8.288. The popularity of this midrash is shown in its being found in *Mek. R. Ish.* Beshallaḥ 1 on Exod 13:21 with the pillar of cloud, including the well of Num 21:17 (Lauterbach 1.184-85); *b. B. Meṣ.* 86b from "the School of Ishmael" (Soncino 498-99; it connects Abraham's "standing" in Gen 18:8

The above midrash on God's repaying Abraham for his very positive behavior towards the three angels in Genesis 18 when his children, the Israelites, later left Egypt and were in the wilderness, is definitely Tannaitic. This is shown in *t. Soṭah* 4:4, where R. Aqiba, a second generation Tanna, and R. Eleazar b. R. Yose the Galilean, a third generation Tanna,[187] contribute to the midrash. R. Meir, another third generation Tanna, also does so in the isolated fragment of it found in *Mek. R. Shim. b. Yoḥ.* Beshallaḥ on Exod 13:21.[188] The Apostle Paul could very well have known of it in an earlier form, for he conflates and slightly alters LXX Gen 18:10 and 14 when citing them in Rom 9:9.[189] Two other occurrences of Ezek 16:9 in Judaic sources are also important in regard to being baptized in 1 Cor 10:2.

with the Lord's "standing" before Moses at the rock of Exod 17:6, resulting in the flow of water, and the water of Gen 18:4 with water coming out of the rock in the same Exodus verse, as well as Miriam's well); *Lev. Rab.* Behar 34/8 on Lev 25:25 (Mirkin 8.164; Soncino 4.432-33 with the well); *Tanḥ.* Vayyera 4 on Gen 18:1 (Eshkol 75; Berman 117-18; it applies the phrases of Genesis 18 to the precept of the paschal lamb and the sukkah); *Tanḥ.* B Vayyera 5 on Gen 18:2-4, with the well of Num 21:17 (Buber 86-87; Eng. Townsend 92-93); *Pesiq. R.* 14/3 on Num 19:2 (Friedmann 57a; Eng. Braude 1.264-65, partly applied to the ritual of the Red Heifer); and *Eliyyahu Rabbah* (12) 13 (Friedmann 59-60; Eng. Braude and Kapstein 176-78).

187 Cf. *Introduction* 79 and 85, respectively.

188 Cf. Nelson 87, and *Introduction* 84. It may also be noted that in the "Testament of Abraham" A, Abraham is represented as himself "washing" the feet of the Commander-in-chief (the archangel) Michael in 3:7-9 and 6:6 (together with those of the other two angels; see *OTP* 1.183 and 185). This was written in Semitizing Greek in Egypt, perhaps Alexandria, probably in the first century CE, at the latest in 117 CE. See Dale Allison, Jr., *Testament of Abraham* 16 and 32-38, as well as George Nickelsburg, *Jewish Literature* 326-27, and E. P. Sanders in *OTP* 1.873-76. It thus shows very early haggadic development of the Genesis 18 narrative in Hellenistic Judaism.

189 Cf. e.g. Robert Jewett, *Romans* (Hermeneia; Minneapolis, MN: Fortress Press, 2007) 577.

5.2 *God's Unusual Behavior Towards the Israelites in the Wilderness*

Exod. Rab. Beshallaḥ 20/11 deals with Exod 13:17, interpreting "not by the way of the land" as "in an unusual manner" regarding God's leading the Israelites in the wilderness:

> God did not conduct Himself with them in the usual manner. Usually when one purchases servants / slaves, it is on the understanding that they wash and anoint him, help to dress him, draw his carriage, and light the way before him. God, however, did not do so, for He did not lead them in the usual way, but He washed them,[190] as it says: "Then I washed you with water" (Ezek 16:9). He anointed them, for it says: "And I anointed you with oil" (ibid.). He clothed them, for it says: "I clothed you also with richly woven work" (v. 10). He bore them, for it says: "And how I bore you on eagles' wings" (Exod 19:4). He illuminated the way before them, as it says: "And the Lord went before them by day in a pillar of cloud ... and in a pillar of fire by night to give them light" (13:21). For this reason it says: 13:17.[191]

A parallel tradition in *Exod. Rab.* Beshallaḥ 25/6 relates this in reference to Exod 16:4, bread from heaven / manna. It applies it to a disciple and his teacher, and to a slave and his master. In addition to the washing of Ezek 16:9 and the clothing / dressing of v. 10, it mentions the slave's putting on his master's shoes, as v. 10 is interpreted: "And shod you with sealskin." Water from the well of Num 21:17 is also noted.[192]

The various Judaic traditions cited above associate the washing of Ezek 16:9 with the motifs of the cloud, water from the well, and manna, all alluded to in 1 Cor 10:1-5.

---

[190] *Tanḥ.* B Beshallaḥ 10 on Exod 13:17 has the interesting variant: God washed "us," with Ezek 16:9 (Buber 58; Eng. Townsend 80-91). Cf. Paul's usage of "our" fathers / ancestors in 1 Cor 10:1.

[191] Cf. Mirkin 5.239; Soncino 3.252, with n. 1. I slightly modify the latter.

[192] Cf. Mirkin 5.279; Soncino 3.306-07. See also *Pesiq. Rav Kah.* 11/8 on Exod 13:17 (Mandelbaum 184; Eng. Braude and Kapstein 207-08). It includes bread from heaven (manna) in Exod 16:4; water from the well of Num 21:17; the cloud of Exod 13:21-22; clothes (Ezek 16:10); and shoes (the sealskin of Ezek 16:10). It is spoken in the name of R. Ḥama b. Ḥanina, a second generation Palestinian Amora (*Introduction* 96).

Judaic comment on Ezek 16:10, next to the important v. 9 with washing, is also very early. In regard to Ps 23:2, "He makes us to lie down in green pastures," R. Eliezer (b. Hyrcanus, a second generation Tanna of the older group,)[193] in what is now a somewhat stylized form asked R. Simeon (b. Yoḥai, a third generation Tanna,):[194] "As the Israelites were going out of Egypt, did weavers' gear go out with them? R. Simeon replied: No. Then how did they clothe themselves those forty years? R. Simeon replied: With garments which the ministering angels gave them for clothing, for God said of Israel in the wilderness, 'I clothed you also with embroidered work' (Ezek 16:10). ... But didn't their garments wear out? [R. Simeon replied:] Have you not read that Moses said to Israel in the wilderness, 'The clothes on your back did not wear out' (Deut 8:4)?" R. Simeon also maintained the garments did not need washing, for the cloud of fire (Exod 13:22) cleansed them and made them shine. In addition, the well (of Num 21:17) brought up "certain plants and certain spices" in which the Israelites lay down (Ps 23:2), thus the garments did not become full of sweat.[195]

Since there was no verse numbering of Scripture at this time, Ezek 16:9 would have almost automatically been considered together with v. 10. The very early comment on v. 10 noted above thus makes it likely that the Judaic comment on v. 9 described above was also quite early.

5.3 *The Unusual Birth of Israelites Just Before the Exodus, and Their Recognizing God after Their Rescue from the Red Sea*

A third early haggadic narrative employs Ezek 16:4 and 9 in regard to the exodus event and is the most important in regard to the verb "being baptized" in 1 Cor 10:2.[196] This charming account explains how the

---

[193] Cf. n. 54.

[194] Cf. *Introduction* 84.

[195] Cf. *Midr. Pss.* 23/4 on Ps 23:2 (Buber 199-200; Braude 1.330-31). A parallel tradition is found in *Cant. Rab.* 4:11 § 2 (Dunski 120; Soncino 9.216-17) in the name of two fourth generation Tannaim. See also *Deut. Rab.* Ki Thabo 7/11 on Deut 29:4 (Eng. 5) in Mirkin 11.119, Soncino 7.144-45.

[196] Again, it should be noted that in the Palestinian triennial lectionary system on the second Sabbath of the month Shevat in the first year, Exod 1:1(ff.) and Ezek

Israelites could leave Egypt over 600,000 strong although Pharaoh tried very hard to decimate their numbers.

Exod. Rab. Shemoth 1/12 on Exod 1:14 relates that Pharaoh decreed upon the Israelites the four harsh commands found in this scriptural verse, thereby "cunningly planning" to prevent their increase by separating the men from their wives. Yet God recalled His promise to Abraham to multiply his descendants like the stars (Gen 22:17). Thus Exod 1:12 states: "But the more they were oppressed, the more they multiplied."

R. Aqiba, a second generation Tanna,[197] commented on the above predicament as follows:

> Israel was redeemed from Egypt on account of the righteous women of that generation. What did they do? When they went to draw water, the Holy One, blessed be He, deposited small fish in their pitchers, with the result that they found them half filled with water and half with fish.[198] These they brought to their husbands, and then put on two pots, one for hot water and one for fish. And they used to feed them, wash them, anoint them and give them to drink, and cohabit with them between the mounds in the field, as it is said: "When you lie between the mounds, the wings of the dove are covered with silver" (Ps 68:14, Eng. 13). Because they lay between the mounds, Israel merited to obtain the plunder of Egypt, as it is said: "The wings of the dove are covered with silver" (ibid.). As soon as they became pregnant, they went back to their homes. When the time of their giving birth was due, they went into the field and gave birth under

---

16:1(ff.) were read together from the Torah and the Prophets. This thus associated Pharaoh's evil decrees of Exod 1:14, but also v. 22, that "every boy that is born [to the Hebrews] you 'shall throw into the Nile,'" with Ezekiel 16 in Judaic tradition. The Israelite women bore their children in the field to avoid the latter. Cf. the art. "Triennial Cycle" by Joseph Jacobs in *JE* (1905 / 1925) 12.254-57, inserted chart, as well as "Triennial Cycle" in *EJ* (2007) 20.142. Exod 1:22 is clearly alluded to in *Targ.* Ezek 16:5 (Sperber 3.292; Eng. Levey 50).

[197] Cf. *Introduction* 79. The parallel account in *b. Soṭah* 11b (Soncino 55-56), also on Exod 1:14, has R. ʿAvira, a Babylonian rabbi active ca. 330 CE (Str-B 6.125). It is a misspelling of ʿAqiva. R. Aqiba finishes his discourse with Exod 15:2, upon which he also comments in 30b (Soncino 149). In *Exod. Rab.* Beshallaḥ 23/8 on Exod 15:1 (Mirkin 5.264; Soncino 3.286), the author of the parallel tradition is R. Judah (b. Ilai), a later student of R. Aqiba and third generation Tanna (*Introduction* 84).

[198] On this motif, cf. *b. Yoma* 75a (Soncino 361).

the apple tree, as it is said: "Under the apple tree I awakened you; there your mother was in travail with you" (Cant 8:5). The Holy One, blessed be He, then sent an angel from on high to cleanse and beautify them, like a midwife who makes the child look beautiful, as it is said: "And as for your nativity, in the day you were born your navel was not cut, nor were you washed in water for cleansing" (Ezek 16:4). He then provided for them two balls, one made of oil and the other of honey, as it is said: "And He made him to suck honey out of the crag, and oil out of the flinty rock" (Deut 32:13). As soon as the Egyptians perceived them, they sought to slay them, but a miracle occurred and they were swallowed into the ground. They then brought oxen and ploughed upon their backs, as it is said: ""The plowers plowed upon my back" (Ps 129:3). But after they [the Egyptians] departed, they burst forth and came out of the ground like the grass of the field, as it is said: "I cause you to increase, even as the growth of the field" (Ezek 16:7). As soon as they grew up, they came in herds to their respective homes, as it is said: "And you came to excellent beauty" (ibid.). Do not read *'adi 'adayin* [excellent beauty], but *be 'edrei 'adarim* [in herds]. When the Holy One, blessed be He, revealed Himself by the Sea, they recognized Him first, as it is said: "This is my God, and I will glorify Him" (Exod 15:2).[199]

The Israelite women's "washing" their husbands in the field is the Hebrew verb רחץ (*rḥṣ*),[200] as in Ezek 16:4[201] and 9. It is the same verb employed in Gen 18:4, where Abraham tells the three angels, "Let a little water be brought, and 'wash' your feet" - interpreted in Judaic tradition by Ezek 16:9 (see section 5.1 above).

This is immediately followed by the Israelite women's "anointing" their husbands. The Hebrew verb סוך (*sukh*) is used here.[202] Of its nine occurrences in the MT, it is coupled with "washing" only in Ezek 16:9, which stands behind this passage.

At the Israelite women's becoming pregnant, they returned home. When the time of their giving birth arrived, they went back to the "field." This is the Hebrew שָׂדֶה (*śadeh*), deriving here from Ezek 16:7, "I made you a myriad like a plant of the 'field.'" This verse is even quoted

---

[199] Cf. Mirkin 5.23-24; Soncino 3.15-16.

[200] Cf. BDB 934: wash, wash off, away, bathe; Jastrow 1468: to bathe, wash.

[201] The *Targum* of this verse also refers it to the situation of Hebrew infants in Egypt, born in the field (Sperber 3.292; Eng. Levey 49-50).

[202] Cf. BDB 691: pour in anointing, anoint; Jastrow 963, with a relevant example in the hiphil.

towards the end of the narrative (see below). Saved from the Egyptians, the newborn infants burst forth (out of the ground which had "miraculously" swallowed them) "like the grass of the field" (Ezek 16:7).

After the Israelite women had given birth to their children, God "sent an angel from on high to 'cleanse' and beautify them, like a midwife who makes the child look beautiful, as is said: As for your birth, on the day your navel cord was not cut, nor were you washed with water to 'cleanse' you (Ezek 16:4)." The angel's "cleansing" the newborn infant here employs the Hebrew verb נקי / נקה (*nqy / nqh*).[203] It is based upon the noun מִשְׁעִי (*mish ʿî*), "cleansing," in the above verse, a very rare noun only found here in the MT and therefore later rendered by a more common term.[204]

It should be noted that it is not God, but an "angel from on high,[205] who (washes) and cleanses the newborn infants. The parallel tradition in *b. Soṭah* 11b says God "sent someone from the high heavens who washed and straightened the limbs...." This someone is also clearly an angel.[206] Elsewhere, when asked who took care of them as newborns, those who were now adults said it was "a fine handsome young man" who came down (from heaven) and did so.[207]

The angel then provided the washed and cleansed newborn infants with "two balls, one made of oil and the other of honey, as it is said: 'He made him to suck honey out of the rock, and oil out of the rock of flint' (Deut 32:13)."[208] The first term "rock" here is סֶלַע (*sela ʿ*), the second צור

---

[203] Cf. Jastrow 932: to be clean. He quotes this passage and its parallels in the piel: to cleanse.

[204] Cf. *Targ*. Ezek 16:4, which employs נקד (*nqd*), "to be clean" (Jastrow 931, and נקר [*nqr*] 935, hiphil, with reference to *b. Soṭah* 11b), in Sperber 3.292.

[205] This may be thought of as Gabriel. Under his name as "Arguer" (פִּיסְקוֹן [*pîsqōn*]: Jastrow 1168), he is connected to Ezek 16:3, the neighboring verse, in *b. Sanh*. 44b (Soncino 290).

[206] In the similar account related to Exod 1:22 in *Pesiq. R*. 47/2 (Friedmann 189a; Eng. Braude 799), it is God who comes down and washes and cleanses the infant, as in the MT.

[207] Cf. *Exod. Rab*. Beshallaḥ 23/8 on Exod 15:1 (Mirkin 5.265; Soncino 3.287). In *Cant. Rab*. 1:7 (ed. Grűnhut 10a-b), it is an angel who washes and anoints the sucklings. In *Deut. Rab*. (ed. Liebermann, p. 14), these tasks are carried out by two angels for each child.

[208] In *t. Shab*. 8:25 (Zuckermandel / Liebermann 121; Eng. Neusner 29), Deut 32:13 is used to show that honey is a drink. Isa 25:6 does the same for oil.

(ṣur). This also can be thought of as a cross-reference to the narrative of the well, where water comes forth from the rock (צוּר [ṣur]) of Exod 17:6, elsewhere called סֶלַע (selaʿ). Deut 8:15-16 refers to the terrible wilderness, where God "made water flow for you from the rock [צוּר - ṣur; LXX πέτρα] of flint, 16) and fed you in the wilderness with manna...."[209] In addition, Psalm 114 deals with Israel's leaving Egypt. Verse 8 notes that God thereby "turns the rock [צוּר - ṣur] into a pool of water, the flint into a spring of water."

It is noteworthy that "honey and oil" are also mentioned in Ezek 16:13 and 19, another link to this chapter from Ezekiel. The *Targum* adds manna to these at v. 13.[210]

After *Targum Neofiti 1* on Deut 32:10 mentions manna, the well and quails from the Sea, it goes on in v. 13[211] to say that He / he suckled them with honey "'and anointed them with oil' [ומשח משח יתהון - *wmshḥ mshḥ ythwn*] from the rock, the rock of flint."[212] *Fragment Targum* MS "P" on the same verse has "He / he anointed them," as does MS "V."[213] Both of these are the verb מְשַׁח (*meshaḥ*), "to anoint."[214] Since the Messiah is in Aramaic מְשִׁיחָא (*meshîḥaʾ*), Hebrew מָשִׁיחַ (*mashîaḥ*),[215] "the Anointed One," a Jew such as Paul who also knew Aramaic[216] if acquainted with an early form of this haggadic narrative, could have

---

[209] It should be noted that in *Somn.* 2.221-22, Philo associates Exod 17:6 and Deut 8:15.

[210] Cf. Sperber 3.293; Eng. Levey 50. The Aramaic term for oil is מְשַׁח (*mshḥ*) in both verses. The noun "fine flour" (סֹלֶת [*sōlet*]) in the Hebrew and Aramaic of these two verses can be viewed as a link to the "fine flour" of Gen 18:6. Fine flour was mixed with honey for the sick according to *Exod. Rab.* Shemoth 5/9 on Exod 4:27, referring to Ezek 16:19 (Mirkin 5.92; Soncino 3.87). In *Tanḥ*. B Shemoth 22 on Exod 4:27, this mixture includes oil, as in Ezek 16:19 (Buber 2.11; Eng. Townsend 21).

[211] As remarked above, there was no versification of the Bible in the first century CE. Deut 32:10 and 13 would probably have been considered together. Cf. Mark 12:26, where Jesus cites "the story about the bush" in Exodus 3.

[212] Cf. Díez-Macho 5.271; Eng. McNamara 153, who notes that VNL have here "He anointed (*mšḥ*) them from the rock..."

[213] Cf. Klein 1.114 and Eng. 2.86, as well as 1.226 and Eng. 2.183, respectively.

[214] Cf. Jastrow 851.

[215] Ibid., 852.

[216] Cf. *marana tha* in 1 Cor 16:22, and the representation of Paul as speaking Hebrew (Aramaic) to the crowd in Jerusalem in Acts 22:2-3.

thought of the angel who bathed with water, cleansed and "anointed with oil" (Ezek 16:9; LXX ἔχρισα) the newborn Israelite babies in the field as the Messiah. Ps 89:21 (Eng. 20) for example has the Lord say: "I have found My servant David, with My holy oil 'I have anointed him' [מְשַׁחְתִּיו - *meshaḥtîw*]."[217] For "oil," the *Targum* has here מְשַׁח (*meshaḥ*).[218] In addition, the "oil of anointing" (שֶׁמֶן הַמִּשְׁחָה [*shemen hammishḥah*]) of Exod 40:9 is associated with "the King Messiah [מלכא משיחא - *mlk ʾ mshyḥ ʾ*] who is destined to redeem Israel at the end of days" in *Targum Pseudo-Jonathan* here.[219] Paul could indeed have also made this association, if he did not borrow it from earlier Christians.

In 1 Cor 10:20 Paul alludes to Deut 32:17, and in v. 22 to Deut 32:21, where "the Lord" is Christ. The Apostle thus seems to have this entire chapter in mind as one scriptural passage while composing 10:1-22. The term "rock" (צוּר [*ṣur*]) occurs in vv. 4, 30 and 31 for the Lord or God, as well as in vv. 13 (LXX πέτρα) and 37. This cluster of five occurrences, especially with the Rock as the Lord in vv. 13 and 30-31, could have been one factor which influenced Paul to maintain Christ (for him the Lord, κύριος) was "the rock" in 1 Cor 10:4.

R. Aqiba's narrative continues with a quotation of Ezek 16:7 regarding the grass of the field. Then it states regarding the rescued infants: "When they grew up [cf. this term in Ezek 16:7], they went in herds [עֲדָרִים עֲדָרִים - *ʿadarîm ʿadarîm*][220] back to their homes, for it is said: 'And you came in excellent beauty [lit., 'ornament upon ornament'; Ezek 16:7).' Do not read עֲדִי עֲדָיִים [*ʿadî ʿadayîm* - excellent beauty],[221] but בְּעֶדְרֵי עֲדָרִים [*be ʿedrē ʿadarîm* - in herds]."[222]

R. Aqiba's account concludes by noting what these adult Israelites saw after they had all passed through the Red Sea and arrived at the far

---

[217] Cf. "Your anointed one" in vv. 39 (Eng. 38) and 52 (Eng. 51).

[218] Cf. Jastrow 851 on the noun, Merino 147 for the Aramaic, and Stec 169 for the English.

[219] Cf. Clarke 117; Eng. Maher 273. See also the "oil of anointing" in association with Ezek 16:9 in *Tanḥ*. Teṣaveh 1 on Exod 27:20 (Eshkol 372; Eng. Berman 539) and *Pesiq. R.* 33/10 on Isa 51:12 (Friedmann 154a; Braude 647).

[220] This is the noun עֵדֶר (*ʿēder* : herd, flock [Jastrow 1046]).

[221] This is the collective noun עֲדִי (*ʿadî,* ornaments [BDB 725]). The NRSV translates it so in Ezek 16:11.

[222] Cf. the remark by the Soncino translator, S. Lehrman (3.16, n. 4): "A favourite and bold Midrashic device to prove a suggestion by altering a Biblical verse."

shore.[223] "When the Holy One, blessed be He, revealed Himself at the [Red] Sea, [it was they who] recognized Him first, as it says: '*This* [זֶה - *zeh*] is my God, and I will glorify Him' (Exod 15:2)."[224]

According to *ʾAvot R. Nat.* B 37, there are ten descents of the Lord in the Torah. That for the (Red) Sea is taught in Exod 15:2.[225] This is the time God performed "miracles" (נִסִּים [*nissîm*]) for the Israelites, and they responded with Exod 15:2.[226] It is also the time a maidservant saw what Isaiah, Ezekiel, and all the prophets never saw. When God "revealed Himself at the Sea, no one had to ask: 'Which one is the king?' As soon as they saw Him, they recognized Him, and 'all of them' [כלן - *kln*] opened their mouths and said: Exod 15:2."[227] This is thus one of the rare occasions on which humans were allowed to see God directly, otherwise punishable by death.[228]

A variant of the above tradition applies it to sucklings and embryos. The Tannaitic Tosefta notes at *Soṭah* 6:4 in the name of R. Yose the

---

223 Connected with this is the assertion that the plunder the Israelites took from the drowned Egyptian soldiers (Exod 14:30) on the far side of the Red Sea was greater than that taken from the Egyptians before departing from Egypt (12:35-36). This is based on the expression "ornament of ornaments" in Ezek 16:7 in *Mek. R. Ish.* Pisḥa 13 on Exod 12:36 (Lauterbach 1.106).

224 *Cant. Rab.* 2:6 (ed. Grünhut, 22a) says that when the children were small, they didn't recognize their Father. Yet when they grew up, they immediately recognized Him and said Exod 15:2 at the Sea. See also *Sifre* Vezot ha-Berakhah 343 on Deut 33:2 (Finkelstein 398; Eng. Hammer 354) for these as adult Israelites.

225 Cf. Schechter 96; Becker 373; Eng. Saldarini 220.

226 Cf. *Exod. Rab.* Yethro 27/4 on Exod 18:1 (Mirkin 6.11; Soncino 3.324).

227 Cf. *Mek. R. Ish.* Shirata 3 on Exod 15:2 (Lauterbach 2.24-25) in the name of R. Eliezer, a second generation Tanna (see n. 54). The parallel tradition in *Mek. R. Shim. b. Yoḥ.* ad loc. (Nelson 129-30) has "all of them" (כולם [*kwlm*]) recognizing God, and "all of them" (כולם [*kwlm*]) opening their mouths and singing Exod 15:2.

228 Cf. Exod 33:20; Judg 13:22; and Isa 6:5. On this in regard to Exod 15:2, see *Exod. Rab.* Beshallaḥ 23/15 (Mirkin 5.269; Soncino 3.292-93). It emphasizes that "each and every one" (כָּל אֶחָד וְאֶחָד [*kol ʾeḥad we ʾeḥad*]) pointed his finger (to God) and said Exod 15:2. In *Pesiq. R.* 47/2 on Lev 16:1 (Friedmann 189a-b; Eng. Braude 799, with the Parma MS), after the citation of Ezek 16:9-10, the Israelites recognized God at the Red Sea, pointed at Him with their fingers and said Exod 15:2. They suffered no harm from seeing God on this occasion, "even as we suffered none when we saw You at the dawn of our life [= birth in the field, called a 'refuse heap' here]."

Galilean, a second generation Tanna[229]: "When the Israelites came up out of the Sea and saw their enemies strewn as corpses on the seashore, they all [כולם - *kwlm*] burst out into song - even a child lying in his mother's lap and an infant sucking at its mother's breast. When they saw the Presence of God [שְׁכִינָה - *shekhînah*], the babe raised its head, and the infant took his mouth off his mother's nipple, and they all [כולם - *kwlm*] responded in song, saying Exod 15:2." R. Meir, a third generation Tanna,[230] then comments: "Even fetuses in their mothers' wombs broke out into song," as he interprets Ps 68:26 and 8:3 (Eng. 2).[231]

There is a great emphasis on "all" the Hebrews' uttering song at the Red Sea in connection with Exod 15:2, including more than 600,000 Israelites,[232] as shown in the texts cited above and in those referred to in the notes. If known to him in an earlier form, this may have partially influenced Paul's own emphasis on "all" (πάντες) our fathers / ancestors" as having gone through the Sea in 1 Cor 10:1, as well as the other four occurrences of the term in vv. 2-4.

Finally, the Palestinian targums on Exod 15:2 link it to the narrative related by R. Aqiba above, including clear allusions to Ezekiel 16. *Targum Pseudo-Jonathan* notes: "From their mothers' breasts the sucklings would indicate with their fingers to their fathers and would say: '*This* is our God who had us suck honey from the rock [כיפא - *kyph* ʾ][233] and oil [משח - *mshḥ*] from the flint rock [טינרא - *ṭynr* ʾ][234] [cf. Deut 32:13] at the time our mothers went out into the open country [cf. Ezek 16:5] and gave birth to us and abandoned us there. He would send an angel who would bathe [מסחי - *msḥy*][235] us and swaddle us [cf. Ezek 16:4]. And now let us praise Him, the God of our fathers, and let us extol Him."[236] Manuscript "V" of the *Fragment Targum* on Exod 15:2 is quite similar, yet it has the variant:

---

[229] Cf. *Introduction* 81, which notes that he disputed "particularly with Aqiba."

[230] Ibid., 84.

[231] Cf. Lieberman, *The Tosefta*. Nashim 184; Eng. Neusner 3.169-70. On the basic motif, see also Wisd Sol 10:21.

[232] Cf. *Exod. Rab.* Shemoth 3/2 on Exod 3:7 (Mirkin 5.68; Soncino 3.60). See also *Midrash Tannaim*, Vezot ha-Berakhah on Deut 33:2 (ed. Hoffmann, 211): "but all of them [כולן - *kwln*] opened their mouths and said: Exod 15:2."

[233] Cf. Jastrow 634 on כֵּפָא (*kēpha* ʾ), and Simon Peter's Aramaic name "Cephas" (the Rock).

[234] Ibid., 533 on טִינָּרָא (*ṭînnara* ʾ), rock, flint.

[235] Ibid., 971 on סְחִי (*seḥî*): wash, bathe.

[236] Cf. Clarke 84; Eng. Maher 203.

"and Who anointed [משח - *mshḥ*] us with oil [משח - *mshḥ*] from the flint rock."[237] Again, for someone like Paul who also knew Aramaic, the Aramaic משח (*mshḥ*) both for "to anoint" and for "oil" could link this targumic tradition to the Anointed One, the Messiah.

* * *

Before the results of the above sections are applied to 1 Cor 10:2 in regard to the motif of being baptized, it is helpful to see how the important base text for the latter, Ezekiel 16, fits the ductus of 1 Corinthians 10 with its emphasis on idolatry.

6. *Idolatry in 1 Corinthians 10, Egypt in the Wilderness, and Ezekiel 16 with its Targum*

6.1 *Idolatry in 1 Corinthians 10*

As noted in the analyses above, passage through the Red Sea, the pillar of cloud, manna, and water from the rock are all positive motifs standing behind 1 Cor 10:1-4. Paul continues in v. 5, however, by stating that "nevertheless, God was not pleased with most of them, and they were struck down in the wilderness."[238] He elucidates this in the following verses.

---

237 Cf. Klein 1.170; Eng. 2.129. Nfmg and VN of *Targum Neofiti 1* also have this tradition, including "oil" (משח [*mashḥ*]). See Díez-Macho 2.97, Eng. McNamara 64, notes "h" and 2. *Pirq. R. El.* 42 (Eng. Friedlander 332, based on the Abraham Epstein MS of Vienna - p. xiv) has the rock at the infants' side "anointing them with oil, like a lying-in woman who anoints her son, as is said: Deut 32:18." It goes on to quote Exod 15:2.

238 The commentators falsely repeat like a mantra that only two people survived here, Caleb and Joshua ben Nun (Deut 1:35-38). Yet they overlook that the children of the first wilderness generation Israelites would definitely enter the promised Land. See "your little ones" and "your children" in v. 39, as well as those under twenty years of age, "the little ones" and "your children," in Num 14:29-33. This is why Paul correctly employs "most of them" in 1 Cor 10:5. Only the *first* wilderness generation (with the exception of Caleb and Joshua) is meant; those born later remained alive.

The Israelites "desired evil" (v. 6) there and some of them became idolaters (the noun εἰδωλολάτρης - v. 7), as Exod 32:6 is interpreted, the incident of the Golden Calf. In v. 8 Paul clearly alludes to the incident of Numbers 25. The Israelite men's sexual immorality with Moabite women was definitely connected to their eating before and sacrificing to their gods, yoking themselves to the Baal of Peor (v. 2). This resulted in 24,000 Israelites dying by the plague (v. 9), which Paul notes in 1 Cor 10:8.[239] These, as well as other events in the wilderness, happened to the Israelites to serve as an example, written down in Scripture to instruct "us" (v. 11), i.e. the Corinthian and other Christians.

In 10:14 Paul tells his addressees to flee from "the worship of idols" (εἰδωλολατρία). After noting baptism in v. 2, he anticipates in vv. 3-4 his later discussion of the bread and wine of the Lord's Supper. The Apostle specifically mentions them as the bread we break / the body of Christ, and the cup of blessing / the blood of Christ in v. 16. To actively partake in the cup and the table of the Lord as well as the table of demons in regard to food sacrificed to idols (εἰδωλόθυτον, and an idol, εἴδωλον, in v. 19)[240] means acknowledging allegiance to them, which one may not do as a Christian (vv. 16-22).[241] One should refrain from eating at a dinner invitation from an unbeliever food specifically mentioned as offered in sacrifice. Yet no offence should be made, in the hope that such people may also be saved (vv. 23-33; 11:1). This is a gentle rebuke of those Corinthian Christians who think they are "standing" (10:12), i.e. who consider themselves strong enough to avoid the dangers of eating food

---

[239] The only occurrence of the number 23,000 in the MT is in Num 26:62, but this is a census number of the Levites. Num 25:9's 24,000 is found in all Judaic sources on this verse. Paul has apparently had a memory slip. Leon Morris in *1 Corinthians* (Tyndale New Testament Commentaries; Grand Rapids, MI: Eerdmans, 1958 / 1979) 143 improbably suggests that "Paul may be making some allowance for those slain by the judges (Num xxv.5)." On other passages in 1 Corinthians dealing with immorality, see chapter 5; 6:9 (fornicators, idolaters, adulterers, male prostitutes, sodomites), and vv. 12-20.

[240] On this issue, cf. especially the studies of Wendell Willis, *Idol Meat in Corinth. The Pauline Argument in 1 Corinthians 8 and 10* (SBLDS 68; Chico, CA: Scholars Press, 1985), and John Fotopoulos, *Food Offered to Idols in Roman Corinth* (WUNT 2.151; Tűbingen: Mohr Siebeck, 2003).

[241] Cf. the recent treatment by Kathy Ehrensperger, "Participation in Christ or with Demons: 1 Cor 10.14-22," in her *Paul at the Crossroads*. Theologizing in the Space Between (LNTS 456; London, etc.: Bloomsbury T & T Clark, 2013 / 2015) 200-05.

said to have been sacrificed to idols and of then also participating in the bread and wine of the Lord's Supper. They should not overestimate their ability to do so, and by implication should not encourage those weaker than they are to follow their example.

Chapter 10 thus deals primarily with the issue of idolatry, as was the case already in chapter 8. It has not been pointed out before, however, that the same issue lies behind vv. 1-4, especially as read in the context of the Judaic interpretation of Ezekiel 16. Yet first it will be helpful to briefly sketch the Israelites' idolatry in Egypt and the wilderness in Judaic tradition.

6.2 *Israelite Idolatry in Egypt and the Wilderness in Judaic Tradition*

When Joseph died, according to Judaic tradition the Israelites in Egypt abolished the covenant of circumcision, wanting to become like the idol worshipers, the Egyptians.[242] Only the tribe of the Levites continued the practice and did not serve idols.[243] In fact, the Israelites became "passionate followers after idolatry in Egypt and used to bring their sacrifices to satyrs," the demons of Deut 32:17.[244] There they were "steeped in idolatry," the law against which "outweighs all other commandments in the Torah." This is because the idol worshiper "breaks off the yoke, annuls the covenant, and misrepresents the Torah."[245] When Israel crossed through the Red Sea, said the second generation Tanna R. Eliezer,[246] an idol crossed over with them, the carved image of Micah.[247] Once they reached the far shore and saw all the dead

---

242 Cf. *Exod. Rab.* Shemoth 1/8 on Exod 1:8 (Mirkin 5.18; Soncino 3.10).

243 Cf. *Sifre* Beha'alothekha 67 on Num 9:5 (Horovitz 62; Eng. Neusner 2.25).

244 Cf. *Lev. Rab.* Aḥare Moth 22/8 on Lev 17:3 (Mirkin 8.39-40; Soncino 4.286-87). See also *Sifre* Ha'azinu 318 on Deut 32:17 (Finkelstein 364; Eng. Hammer 327): "What does a demon do? He enters into a person and compels him [to sin - through idolatry]." See the fourfold mention of "demons" by Paul in 1 Cor 10:20-21, the allusion in v. 20 to Deut 32:17, and making the Lord "jealous" in v. 22 in regard to Deut 32:16 and 21.

245 Cf. *Mek. R. Ish.* Pisḥa 5 on Exod 12:6 (Lauterbach 1.36-37).

246 Cf. n. 54.

247 *Cf. Sifre* Beha'alothekha 84 on Num 10:35-36 (Horovitz 82; Eng. Neusner 2.74). This is not the prophet Micah, but that of Judg 17:1-6.

Egyptians, the Israelites thought Egypt was now empty. Therefore they said: "Let us make an idol to march at the head of us, and let us return to Egypt."[248]

Paul explicitly refers to the making of the Golden Calf as an idol in the wilderness in 1 Cor 10:7 by quoting Exod 32:6. The third generation Tanna R. Eliezer b. Jacob[249] said regarding this: "For this iniquity there is enough to punish Israel from now until the dead are raised."[250] The "reveling" of Exod 32:6 is interpreted in Judaic sources both as sexual immorality and as idolatry.[251] *Mek. R. Ish.* Baḥodesh 8 on Exod 20:12-14 also connects idolatry and immorality. It states regarding the arrangement of the Ten Commandments: "On one tablet was written: 'You shall have no other god.' And opposite it on the other tablet was written, 'You shall not commit adultery.' This says that if one worships idols, it is accounted to him as though he committed adultery, breaking his covenant with God. For it is said: 'Adulterous wife, who receives strangers instead of your husband' (Ezek 16:32)" and Hos 3:1.[252] In *Test. Reuben* 4:6 Jacob also tells his firstborn son that unchastity leads to idolatry.[253] As if the Golden Calf incident were not sufficient, the Israelites "even took the manna and offered it to idols," as Ezek 16:19 is interpreted.[254] It was simply hard for the Israelites to part with their idols, as Ezek 20:7 is explicated by the second generation Tanna R. Judah b. Bathyra.[255] This included the entire forty year period in the wilderness. The importance of the Israelites' idolatry as also based on Ezekiel 16 will now be pointed out.

---

248 Cf. *Mek. R. Ish.* Vayassa 1 on Exod 15:22 (Lauterbach 2.86).

249 Cf. *Introduction* 85.

250 Cf. *ʾAvot R. Nat.* A 34 (Schechter 99; Becker 242; Goldin 137). The next paragraph lists ten names of contempt by which idolatry was called.

251 Cf. for example *t. Soṭah* 6:6 for fornication in connection with Gen 21:9 and this verse (Zuckermandel / Liebermann 304; Eng. Neusner 3.172), coupled with idolatrous worship, as well as *Sifre* Balak 131 on Num 25:1 (Horovitz 169; German in Kuhn, 502).

252 Cf. Lauterbach 2.262-63.

253 Cf. Charles 9; *OTP* 1.783 with "promiscuity" for the first.

254 Cf. *Exod. Rab.* Ki Thissa 4/1 on Exod 31:8 (Mirkin 6.133; Soncino 3.469). *Tanḥ.* Ki Thissa 14 on Exod 31:18 (Eshkol 407; Eng. Berman 590) maintains that even "on the day that Israel erected the golden calf, manna descended. They took it and brought it as an offering to the calf, as it is said: 'My bread...' (Ezek 16:19)."

255 Cf. *Mek. R. Ish.* Pisḥa 5 on Exod 12:6 (Lauterbach 1.38), and *Introduction* 83.

6.3 *Idolatry in Ezekiel 16*

Ezekiel 16, quoted or clearly alluded to a number of times in the Judaic narratives analyzed in section 5. above, is generally described as a kind of allegory. The prophet is told by the Lord to "make known to Jerusalem her 'abominations'" (v. 2).[256] She is depicted as a foundling, "thrown out in the open field" by her parents on the day she is born (v. 5). The standard things done for a newborn are not performed for her, including washing her with water to cleanse her (v. 4).[257] When the Lord passes by her, He sees her flailing in her blood (v. 6), which can be interpreted as the Lord's "finding" Israel in the wilderness (Deut 32:10).[258]

Verses 6-7 describe how the girl grows to maturity. When she is ready to marry the Lord, He bathes her with water and anoints her with oil (v. 9), clothing her in exquisite garments and giving her "choice flour, honey and oil for food." All of this makes her "fit to be a queen" (v. 13). For this reason Daniel Block speaks here of "this remarkable rags-to-riches story."[259]

Yet the exceedingly beautiful wife (Jerusalem) now begins to play the whore. She turns gold and silver gifts from her husband into male images (v. 17), which recalls the incident of the Golden Calf of Exod 32:2-4, 24.[260] The choice flour, oil and honey her husband had given her she dedicates to idols (v. 19), even sacrificing her own children (vv. 20-21).

---

256 These are emphasized in the chapter by the occurrence of the noun תּוֹעֵבָה (*tō ʿēbhah*) nine times, and the verb תָּעַב (*ta ʿabh*) twice.

257 Moshe Greenberg in *Ezekiel 1-20* (AB 22; Garden City, NY: Doubleday, 1983) 275 is the only commentator who calls attention to the haggadic narrative in *b. Soṭah* 11b based on these verses. It should be noted that here the newborn infant is male, rather than female.

258 Cf. v. 13, where the Lord nurses (Israel) with honey from the rock and with oil from the flint. See Greenberg, *Ezekiel 1-20*, 299. See also Hos 9:10, where the Lord "finds" Israel in the wilderness, yet it sins at Baal-Peor.

259 Cf. his *The Book of Ezekiel. Chapters 1-24* (Grand Rapids, MI: Eerdmans, 1997) 485. He correctly maintains that "vv. 6-14 offer one of the most vivid pictures of the grace of God in the entire Bible" (521). Leslie Allen calls the girl "Cinderella" in this regard. See his *Ezekiel 1-19* (WBC 28; Dallas, TX: Word Books, 1994) 223. He describes the narrative as "the powerful allegory of a foundling, whom Yahweh rescued, married, and marvelously provided for" (247).

260 So too Block, *The Book of Ezekiel. Chapters 1-24*, 488, as well as Greenberg, *Ezekiel 1-20*, 298.

This recalls the Israelites' sacrificing their own children as burnt offerings to Baal.[261] The explicitly sexual imagery employed by Ezekiel to describe the adulterous wife is indeed shocking.[262]

The "longest single prophecy in the OT prophetic books,"[263] with its sixty-three verses, then continues in various ways to accuse the adulterous wife of adultery (vv. 35-58). She refuses to recall the days of her youth, when the Lord had cared for her (vv. 22, 43, 60).

The drastic imagery and the repeated emphasis on various kinds of idolatry caused the second generation Tanna R. Eliezer[264] not to want Ezekiel 16 to be read as a *hafṭarah* or prophetic reading.[265] Yet his harsh attitude was not prevalent. The chapter was allowed to be read if the *Targum* was read concomitantly.[266] Leslie Allen states in this regard: "It is not surprising that the Targum completely rewrote it, removing any slur against Jerusalem and turning it into a wholesome presentation of Jewish orthodoxy."[267] To this I now turn.

6.4 *Targum Ezekiel 16, Including Idol Worship*

The *Targum* of Ezekiel 16[268] understands it as "poetic allegory" and is a "remarkable exposition interpolated into MT." Its "exegetical genius" is

---

[261] Cf. Jer 7:31; 19:5; and 32:35.

[262] Cf. Block, *The Book of Ezekiel. Chapters 1-24*, 404, n. 18: "Flailing about in blood, engaging in harlotry with male images, slaughtering children as food, spreading the legs for every passerby, pouring out 'your juice,' Egypt's swollen member, a bloody victim of wrath and jealousy, hacking in pieces with swords, paying clients to receive sexual favors." It is " a story of unmitigated depravity" (471). See for example *Lev. Rab.* Qedoshim 25/7 on Lev 19:23, dealing with Ezek 16:26, "You have also played the harlot with the Egyptians, your neighbors, great of flesh" : "They had an abnormally large *membrum virile*" (Mirkin 8.69; Soncino 4.321).

[263] Cf. Block, *The Book of Ezekiel. Chapters 1-24*, 520.

[264] Cf. n. 54.

[265] Cf. *m. Meg.* 4:10 (Albeck 2.368; Danby 207; Neusner 324).

[266] Cf. *t. Meg.* 3:34 (Zuckermandel / Liebermann 228; Eng. Neusner 2.296), as well as *b. Meg.* 25b (Soncino 151).

[267] Cf. his *Ezekiel 1-19*, 246-47.

[268] Cf. Sperber 3.292-99, and the English translation by Samson Levey, *The Targum of Ezekiel* 49-54.

"an amazing feat of the use of Scripture."[269] Already in v. 3 it refers to the Lord's revealing Himself to Abraham "your father between the pieces of the covenant-offering" (Genesis 15), informing him that the inhabitants of Jerusalem (the Israelites) would go down to Egypt, but that He would redeem them from there.[270] Verse 4 states that "the congregation of Israel was enslaved and oppressed. It was like a new-born child who is abandoned in the field," for whom the usual things were not done at its birth.[271] Verse 5 clearly alludes to Pharaoh's decree to throw Hebrew male children into the Nile in Exod 1:22.[272] The Lord in v. 6 promises to have pity on them by the blood of circumcision, and to redeem them by the blood of the Passover lamb.[273] The Lord caused the Israelites to increase greatly (in Egypt), becoming "families and tribes" (v. 7). When their time of redemption arrived (v. 8), the Lord indeed redeemed them and led them into freedom (v. 9, an allusion to the exodus event with the crossing of the Red Sea).[274] Verse 12 states that the Lord's "cloud of glory" covered them, and "an angel, sent from before Him, led the way ahead of them." This clearly alludes to Exod 13:21. The next verse (13) notes that the Lord fed them "with manna, which was as good as fine flour and honey and oil."[275]

The *Targum* thus haggadically rewrites the Hebrew text of Ezek 16:1-12 to refer to the cruel suppression of the Israelites in Egypt, their becoming numerous and strong there, the Lord's redeeming them and leading them into freedom (the exodus event, including the crossing of the Red

---

[269] Cf. Levey 51, n. 5, specifically referring to vv. 3-4, but also to the rest of the chapter.

[270] Cf. Sperber 3.292; Eng. Levey 49.

[271] Ibid.

[272] In reference to Exod 1:22, *Cant. Rab.* 2:15 § 2 (Dunski 77; Soncino 9.136) asks how many infants altogether were thrown into the River (Nile). The answer is ten thousand, the רְבָבָה (*rebhabhah*) of Ezek 16:7.

[273] Cf. Sperber 3.292; Eng. Levey 50. The dittography of the phrase with "in your blood" allows this, or the Hebrew "bloods" is interpreted so. All other MSS have "lamb," only SP the plural. As Levey points out (51, n. 8), this could be its later attempt to avoid a possible allusion to Jesus as *the* lamb of God. In *Mek. R. Ish.* Pisḥa 5 on Exod 12:6 (Lauterbach 1.33-34), R. Mattyah b. Ḥeresh, a second generation Tanna (*Introduction* 83), first expounds Ezek 16:8, and then the "bloods" (the dual form, as well as the repetition of the word) of v. 6 as the paschal sacrifice and circumcision.

[274] Cf. Sperber 3.293; Eng. Levey 50.

[275] Ibid.

Sea), the Lord's cloud of glory, an angel leading the way ahead of them, and manna. I suggest that the Apostle Paul was aware of this targumic reinterpretation of the Hebrew text, at least in an earlier form, just as the haggadic narrative of R. Aqiba related above in section 5.3 was based to a great extent on the same verses of Ezekiel. There are four reasons for the above assertion. I will leave a discussion of the fourth, "being washed" in regard to "being baptized," until the next section, 7.

1. Paul also employs the cloud, the (Red) Sea, and spiritual food (manna) in 1 Cor 10:1-3.

2. The *Targum* adds "Abraham your father" and "the merit of your fathers" (Abraham, Isaac and Jacob) in v. 3, and "your (fore)fathers" (אבהתכון [*ʾbhtkun*]) in vv. 6, 7 and 8.[276] I suggest that in addition to the material now found in *m. Pesaḥ* 10:5-6, Paul's emphasizing in 1 Cor 10:1 all our "fathers" (πατέρες), meant as "(fore)fathers," was also in part influenced by the cluster of this terminology in *Targ.* Ezek 16:3-8.

3. *Targum* Ezekiel 16 as of v. 14 greatly emphasizes the motif of idol worship, including ritual offerings / sacrifices. Although this is already in part present in the MT (cf. v. 36), the *Targum* adds it and expands it again and again: vv. 15, 16, (17), 19, 20, 22, 25, 26, 29, 33, 34 and 36. 1 Cor 10:1-4, partially informed by the Judaic traditions still found in *Targ.* Ezek 16:1-14, by itself does not openly refer or allude to idolatry. Therefore some commentators consider 10:1 to be a new topic. Yet it begins with "for" (γάρ) and picks up on the discussion of idol worship in chapter 8. As noted before, in 10:7 Paul specifically mentions "becoming idolaters," which he finds within the "playing" of Exod 32:6. The "sexual immorality" of 10:8 alludes to Num 25:1-9, yet it also involved idolatrous worship of Baal Peor. Paul warns the Corinthians to "flee from the worship of idols" in v. 14, and mentions them again in v. 19, with demons in vv. 20-21. He continues with a discussion of Christians' eating food sold in the market which has been offered to an idol (vv. 23-33; 11:1).

Read in the context of Judaic tradition on Ezek 16:1-13, 1 Cor 10:1-4 thus fits Paul's following discussion of idol worship very well. The *Targum* of this Ezekiel chapter strongly emphasized the same motif.

The dating of the *Targum* should now be addressed. "Its language is basically Palestinian Aramaic, revised and edited in Babylon."[277] While

---

[276] Cf. also "your father Abraham" in v. 45. The MT has "your father an Amorite" here. See Sperber 3.292-93; Eng. Levey 49-50.

[277] Cf. Levey 1.

the rest of the *Targum* may at least in part have been revised by R. Yoḥanan b. Zakkai, a first generation Tanna who survived the Jewish-Roman War of 66-70 CE and founded a school at Yabneh,[278] this will not have pertained to chapter 16. The English translator Levey himself points to the *Targum*'s rendering of 16:61 as possibly reflecting the historical situation of 165-104 BCE.[279] If so, at least this section is very early.

More important is an argument regarding the entire chapter, especially the basic rewriting of vv. 1-14 back into the wilderness period, important for 1 Cor 10:1-4. As noted before, Ezekiel 16, labeled "Make known to Jerusalem her abominations" in *t. Meg.* 3:34,[280] or in the Erfurt MS its "reproof" (תּוֹכַחַת [*tōkhaḥat*]),[281] with its shocking sexual imagery was certainly considered even before 70 CE too revolting to be read alone in Hebrew in the synagogue service. It should be recalled that R. Eliezer, a second generation Tanna of the older group, therefore did not want it to be read at all. Yet it was considered holy Scripture and therefore should also be read. For this reason, like the similarly sexually shocking accounts of Amnon and Tamar (2 Samuel 13), Absalom and his father's concubine (2 Sam 16:20-23), and the concubine of Gibeah (Judges 19), Ezekiel 16 is both "read and translated [into Aramaic]."[282] This is because "Verses referring to warnings and punishments in the Torah[283] are read and translated."[284]

This is precisely what Paul states in 1 Cor 10:6, "Now these things [in vv. 1-5] occurred as [negative] examples[285] for us, so that we might not desire evil as [the Israelites in the wilderness] did." He adds more negative examples and then states in v. 11: "These things happened to

---

278 Cf. *Introduction* 74. On this, see Levey 2, 4 and 51, n. 5.

279 Cf. Levey 55, n. 30, for details.

280 Cf. Lieberman, *Tosefta*. The Order of Moʿed, 363.

281 Cf. Jastrow 1652: "reproof, admonition, threat of punishment," "rebuke." In *b. Shab.* 129b (Soncino 647) it is simply called "the chapter of rebuke" (פרשת תוכחה [*prsht twkhḥh*]).

282 Cf. *t. Meg.* 3:32-34 (Zuckermandel / Liebermann 228; Eng. Neusner 2.296). In 3:31 the similar narrative of Lot and his two daughters (Gen 19:30-38) is also read and translated, as well as the first part of the Golden Calf account.

283 This is meant here in its broader sense.

284 Cf. *t. Meg.* 3:31 in Lieberman, *Tosefta*. The Order of Moʿed, 362; Eng. Neusner 2.296.

285 Cf. τύπος in BAGD 830, 5. b.

them to serve as a [warning] example,[286] and they were written down to instruct us, on whom the ends of the ages have come." Paul's intention is the same as that found in the Tosefta in connection with Ezekiel 16: to warn the Corinthian Christians by citing negative examples from Scripture.

For the above reasons I consider *Targum* Ezekiel 16 basically to be pre-70 CE and to have been known at least in an earlier form to Paul. The shocking chapter was not allowed to be read aloud publicly without being reinterpreted at least partially in a positive manner, especially vv. 1-14. And it is precisely verses from this section which inform 1 Cor 10:1-4.

7. *Being Baptized into Moses in the Cloud and the Sea*

Paul writes in 1 Cor 10:2 that "all 'were baptized' into Moses in the cloud and in the Sea." Nestle-Aland[28] has the aorist passive form ἐβαπτίσθησαν here, which I agree is preferable to ἐβαπτίσαντο, the aorist middle, found in some manuscripts. The verb βαπτίζω primarily means to "dip, immerse," only later in Christian usage such as in Paul to "baptize."[287] The Israelites were baptized "into Moses," εἰς τὸν Μωϋσῆν. Paul certainly models this on being baptized "into" (εἰς) Christ, as in Rom 6:3 and Gal 3:27. The fuller form is "into the name of," as in 1 Cor 1:13 and 15. It is this phrase regarding the Israelites, "being baptized into Moses," which has puzzled the commentators for centuries. I would thus like to propose a new solution to this conundrum based on the text analyzed above, Ezekiel 16.

As pointed out in section 1., the Israelites could not have been baptized "in the [Red] Sea" because Scripture and Judaic tradition repeat again and again that they remained dry the entire time, not touched by a drop of water. Secondly, they were also baptized "in the cloud." This is definitely not thought of as a heavy rain cloud, which produced a shower of water

---

286 Cf. τυπικῶς in BAGD 829: "typologically, as an example or warning," only here in the NT.

287 Cf. BAGD 131, who prefer the middle here, "dip oneself, wash." Yet the Israelites did not voluntarily let themselves be "dipped / washed / baptized" in the Red Sea. See also LSJ 305: "dip, plunge." They also read the middle here: "get oneself baptized" (306).

upon the fleeing Israelites, thus "baptizing" them.[288] I therefore proposed that ἐν, "in," should be read as "in (the time of)," that is, a) when they were led by a cloud (Exod 13:21-22) before they crossed the Red Sea, as well as from the far shore onwards; and b) when the newborn Israelites according to the early haggadic narrative described above were "washed with water" at their birth in the field, abandoned by their mothers, grew up, returned home, and after crossing the Red Sea, on the far side saw the Lord, pointed up to Him and declared: "*This* is my God, and I will praise Him, my father's God, and I will exalt Him" (Exod 15:2).[289] The accompanying cloud is assumed to be present also at this time. Ezek 16:4 and 9 are the background of this "washing with water," as will now be argued.

Ezek 16:4 states of the newborn girl (Jerusalem): "and you were not washed with water for cleansing." Verse 9 says regarding the Lord's activity: "And I washed you with water, and washed off the blood from upon you, and I anointed you with oil." The Hebrew for "to wash" with water in both instances is רָחַץ (*raḥaṣ*): to wash, wash off, away, bathe.[290] While the *Targum* has a completely different text in v. 9, in v. 4 it employs the verb שְׁטֵף (*sheṭēph*), to wash, rinse.[291] The LXX renders the Hebrew רחץ (*rḥṣ*) both times by the verb λούω, to wash,[292] as it almost exclusively does elsewhere,[293] usually with ὕδατι, with / by water. The verb רחץ (*rḥṣ*) also stands behind βάπτω, to dip,[294] once in the LXX.[295] This in turn is a synonym of βαπτίζω,[296] usually employed in the NT. It is also noteworthy that Paul employs the verb ἀπολούω in the aorist

---

[288] Cf. again the remarks of Meyer and Zeller in n. 90.

[289] As noted earlier, another tradition says these were still infants. It should be noted that this "washing with water" by the Lord or an angel occurs only once for each infant, just as baptizing with water also occurs only once.

[290] Cf. BDB 934. One occurrence is found in Gen 18:4, connected to Ezek 16:9 in section 5.1 above. See also Jastrow 1468, with examples of "they were 'cleansed' of their sins."

[291] Cf. Jastrow 1554.

[292] Cf. LSJ 1062; BAGD 480: wash, bathe. See the variant reading of Rev 1:5, "him who washed / cleansed us from our sins through his blood" (see n. 290).

[293] Cf. thirty-nine more times for רחץ (*rḥṣ*), and only once for שחה (*śḥh* - Ps 6:7). It is rendered by the verb ἀπολούω in Job 9:30.

[294] Cf. LSJ 306. In Arrianus, a second century CE writer, it can mean to baptize.

[295] Cf. Ps 67:24.

[296] Cf. LSJ 305: dip, plunge.

middle form in 1 Cor 6:11. The Corinthian Christians were "washed" and sanctified, certainly a reference to baptism.[297]

The cognate noun רַחְצָה (*rahṣah*), washing,[298] occurs only at Cant 4:2 and 6:6, where the LXX renders it by λουτρόν, which also occurs only in these two verses in the LXX. Its basic meaning is "bath."[299] In the NT it has the meaning "bath, washing" of baptism,[300] and occurs only twice, both times within the Pauline School. Titus 3:5 says God saved us (in baptism) "through the 'washing' of rebirth and renewal by the Holy Spirit." Eph 5:25 says husbands should love their wives, "just as Christ loved the church and gave himself up for her, 26) in order to make her holy by cleansing her with the 'washing' of water by the word." The "washing" here is λουτρόν. Nestle-Aland[28] refer here significantly to Ezek 16:9, yet they could also have noted v. 4. This is because the latter adds in the Hebrew "for cleansing," the very rare מִשְׁעִי (*mish ʿî*), only occurring here in the MT. This is probably why the LXX omitted it. Yet the *Targum* renders it with אתנקדא (*ʾtnqd ʾ*),[301] "to be cleansed." This could very well have influenced the author's choice of the verb καθαρίζω, to cleanse,[302] along with λουτρόν in Eph 5:26 in reference to baptism.

Eph 5:26 also appears to be an allusion to Ezek 16:(4 and) 9, as also maintained by the commentators.[303] The author may have known that Paul himself associated Ezek 16:4 and 9 with baptism, as I have proposed for 1 Cor 10:2.[304]

---

[297] Cf. LSJ 208 and BAGD 96 on the verb, employed elsewhere in the NT only at Acts 22:16, "Get up, be baptized, and have your sins 'washed away,' calling on his name." See also n. 292.

[298] Cf. BDB 934.

[299] Cf. LSJ 1061.

[300] Cf. BAGD 480.

[301] Cf. Sperber 3.292; Eng. Levey 50. See Jastrow 935 on נקר / נקד (*nqr* / *nqd*) II.

[302] Cf. BAGD 387: make clean, cleanse, purify.

[303] Cf. for example Andrew Lincoln, *Ephesians* (WBC 42; Dallas, TX: Word Books, 1990) 375, who calls attention not only to 1 Cor 6:11, but also to the "bridal bath" of Ezek 16:9. See also Petr Pokorný, *Der Brief des Paulus an die Epheser* (THNT 10/II; Leipzig: Evangelische Verlagsanstalt, 1992) 222: "Die Taufe als Reinigung paβt ... zur Metapher für die Ehe, da das Baden der Braut vor der Hochzeit ein allgemein verbreiteter Brauch was (z. B. Ez. 16,8-14 - von Jahwe u. Israel)."

[304] Andrew Bandstra strangely rejects the basic Christian meaning of βαπτίζω in 1 Cor 10:2 and refers it instead to a "judgment ordeal," interpreting the cloud and the sea as "the two elemental ordeal powers, fire and water." Cf. his "Interpretation in 1 Corinthians 10:1-11" in *Calvin Theological Journal* 6 (1971) 8.

In *Exod. Rab.* Beshallaḥ 20/11 on Exod 13:17 and its parallel traditions (see section 5.2 above), it is the Lord (God) who washes the Israelites with water in the wilderness, for which Ezek 16:9 is quoted. It is also He who anoints them with oil (ibid.). In *Exod. Rab.* Shemoth 1/12 on Exod 1:14 (and its parallel traditions; see section 5.3 above), God sends an angel from on high to cleanse (with water - Ezek 16:4) the newborn Hebrew infants in the field. I suggest that Paul was acquainted with at least one of these narratives in an earlier form and thought of Christ being active here, either described as an angel,[305] or as the Lord. If the latter, Paul as a Hellenistic Jewish Christian could have perceived the κύριος of the LXX in these Ezekiel 16 passages not as the Lord (God), but as Christ the Lord. Such usage is shown in 1 Corinthians 10 itself. Referring to Num 21:5-6, Paul in v. 9 says, "We must not put Christ to the test, as some of them did, and were destroyed by serpents." This presupposes that Christ was present in the wilderness on that occasion. The variant reading for "Christ" here, also relatively well attested, is "Lord," κύριος. However, as shown by the better reading "Christ," the Lord here is not God but Jesus Christ as Lord. In the nearby v. 21, Paul also speaks of the "cup of the Lord" and the "table of the Lord," both times with κύριος. He clearly means Christ here, as in the phrases "the blood of Christ" and "the body of Christ" in the Eucharist in v. 16. In addition, at least one Palestinian Semitic tradition could describe the Messiah as "the Lord."[306] The imagery of "anointing" and "oil" in Judaic interpretation of Ezek 16:9 also may have encouraged a bilingual (Greek and Hebrew / Aramaic) Jewish Christian, even Paul himself, to think of the Messiah, the "anointed one with oil," as present here.

The Lord (now thought of as Christ) washed the newborn Israelite infants with water when they were born in the field in Egypt. When they as adults (or in another tradition still as infants) had passed through the Red Sea to the far shore, they recognized him as their Lord and praised / exalted him (Exod 15:2).

As described in section 4. above, the well which accompanied the Israelites in the wilderness was thought to have done so from the very

---

305 Two recent studies of angel christology are by Charles Gieschen, *Angelomorphic Christology: Antecedents and Early Evidence* (AGAJU 42; Leiden: Brill, 1998), and Darrell Hannah, *Michael Traditions and Angel Christology in Early Christianity* (WUNT 2.109; Tűbingen: Mohr Siebeck, 1999). Neither deals with Ezekiel 16 in Judaic tradition as related to 1 Cor 10:2.

306 Cf. Appendix II. above.

outset, thus retroactively, for the entire forty years.[307] It provided them with water in abundance for all their needs, including for washing themselves.[308] In addition, the well and the rock could be thought of as equivalent, certainly in part because of how the shape of the well was described in Judaic thought. This makes the statement in 1 Cor 10:4, "and the rock was Christ," much less striking. It associates Christ with the rock / well, and thus with the source of the water needed by the Israelites during the exodus / wilderness wandering period.

Yet what does being baptized "into Moses" at the time of the cloud (already in Exod 13:21-22) and the Red Sea mean in 1 Cor 10:2? In the NT baptism was always voluntary, and in the beginning presumably only adults were baptized. That is, the person desiring to be baptized renounced adherence to a former life of sin (for Jews), or to other gods (for Gentiles). One's new life as a Christian was under the leadership of Christ,[309] who now mediates between God and man, as Moses did between God and the Israelites.[310] This is the simplest and most satisfying explanation for being baptized "into Moses." It was into his

---

307 Other Judaic traditions have the well go back even to the time of the Patriarchs. One example is Jacob's well in Gen 29:1-14, which provided the background (e.g. rolling away a large stone from the opening) for the Gospel narrative of the empty tomb. Cf. the extensive discussion in my *The Death, Burial, and Resurrection of Jesus, and the Death, Burial, and Translation of Moses in Judaic Tradition* (Studies in Judaism; Lanham, MD: University Press of America, 2008) 179-97.

308 Cf. *Midr. Pss.* 23/4 on Ps 23:2, "He leads me beside refreshing waters." R. Samuel (probably bar Naḥman, a third generation Palestinian Amora: *Introduction* 97,) stated: "the waters of the well were fit to drink and fit 'to wash in' [לרחוץ - *lrḥwṣ*]. They brought refreshment to the body and health to the soul, as it says: Ps 23:2" (Buber 200-01; Braude 1.331). Just before this it is stated that the Israelites' garments did not have to be washed (כִּבֵּס [*kabhas*]: Jastrow 609, of clothes) because the pillar of fire (Exod 13:21) cleansed them and made them shine.

309 Cf. the statement of Cyril of Jerusalem (d. ca. 386 CE) in his "Mystagogical Lectures I 1. 3" in regard to 1 Cor 10:2 : "Moses' mission was to lead out of Egypt a persecuted people; Christ's was to rescue all the people of the world who were under the tyranny of sin." See *1-2 Corinthians*, ed. Bray (Ancient Christian Commentary on Scripture, New Testament VII) 89.

310 Cf. also believing in God and His servant Jesus (as in Phil 2:7) with the rescued Israelites' "believing in the Lord and in His servant Moses" (Exod 14:31).

leadership for the entire time of the exodus / wilderness wandering.[311] This was considered by Paul (or possibly by the Jewish-Christian tradition informing him) to be analogous to being baptized into the authority and domination of Christ.

Christ is thus considered to have been already present at the events of the exodus and the wilderness wandering, i.e., as "pre-existent." This motif is found elsewhere in Paul, the rest of the NT, and in Judaic sources for the Messiah, as I now point out.

8. *Christ Considered as Pre-existent*

Paul asserts that the Israelites in the wilderness drank from the spiritual rock which accompanied them, and it was Christ (1 Cor 10:4). This means that he existed and was active many centuries before he was crucified, died, was buried, rose from the dead, and then appeared to various people, including Paul (15:3-8). As proposed above, the Apostle also asserts in 10:9 that some Israelites put Christ (as the Lord) to the test in the incident of Num 21:5-6, which also took place in the wilderness. Paul clearly pictures Christ as pre-existent in these verses.[312]

Hymnic elements in the greater Pauline Corpus also present Christ as pre-existent. In the so-called "Christ Hymn" of Phil 2:6-11, generally thought to have been appropriated by Paul from elsewhere at this point, he is described as being "in the form of God" (v. 6), that is, of heavenly nature. Yet he "emptied himself,"[313] "being born in human likeness" (v.

---

311 Cf. Acts 7:35, where God sent Moses as a "ruler and liberator," who then led the Israelites out, including the wilderness (v. 36).

312 Cf. also 8:6, "Jesus Christ, through whom are all things...." I find it difficult to follow Richard Jeske, who maintains the phrase "and the rock was Christ" refers to "the pre-existence of the corporate body of Christ, the church." See his "The Rock was Christ: The Ecclesiology of 1 Corinthians 10," in *Kirche*. Festschrift für Günther Bornkamm zum 75. Geburtstag, ed. Dieter Lührmann and Georg Strecker (Tübingen: Mohr, 1980) 248.

313 Cf. also 2 Cor 8:9, "though he was rich, yet for your sakes he became poor...."

7).[314] After his death on a cross (v. 8), God exalted him and gave him the name above every name (v. 9), "Lord" (κύριος - v. 11).[315]

From the Pauline School, Col 1:15-20 contains another early hymn. It states that Christ is "the image of the invisible God, the firstborn of all creation" (v. 15). "All things were created through him and for him" (v. 16), and "he himself is before all things" (v. 17), i.e., he existed before the creation of the world.[316]

The latter is also true for the name of the Messiah in Judaic sources. *Gen. Rab.* Bereshith 1/4 deals with Gen 1:1, "In the beginning God created." It relates that "six things preceded the creation of the world; some of them were actually created, while the creation of the others was already contemplated." Among the latter was "the name of the Messiah," for it is written: "His name existeth ere the sun" (Ps 72:17).[317]

Another Judaic source also connects the Messiah with the creation of the world. In *Gen. Rab.* Bereshith 2/4 on Gen 1:2, "And the spirit of God hovered," these words are interpreted in the following manner: "this alludes to the Messiah, as you read: 'And the spirit of the Lord shall rest upon him' (Isa 11:2)."[318] The latter verse is frequently interpreted messianically.[319]

---

314 Cf. Rom 8:3, "by sending His own Son in the likeness of sinful flesh," and Gal 4:4, "God sent His Son...."

315 Cf. 2 Cor 4:4-5, where Christ as Lord is the image of God. Thiessen in "The Rock Was Christ" 120 states that Paul's "frequent references to Christ as κύριος suggests that he identifies Christ with Yhwh."

316 The author of Jude in v. 5 also portrays Jesus Christ as pre-existent at the time of the exodus: "Jesus once and for all saved a people out of the land of Egypt, afterwards he destroyed those who did not believe." Is this a faint echo of 1 Cor 10:4-5? Cf. Hannah, *Michael Traditions and Angel Christology* 139-40.

317 Cf. Theodor and Albeck 6, with parallels in the note on line 4; Soncino 1.6. For the name "Yinnon" from Ps 72:17 as a name of the Messiah, see the passages cited in Str-B 1.65.

318 Cf. Theodor and Albeck 17; Soncino 1.17. In a parallel tradition, *Pesiq. R.* 33/6 on Isa 51:12 (Friedmann 152b; Braude 642-43), this is stated as proof that "the King Messiah existed from the beginning of God's creation of the world." This work at 36/1 on Isa 60:1-2, dealing with Ps 36:10 (Friedmann 161b; Braude 677), also interprets the light of the latter verse as the light of the Messiah, referred to in Gen 1:4, "And God saw the light that it was good." See also *Lev. Rab.* Thazria 14/1 on Lev 12:2 (Mirkin 7.154; Soncino 4.178): "i.e., the spirit of the Messianic King."

319 Cf. e.g. *Gen. Rab.* Yayechi 97 on Gen 49:8 (Theodor and Albeck 1213; Soncino 2.902); *Num. Rab.* Naso 13/11 on Num 7:13 (Mirkin 10.62; Soncino 6.523); *Ruth*

Such passages show that a "wisdom christology" as found elsewhere in the NT[320] is not necessary to elucidate the motif of the Messiah's (the Christ's) pre-existence as described by Paul in 1 Cor 10:1-4 and 9. Both in Hellenistic Jewish Christianity (Phil 2:6-11) and in Palestinian Judaic sources the Messiah / the Christ was considered to have already existed before the creation of the world. Paul's assertion that Christ was present in the later wilderness wandering of the Israelites was another example of this tradition.

9. *The Form of 1 Cor 10:1-5*

1 Cor 10:1-5 is part of Paul's first *letter* to the Corinthians. Before discussing vv. 1-5, it is appropriate to consider the nature of the entire unit, vv. 1-13.

Over a hundred years ago Johannes Weiss employed the term "midrash" for these verses.[321] He has been followed by many others. Nils Dahl, for example, labeled vv. 1-13 a Christian midrash containing more or less "fest geprägte Lehrstücke," which Paul had already employed before in congregational meetings for the purpose of exhortation or polemic.[322] Jean Héring called vv. 1-5 "ce petit traité midrashique."[323] Raymond Collins speaks of vv. 1-13 as "a sustained midrashic exposition" which "has its roots in a pre-Pauline, perhaps even a pre-Christian, tradition."[324] Gary Collier believes vv. 1-13 are "a self-contained midrash on ἐπιθυμία in Numbers 11," "a small but pointed

---

Rab. 7/2 on Ruth 3:15 (Vilna, Ruth 22; Soncino 8.83); and *Targ.* Isa 11:1-2 (Stenning 40-41).

320 Cf. John 1:1-3, 10, 14; 1 John 1:2; as well as OT / LXX passages such as Prov 8:22 and Sir 24:9.

321 Cf. his *Der erste Korintherbrief* 250. On p. 251 he speaks of "a special midrashic exegesis" in this unit.

322 Cf. the dissertation of one of my Yale professors, *Das Volk Gottes.* Eine Untersuchung zum Kirchenbewußtsein des Urchristentums (Oslo: Dybwad, 1941) 210 and 322, n. 8.

323 Cf. his *La première épitre de Saint Paul aux Corinthiens* (Neuchâtel: Delachaux & Niestlé, 1959²) 77.

324 Cf. his *First Corinthians* (Sacra Pagina 7; Collegeville, MN: The Liturgical Press, 1999) 364.

midrash on craving evil."[325] Alexander Wedderburn thinks one tradition informing 10:1-4 is "an already existing Christian midrash or midrashim on the Exodus events."[326]

Other scholars could be cited here who maintain that 1 Cor 10:1-13 or at least vv. 1-5 are a midrash or "midrash-like." Yet the term is inappropriate at this point. Strictly speaking, one should only speak of a "midrash" when a specific OT verse or verses are expounded as to their meaning, either for the past, or, more commonly, for the present.[327] Examples in this study are the narrative of the angels' rewarding Abraham for his behavior in light of the verses of Genesis 18 (section 3.1 above), as well as the unusual birth of Israelites just before the exodus, explained on the basis of verses from Ezekiel 16 (section 3.3 above). In 1 Cor 10:1-13, only Exod 32:6 is expressly quoted in v. 7. Verse 8 clearly alludes to Num 25: 1-9, and v. 9 to Num 21:5-6. Other verses, however, only have subtle allusions to passages in Exodus and Numbers. Thus the term "midrash" in its narrower sense should not be employed here.[328]

Other commentators characterize 1 Cor 10:1-13 as a "homily." Wayne Meeks believes it is of Christian origin and was "very carefully composed prior to its use in its present context."[329] Christophe Senft also labels it

---

[325] Cf. his "'That We Might Not Crave Evil.' The Structure and Argument of 1 Corinthians 10.1-13" in *JSNT* 55 (1994) 74.

[326] Cf. his *Baptism and Resurrection* 244.

[327] Cf. the first meaning of מִדְרָשׁ (*midrash*) in Jastrow 735: textual interpretation. See also the verb דְּרַשׁ (*darash*) in Jastrow 325, 2): to expound, interpret. Moshe David Herr in the art. "Midrash" in *EJ* (2007) 14.182-85 differentiates between midrash and pesher in the Dead Sea Scrolls. Midrash usually forms "a running commentary on specific books of the Bible" (182). In contrast to the homiletical midrashim, *Genesis Rabbah*, the oldest aggadic midrash, is typical of the exegetical kind (183). See also Klaus Berger, *Formen und Gattungen im Neuen Testament* (UTB 2532; Tűbingen / Basel: A. Francke, 2005) 172, who differentiates between various types of midrash, beginning with the exegetical kind.

[328] This is also true for the term "pesher," which should be reserved for the Dead Sea Scrolls. Against Alastair McEwen, "Paul's Use of the Old Testament in 1 Corinthians 10:1-4" in *Vox Reformata* 47 (1986) 6 and 8, where he strangely combines it with "midrash." See the Herr article in n. 327.

[329] Cf. the essay of my Yale doctoral advisor, "'And Rose Up to Play': Midrash and Paraenesis in 1 Corinthians 10:1-22," in *JSNT* 16 (1982) 65, as well as 73.

"une brève homélie."[330] Peter von der Osten-Sacken argues that there was no "Vorlage," supplemented in a minor way by Paul, yet the unit is nevertheless a homily.[331] J. Smit, however, argues that Paul didn't use a pre-existing homily at all because "his presentation of this story is completely adapted to the actual rhetorical situation."[332] If one accepts as I do 10:1-13 as an integral part of the letter First Corinthians, and one does not see a seam either at v. 1 (loosely connected by γάρ , "for," to the preceding, especially chapter 8),[333] or at v. 14 (the idolatry theme continues here: "therefore"), there is no compelling reason to consider vv. 1-13 to be a separate homily inserted at this point.

While it cannot completely be excluded that Paul borrowed from elsewhere as pre-formulated some of the material he employs in 1 Cor 10:1-13, or that he himself now used certain motifs he had emphasized elsewhere in his teaching, I find this improbable. We have no evidence for the latter in his extant writings. And although Paul definitely employs motifs in vv. 1-4 which, for example, are in part based on Judaic tradition regarding the first verses of Ezekiel 16, the Apostle to the Gentiles most probably is composing completely on his own at this point. I argue for this because of his bilingual early training in Judaic traditions,[334] and because he demonstrates great skill throughout his letters by combining such traditions with citations of, and allusions to, the OT (primarily the LXX, only at times the MT).[335]

---

330 Cf. his *La Première Épitre de Saint Paul aux Corinthiens* (CNT 2. VII; Geneva: Labor et Fides, 1990²) 127. Collier in "That We Might Not Crave Evil" 74 also sees the possibility of an independent "homily" of some kind being employed here.

331 Cf. his "Geschrieben zu unserer Ermahnung" 64.

332 Cf. his "'Do Not Be Idolaters.' Paul's Rhetoric in First Corinthians 10:1-22" in *NovTest* 39 (1997) 49.

333 It is very improbable that Paul dictated (16:1) this letter of sixteen chapters all at one time. He could very well have taken a break at the end of chapter 9 before commencing again at 10:1.

334 Cf. again Acts 22:3; 26:4; and Gal 1:14.

335 The Jewish converts Paul made in Corinth (and probably also proselytes to Judaism) would have recognized the exodus and wilderness events to which Paul alluded in 1 Cor 10:1-5. They knew their holy Scriptures very well. In his stay of one and a half years in the city (Acts 18:11), he would also have attempted to show the Gentiles that Christ was the fulfilment of the OT promises. He thus also acquainted such people with basic or key biblical narratives, especially as interpreted in Judaic tradition. Cf. Werner Klaiber, *Der erste Korintherbrief* (Die Botschaft des Neuen Testaments; Neukirchen-Vluyn: Neukirchener, 2011) 151:

In light of the above, I consider a characterization of 1 Cor 10:1-13 as "haggadic paraenesis" to be most appropriate.[336] The Greek term παραίνεσις means "exhortation," "advice or counsel given" by someone to another.[337] This is precisely what Paul is doing in chapter 10. He exhorts the Corinthian Christians to flee from the worship of idols (v. 14). They should not believe participation in idolatrous practices such as drinking the wine and eating the food dedicated to an idol is compatible with drinking (wine) from the cup of blessing, the blood of Christ, and eating the bread, sharing in the body of Christ, at the Eucharist (vv. 14-22).

To make the above points, Paul enumerates various events in early Israelite history, those in vv. 1-4 already being found in a number of scriptural passages and in early Judaic traditions in a cluster. These events occurred as warning "examples" (τύποι, v. 6; τυπικῶς, v. 11). They were written down in the Scriptures for the νουθεσία (admonition, instruction, warning)[338] of present-day Christians, who live at the ends of the ages (v. 11).

One of the purposes of Judaic haggadah is to aid in driving home the point a writer / speaker is making through the use of appropriate illustrations.[339] The listing of examples is exactly what Paul does in 1 Cor 10:1-10. He begins in vv. 1-4 by adducing examples from the exodus,

---

Paul presumes knowledge of the OT narratives to which he refers. See also Luise Schottroff, *Der erste Brief an die Gemeinde in Korinth* (TKNT 7; Stuttgart: Kohlhammer, 2013) 178: "Paulus tippt hier die Exodusgeschichte wie in einer Zusammenfassung von Bekanntem an...."

[336] In this regard cf. Wolff, *Der erste Brief an die Korinther* 39 on vv. 1-10: It can be called an "haggadic midrash." Collins in *First Corinthians* 364 notes regarding vv. 1-13: "Paul's use of the Exodus account bears similarity to rabbinic *haggadah* (the story) and *halakhah* (the behavioral imperative)." In *Der erste Brief an die Korinther* 2.381, Wolfgang Schrage labels 10:1-13 an "*exemplum* mit paränetischer Funktion."

[337] Cf. LSJ 1310. The verb παραινέω means to exhort, recommend, advise.

[338] Cf. BAGD 544. The noun occurs only here, Eph 6:4, and Titus 3:10 in the NT. Berger in *Formen und Gattungen* 86 (see also 159) speaks of the wilderness generation as a deterrent "example" in 1 Cor 10:1-12. It is a "warning" for the Christian congregation (175).

[339] A major discussion of the term "haggadah / aggadah" cannot be given here. One example is Jacob Neusner, *The Halakhah and the Aggadah* (Studies in Ancient Judaism; Lanham, MD: University Press of America, 2001). For a full description, with relevant secondary literature, see my *The Death, Burial, and Resurrection of Jesus* 283-91.

Judaism's core event of salvation, and the wilderness wandering period of forty years. Yet in addition he employs Judaic traditions regarding these events, including the well, applying them to the present by maintaining that all the Corinthian Christians (not just those of Jewish background) were then already present. Even Christ was there.[340] Such statements are typically haggadic.

For the above reasons I prefer the designation "haggadic paraenesis" for 1 Cor 10:1-13, including vv. 1-5, the main object of this entire study.

---

340 Cf. also the Judaic tenet that "no strict order as to 'earlier' and 'later' is observed in the Torah" in *Mek. R. Ish.* Shirata 7 on Exod 15:9 (Lauterbach 2.54-55), as well as *Eccl. Rab.* 1:12 § 1 (Vilna, Eccl. 9; Soncino 8.37-38).

II. PAUL'S TOLERATION IN CORINTH OF BAPTISM ON BEHALF OF THE DEAD (1 COR 15:29), AND INTERCESSION FOR THE DEAD IN EARLY JUDAISM

Introduction

While Paul already spoke of the resurrection of the dead in his earliest letter (1 Thess 4:13-18), his major description of it is now found in 1 Corinthians 15. It was written from Ephesus (16:8), probably around 54 CE.[1] In this long chapter of fifty-eight verses, Paul argues fervently against some of the Corinthian Christians who maintained there is no resurrection of the dead (15:12). In part, he describes how Christ is the first fruits of the resurrection. When he returns, those who belong to him will be raised, and the end will then come (vv. 20-28).

---

[1] Cf. e.g. Roy Ciampa and Brian Rosner, *The First Letter to the Corinthians* (Pillar New Testament Commentary; Grand Rapids, MI: Eerdmans, 2010) 3: "in the spring of 54 or 55 A.D." The dating is connected with Gallio's being proconsul of Achaia in Corinth (ca. 51-52 CE) when Paul was brought before his tribunal (Acts 18:12). Before this, v. 11 states that he had taught the word of God in Corinth for a year and six months.

Paul adds another argument, now a practical one, for the resurrection in v. 29, correctly separated from the preceding by being made a new paragraph in the NRSV, and from the new personal argument in vv. 30-34. Verse 29 reads: "Otherwise, what will those people do who receive baptism on behalf of the dead? If the dead are not raised at all, why are people baptized on their behalf?" These rhetorical questions are the Greek: Ἐπεὶ τί ποιήσουσιν οἱ βαπτιζόμενοι ὑπὲρ τῶν νεκρῶν; εἰ ὅλως νεκροὶ οὐκ ἐγείρονται, τί καὶ βαπτίζονται ὑπὲρ αὐτῶν.[2]

Martin Luther in 1544 already called v. 29 an *obscurus locus*.[3] Roy Ciampa and Brian Rosner maintain it is "undoubtedly the most difficult verse to interpret in the entire letter...."[4] Michael Hull in his recent monograph on the verse notes that it "remains one of the most contested and controversial verses in the NT."[5] Christophe Senft is of the opinion: "The verse is embarrassing and has given birth to a bizarre efflorescence of interpretations."[6] With tongue in cheek, Hans Conzelmann maintained that ever since the early Church Fathers "the ingenuity of the exegetes celebrates triumphs" over it.[7] Richard De Maris labels it an "exegetical puzzle."[8] Richard Hays thinks the contents are "notoriously puzzling,"[9] and Raymond Collins speaks of the verse as "this enigmatic reference."[10] James Patrick notes that baptism for the dead is a "mysterious practice."[11]

---

[2] I accept the text as found in Nestle-Aland's *Novum Testamentum Graece*[28].

[3] Cited from the Weimar edition of Luther's works by Mathis Rissi in *Die Taufe für die Toten: Ein Beitrag zur paulinischen Tauflehre* (ATANT 42; Zurich / Stuttgart: Zwingli, 1962) 16.

[4] Cf. their *The First Letter to the Corinthians* 780.

[5] Cf. his *Baptism on Account of the Dead (1 Cor 15:29).* An Act of Faith in the Resurrection (Academia Biblica 22; Atlanta: Society of Biblical Literature, 2005) 2. On p. 21 he speaks of its "abstruse nature," and on p. 226 of "this opaque verse."

[6] Cf. his *La Première Épître de Saint Paul aux Corinthiens* 201.

[7] Cf. his *Der erste Brief an die Korinther* 338.

[8] Cf. his "Corinthian Religion and Baptism for the Dead (1 Corinthians 15:29): Insights from Archaeology and Anthropology," in *JBL* 114 (1995) 661.

[9] Cf. his *First Corinthians* (Interpretation, New Testament 7; Louisville, KY: John Knox, 1997) 267.

[10] Cf. his *First Corinthians* (Sacra Pagina 7; Collegeville, MN: The Liturgical Press, 1999) 557.

[11] Cf. his "Living Rewards for Dead Apostles: Baptism for the Dead in 1 Corinthians 15.29" in *NTS* 52 (2006) 84.

Ben Witherington III speaks of its "magical view of baptism's efficacy."[12] Other scholars are more negative. Johannes Weiβ labeled it "that offensive matter."[13] Finally, in 1888 Frédéric Godet called it "such a meaningless, superstitious practice."[14] Archibald Robertson and Alfred Plummer also called it "such a superstitious rite,"[15] and Jerome Murphy-O'Conner "a superstitious practice."[16]

Scholarly opinions regarding 1 Cor 15:29 thus range from its being puzzling and controversial to being meaningless and superstitious. Because the verse has been so perplexing, two monographs have been devoted to it,[17] as well as several research reports. These include those of Karl Staab in regard to the Greek Church Fathers,[18] as well as the general overviews by Bernard Foschini,[19] Christian Wolff,[20] Michael Hull,[21] and most recently Joel White.[22]

---

[12] Cf. his *Conflict and Community in Corinth*. A Socio-Rhetorical Commentary on 1 and 2 Corinthians (Grand Rapids, MI: Eerdmans, 1995) 305-06. See also Alexander Wedderburn, *Baptism and Resurrection:* Studies in Pauline Theology against its Graeco-Roman Background (WUNT 44; Tűbingen: Mohr, 1987) 288, where he calls the practice "a quasi-magical interpretation of the Christian rite."

[13] Cf. his *Der erste Korintherbrief* 361, n. 1.

[14] Cf. his *Kommentar zu dem ersten Briefe an die Korinther, Zweiter Teil, Kapitel 8-16* (Hannover: Meyer, 1888) 212. On p. 213 he maintained it belongs to "the coarsest religious materialism."

[15] Cf. their *A Critical and Exegetical Commentary on the First Epistle of St Paul to the Corinthians* 359-60.

[16] Cf. his "'Baptized for the Dead' (I Cor. XV, 29). A Corinthian Slogan?" in *RB* 88 (1981) 541.

[17] Cf. those of Mathis Rissi and Michael Hull.

[18] Cf. his "1. Korinther 15,29 im Lichte der Exegese der griechischen Kirche" in *Studiorum Paulinorum Congressus Internationalis Catholicus* (AnBib 17/18; Rome: Ponticical Biblical Institute, 1963) 1.443-50. Andreas Reichert in *Das Verständnis der Taufe im 1. Korintherbrief* 197-208 also reviews them.

[19] Cf. his "'Those Who Are Baptized for the Dead,' I Cor. 15:29; An Exegetical Historical Dissertation," in *CBQ* 12 (1950) 260-76, 379-88, and 13 (1951) 46-78, 172-98, 276-83. Interestingly, he maintains that Paul "knew that no such 'Baptism for the dead' existed, and that it was a complete absurdity which he fabricated merely as an instrument of argumentation" (13.281). He is alone in this opinion.

[20] Cf. his *Der erste Brief des Paulus an die Korinther. Zweiter Teil, 7/II,* 185-89.

[21] Cf. his *Baptism* 7-49 on "Contemporary Readings of 1 Corinthians 15:29."

[22] Cf. his "Recent Challenges to the Communis Opinio on 1 Corinthians 15.29" in *Currents in Biblical Research* 10 (2012) 379-95, with bibliography on pp. 394-95.

Most interpretations of 1 Cor 15:29 depend on the meaning of the preposition ὑπέρ in its two occurrences: ὑπὲρ τῶν νεκρῶν and ὑπὲρ αὐτῶν.[23] While this preposition with the genitive elsewhere can mean "in place of, instead of," "because of," and "about, concerning," its first and major meaning is "on behalf of, for the sake of someone or something."[24] This is the way Paul himself employs it in 1 Cor 1:13; 4:6; 11:24; 12:25; and in the resurrection chapter at 15:3. Thus I follow the NRSV and the great majority of commentators in maintaining that some of the Corinthian Christians had themselves baptized again "on behalf of" the dead.[25] This means they did so vicariously, by proxy. In spite of attempts again and again to read the text differently, vicarious baptism has now become the interpretation with a broad consensus.[26]

Yet where did this practice come from? Joel White flatly states regarding vicarious baptism: "Its supporters cannot point to even one instance of a truly analogous phenomenon - one in which a water rite or ritual cleansing is performed on a living human being and designed to affect the fate of a dead individual - anywhere in the ancient world prior to or contemporaneous with Paul."[27] This is also the opinion of James Patrick[28] and others.[29] Nevertheless, scholars have pointed to the pagan

---

[23] Cf. Anthony Thiselton in *The First Epistle to the Corinthians* 1241: "the key issues depend on the use of ὑπέρ with the articular genitive plural noun τῶν νεκρῶν."

[24] Cf. BAGD 838-39 as 1. a. All the Greek Church Fathers also interpreted ὑπέρ as "on behalf of." See Karl Staab, "1. Korinther 15,29" 449.

[25] Cf. e.g. Raymond Collins in *First Corinthians* 557: "The obvious meaning of Paul's words in the Greek text is that some Christians at Corinth practiced a kind of vicarious baptism." In addition, "'On behalf of' (*hyper*) suggests some kind of transferred application of benefits, a vicarious effect (cf. 11:24)" (p. 559).

[26] Cf. the statement to this effect by Helmut Merklein and Marlis Gielen in *Der erste Brief an die Korinther. Kapitel 11,2 - 16,24* (ÖTKNT 7/3; Gütersloh: Gütersloher Verlagshaus, 2005) 331. See already the emphatic words of Hans Conzelmann in *Der erste Brief an die Korinther* 338-39: "the wording requires its interpretation as vicarious baptism." See also Michael Hull, *Baptism* 11, n. 14, on the large number of those who maintain vicarious baptism is meant here.

[27] Cf. his "Recent Challenges" 384.

[28] Cf. his "Living Rewards" 78, where he maintains that there are no "parallels or precedents of some sort which may be cited as evidence for this type of baptism, whether in Jewish, pagan, orthodox Christian or heretical religious practice."

[29] Cf. e.g. Gordon Fee, *The First Epistle to the Corinthians* (Grand Rapids, MI: Eerdmans, 1987) 764: "This is a genuinely idiosyncratic historical phenomenon," and Roy Ciampa and Brian Rosner, *The First Letter* 781: "there is no biblical or

initiation rites of the mystery cults,[30] as well as to the pagan Greco-Roman cult sites in Corinth connected with offerings for the dead, an area of activity dominated by women.[31]

Yet if baptism for the dead practiced by some Corinthian Christians had had its origin in a pagan rite, Paul would certainly have castigated it. Elsewhere in his first letter to the Corinthians he deals very forcefully with them.[32] It is significant that Paul *tolerates* the practice of believers' having themselves baptized again on behalf of the dead. He neither openly espouses it, nor does he criticize it.[33] I suggest that his tolerance in this regard is due to analogous[34] phenomena in early Judaism, at least

---

historical evidence of any precedent or equivalent practice in the early church or in its pagan context."

30 Cf. e.g. the passages cited by Wolff, *Der erste Brief* 190, who favors this view.

31 Cf. the very instructive article by Richard De Maris, "Corinthian Religion" 661-82. He calls this "a local preoccupation with the underworld, such that Christians of first-century Corinth were pushed to innovate" (671-72). See also the remarks of Markus Öhler in *Taufe* 57: "Since ... the pagan veneration of one's ancestors, or the cultic rites on their behalf, were no longer continued, the Christians [in Corinth] adapted the rite [baptism, including vicarious baptism,] which they considered to be the 'salvific' one."

32 Cf. 4:21, where he says he could come to the Corinthians "with a stick." He also accuses them of jealousy and quarreling (3:3), of deceiving themselves (v. 18). They are arrogant (5:2) and boastful (v. 6). He states something to their shame (6:5); they themselves wrong and defraud (v. 8). Believers who consider themselves strong and eat in the temple of an idol "sin against members" of their family who are weak in this regard (8:12). In addition, those who eat well at the Lord's Supper "show contempt for the church of God and humiliate those who have nothing" (11:22).

33 Cf. William Orr and James Walther, *1 Corinthians* (AB 32; Garden City, NY: Doubleday, 1976) 337: "He attaches neither praise nor blame to the custom." Gordon Fee in *The First* 767 speaks of "Paul's apparently noncommittal attitude toward it...."

34 I purposely avoid the term "parallel," for there was obviously no direct parallel elsewhere to vicarious baptism with water. An "analogy" implies correspondence in function between two things; thus I prefer this term. Two matters may first appear to be different, yet if they function in the same way (here, aiding in helping a dead person to attain the resurrection), they are analogous. In regard to 1 Cor 15:29, the Jewish scholar Arthur Marmorstein in "Paulus und die Rabbinen" in *ZNW* 30 (1931) 281 correctly states about early Jewish practices: "Sacrifice or prayer may have been very easily supplanted by baptism. Basically, the concern here as well as there is with the same teaching or idea." He deals with 1 Cor 15:29 on pp. 277-85, with a number of references to early Jewish sources. The latter is

some of which he was certainly acquainted with: offering a sacrifice in the Jerusalem Temple and praying on behalf of the dead so that they could participate in the resurrection; placing food and beverage on the grave of a person for its journey to Sheol, the underworld; intercessory prayer on behalf of a wicked person so that he/she may participate in the resurrection; almsgiving on behalf of the dead; and the late example of circumcising an infant boy who had died before the eighth day, on which he was to be circumcised according to tradition. These analogies will be treated in sections 1. to 9. In the Summary and Conclusion I will suggest how at least some of these practices, mediated via the Jewish members of the Corinthian church, caused some of them and later some of the Gentile members to introduce and carry out the practice of having oneself baptized on behalf of the dead.[35]

Although there are more, I shall now confine myself to what I consider the most relevant nine Judaic sources, treating the first eight chronologically from before 168 BCE, up to the Tannaitic and Amoraic periods. Another late analogous practice from ninth century CE Babylonia is then cited in section 9.

---

also true for Solomon Schechter, *Aspects of Rabbinic Theology*. Major Concepts of the Talmud (New York: Schocken Books, 1909 / 1961) 195-98 on "The Zachuth of a Pious Posterity, or the sin of a wicked posterity which has a retrospective influence upon their progenitors." Finally, Ephraim Urbach in *The Sages*. Their Concepts and Beliefs (Cambridge, MA: Harvard University Press, 1987, original 1975) 508-11 also deals with how "the living endowed the dead with merit" (508, with the relevant notes on pp. 915-17).

[35] It should be noted that Josephene Ford in her "Rabbinic Humour behind Baptism for the Dead (1 Cor. XV. 29)" in *Studia Evangelica* IV, ed. F. Cross (TU 102; Berlin: Akademie-Verlag, 1968) 402 proposes that Paul "refers to the purificatory rites performed after contact with dead bodies." She did not acknowledge that John Lightfoot had already proposed this in the seventeenth century. See his *A Commentary on the New Testament from the Talmud and Hebraica*. Volume 4, Acts - 1 Corinthians (Peabody, MA: Hendrickson, 1989; Latin original 1658-74, Eng. translation 1859) 270-71. Where the humor is in this regard is Ford's own secret.

1. *Tobit 4:17*

The apocryphal writing "Tobit," now in Greek, was probably originally in Aramaic and later translated into Hebrew.[36] Likely Palestinian, it derives from a time before 168 BCE.[37] In 4:16 Tobit instructs his son Tobias: "Give some of your food to the hungry, and some of your clothing to the naked. Give all your surplus as alms, and do not let your eye begrudge your giving of alms." It then continues in v. 17: "Place your bread on the grave of the righteous, but give none to sinners." The first clause in the Greek MSS BA is: ἔκχεον τοὺς ἄρτους σου ἐτὶ τὸν τάφον τῶν δικαιῶν. The question in this regard is the reason for the practice at this early time of placing food on the grave of the deceased who was considered to be righteous. Was the food intended as provisions for the departed's spirit on its way to Sheol, without which it would not fare as well, or also for its stay there? A passage from the Pentateuch, as well as post-biblical Judaic sources, appear to speak strongly for the first or both.[38]

1.1 *Deut 26:14*

This verse states that the person who has paid the tithe of his produce should say:

> I have not eaten of it while in mourning;
> I have not eaten any of it while I was unclean;
> and I have not given any of it to the dead.

The last phrase, "to the dead," is the singular Hebrew לְמֵת (*lemēt*), LXX τῷ τεθνηκότι. It most probably refers not to food for mourners, but to placing food in the grave of a dead person for its journey to Sheol, the

[36] There are four Aramaic MSS of Tobit in the Dead Sea Scrolls, and only one Hebrew MS. Cf. *The Dead Sea Scrolls, Study Edition,* ed. Florentino Martínez and Eibert Tigchelaar, 382-99 for 4Q196-99.

[37] Cf. George Nickelsburg, *Jewish Literature between the Bible and the Mishnah* 35, as well as Joseph Fitzmyer, *Tobit* (CEJL; Berlin: de Gruyter, 2003) 25; on p. 52 he prefers a date slightly before 175 BCE, with p. 54 on the provenance.

[38] They are all mentioned by the commentators on Deut 26:14 and elsewhere, but succinctly by my former teacher at Yale, Joseph Fitzmyer, in his *Tobit.*

underworld, or also for its stay there. This was known, for example, as a common practice in Thebes and elsewhere in ancient Egypt.[39] However, holes in the floors of some graves found in Samaria are also thought to have "served as receptacles for food and drink offerings to the dead" in Sheol.[40] The term "to" (ל [*l*]) can just as well mean "for" or "on behalf of"[41] the dead, i.e. for their consumption. As will be pointed out below, this practice continued in some Jewish circles even into Talmudic times.

1.2 *Ahiqar*

"The Words of Ahiqar" consists of a narrative folk tale adjoined to proverbial sayings. The proverbs probably originated in northern Syria in Aramaic, at the latest in the early sixth century BCE. An Aramaic version was found among the Elephantine Papyri of the fifth century BCE in Egypt. The originally non-Jewish text was later expunged of most heathen references, and in this form it was known to the author of Tobit.[42]

The version of 2:10 now found in Syriac appears to have influenced Tobit 4:17. It reads: "My son, pour out your wine on the graves of the righteous, rather than drink it with evil men."[43] Here "wine" is mentioned as the "food" of Tobit. It too is meant to be consumed by the deceased person on its way to and / or in the underworld, Sheol.

---

[39] Cf. S. R. Driver, *Deuteronomy* (ICC 5; Edinburgh: T. & T. Clark, 1895 / 1960) 292.

[40] Cf. Duane Christensen, *Deuteronomy 21:10 - 34:12* (WBC 6B; Nashville, TN: Thomas Nelson, 2002) 542. He notes that "The Torah did not forbid this practice, but because contact with the dead is ritually defiling, it prohibits the use of the tithe for it" (ibid.). Later Judaism interpreted Deut 26:14 to mean that no money should be taken from the tithe to use for a coffin or a shroud for the dead. See *Sifre* Ki Tabo' 303 on this verse (Finkelstein 322; Eng. Hammer 293), as well as targums *Pseudo-Jonathan* (Clarke 239; Eng. Clarke 71), *Neofiti 1* (Díez-Macho 5.215; Eng. McNamara 121), and *Fragment Targum "V"* (Klein 1.220; Eng. Klein 2.178).

[41] Cf. BDB 515, 5. h: for, for the sake of, on behalf of.

[42] Cf. J. Lindenberger in *OTP* 2.479-93, esp. 488-89. See Tobit 1:21-22; 2:10; 11:18; and 14:10 for Ahiqar.

[43] Cf. the English of the Syriac A version (it is lacking in B) in R. H. Charles, *Pseudepigrapha* 730. The Arabic 2:13 (p. 731) reads: "O my son, pour out your wine on the tombs of the just, and drink not with ignorant, contemptible people." On this individual saying, see also J. Lindenberger in *OTP* 2.490.

1.3 *Sirach 7:33 and 30:18*

"The Wisdom of Jesus Son of Sirach" was first written in Hebrew in Palestine in the first quarter of the second century BCE, then later translated by the author's grandson into Greek.[44] Two passages deal with gifts of food to the dead.

Sir 7:33 reads: "Give graciously to all the living; do not withhold kindness even from the dead." The LXX rendering of the latter is: καὶ ἐπὶ νεκρῷ μὴ ἀποκωλύσῃς χάριν, whereby "the dead" is singular. The singular is also used in the extant Hebrew: וגם ממת אל תמנע חסד *(wgm mmt ʾl tmnʿ ḥsd)*.[45]

The second text is Sir 30:18 : "Good things poured out upon a mouth that is closed are like 'offerings of food placed upon a grave.'" The latter phrase in Greek is θέματα βρωμάτων παρακείμενα ἐπὶ τάφῳ .[46]

These two passages attest the early Jewish practice of putting food upon a deceased person's grave. It is clearly meant for that person's consumption, not the donor's, nor for a mourners' meal.

1.4 *Letter of Jeremiah 27*

The Letter of Jeremiah was composed in Hebrew (now lost), probably in Palestine, at the end of the fourth or beginning of the third century BCE. It was translated into Greek sometime between 167-163 BCE, probably in Egypt.[47]

The author ridicules the efficacy of idols in v. 27. If one falls down, it has to be picked up; if set upright, it cannot move itself; if tipped over, it cannot straighten itself. It continues: "Gifts are placed before them just as

---

[44] Cf. George Nickelsburg, *Jewish Literature* 62-63. Hebrew fragments have been found at Qumran and Masada.

[45] Cf. Pancratius Beentjes, *The Book of Ben Sira in Hebrew* 31. Only MS A has this.

[46] The extant Hebrew is difficult to interpret. It is only found in MS B, cited in Beentjes 54.

[47] Cf. Carey Moore, *Daniel, Esther and Jeremiah: The Additions* (AB 44; Garden City, NY: Doubleday, 1977) 326-29. Moore refers to Tobit 4:17 and Sir 30:18-19 on p. 344. In some circles the writing is considered the sixth chapter of Baruch; I follow the NRSV at this point.

before the dead." This is the Greek 26: ἀλλ' ὥσπερ νεκροῖς τὰ δῶρα αὐτοῖς παρατίθεται.

The author of the Letter of Jeremiah clearly writes to Jews (v. 1). When he states that gifts are placed before idols by those worshiping them, it thus seems probable that he first means them, the idolaters, when he adds "just as before the dead." Yet in light of the texts cited above in 1.1-3, he probably at the same time points to a Jewish practice with which he is familiar. It is his fellow Jews who also place gifts (probably of food and drink) upon the grave of a deceased person.

1.5 *Mourning Customs for Bridegrooms and Brides Who Died Before Marriage*

The tractate "Mourning" (*ʾEbel Rabbati*) is one of the minor tractates of the Babylonian Talmud. Euphemistically called *Śemaḥot* ("Rejoicings"), its final redaction was probably in the eighth century CE. Yet the authorities it cites are all Tannaitic, pointing to the basic work as having been gathered from its sources and composed in the third century CE.[48] Several passages dealing with Tannaitic mourning customs show how deeply embedded the belief cited above in sections 1.1-4 of caring for the later welfare of a deceased person was by providing him / her with provisions.

Before the burial, when a dead person is lying before a mourner who will make these arrangements, the latter does not need to recite the *Shema* ʿ and pray the *Tefillah* (Eighteen Prayer or ʿAmidah). When others stand to pray, he utters a kind of confession. R. Simeon b. Eleazar, a fourth generation Tanna who was a student of R. Meir,[49] stated in this regard in 10:2, 48b: "He also prays [lit., 'asks'] for all the needs of the dead person."[50] In other words, he seeks the well-being of the deceased by requesting God to now supply those needs - on the way to or in the underworld, Sheol.

---

48 Cf. Dov Zlotnick, *The Tractate "Mourning"* 1-9. The vocalized Hebrew text is found at the end of the volume. I basically employ, however, the English translation of J. Rabbinowitz in the Soncino edition of *The Minor Tractates of the Talmud* 1.325-400.

49 Cf. Hermann Strack and Günter Stemberger, *Introduction to the Talmud and Midrash* 88. This is cited hereafter as *Introduction*.

50 Cf. Zlotnick, Hebrew 29; Soncino 1.380.

R. Simeon b. Eleazar's teacher, R. Meir, was a third generation Tanna.[51] He maintained in 8:2, 47a that if a bridegroom and a bride die before their marriage, "We erect a canopy for bridegrooms and brides and suspend from it articles which have and have not reached the edible stage." These articles are then enumerated. In regard to the mourners' themselves later not being allowed to appropriate these items, it is stated: "The general rule is: no benefit may be derived from anything that is suspended from the canopy."[52] Here nuts, bread and flasks of perfumed oil are placed on the graves of those who died early in life to accompany them in the afterlife.

In a similar vein, 8:3, 47a states: "We scatter before [early deceased] bridegrooms and brides strings of fish and pieces of meat in summer but not in winter." "One takes roasted ears of grain and nuts and throws them. The general rule is: we do not scatter before them anything that is perishable."[53] Here provisions are also provided for the afterlife of those who have died before they could marry.

Finally, 8:4, 47a notes: "We may let wine and oil flow through pipes before bridegrooms and brides, and we do not fear [being suspected of] the ways of the Amorites [superstitious practices]. Nor do we fear sinning by putting food to shame [wasting it]."[54] This was not only a measure designed to dispel the stench of a corpse rapidly decaying, especially in the scorching summer sun of Palestine.[55] It also recalls the holes in the floors of some graves found in Samaria thought to have "served as receptacles for food and drink offerings to the dead" in Sheol.[56] Here Sages in the Tannaitic period in Palestine have no fear of such a practice reminding others of pagan superstition. This is because there was good precedent for it, as indicated already in Deut 26:14 analyzed above.

* * *

---

[51] Cf. *Introduction* 84.

[52] Cf. Zlotnick, Hebrew 19; Soncino 1.363. The canopy is the ceremonial baldachin spread above the couple to be married.

[53] Cf. Zlotnick, Hebrew 19; Soncino 1.364-65.

[54] Cf. Zlotnick, Hebew 19; Soncino 1.364. In *b. Ber.* 50b (Soncino 306) the first is said of bridegroom and bride at an actual wedding. Here in "Mourning" they are already deceased, as the previous paragraphs show. The incident with the sons of Rabban Gamaliel at the end of 8:4 takes place while they are alive. It was simply added here because of the catchword phrase "wine, oil and pipes."

[55] Cf. John 11:39 of Lazarus.

[56] Cf. n. 40 above on Deut 26:14.

When Tobit 4:17 states, "Place your bread on the grave of the righteous," in light of the above five passages, from the sixth century BCE to ca. 230 CE, this very probably means the donor or mourner is represented as trying to positively influence the fate of the deceased person by providing him / her with food (and drink) for that person's journey to, or stay in, Sheol. This concrete practice of trying to positively influence the fate of a deceased person (here only if "righteous") is thus analogous to the practice of some Corinthian Christians' having themselves baptized again. They also did it with the same motivation. It was "on behalf of the dead" in the Hereafter.

2. 2 *Macc 12:38-45*

The earliest testimony to Jewish belief in the resurrection of the dead is found in Dan 12:2-3.[57] This is generally thought to deal with the severe persecution of Antiochus IV Epiphanes, which began in 167 BCE with the destruction of the Jerusalem Temple. The book was probably completed before his death in 164 BCE.[58] This is important for dating belief in the resurrection as attested in 2 Maccabees.

The writing 2 Maccabees is a condensation of the (lost) five volumes composed in Greek by Jason of Cyrene (2:23), also dealing with Jewish resistance to the same Antiochus IV Epiphanes and his son Eupator (2:20). In its final form it was sent by the Jews of Jerusalem and Judea to those of Egypt (1:10) in the year 124 BCE (1:7), only some forty years after the book of Daniel was composed.[59] In part it deals with the fate of those Jews who unjustly lost their lives in the time of great persecution. The author's answer to this theological problem is that God will *raise* such martyrs to new life.

---

[57] Cf. the art. "Resurrection" by Moshe Greenberg, Daniel Boyarin and Seymour Siegel in *EJ* (2007) 17.240-42, with Dan 12:2-3 on p. 241.

[58] Cf. e.g. Louis Hartman and Alexander Di Lella, *The Book of Daniel* (AB 23; Garden City, NY: Doubleday, 1978) 14 on Dan 10:1 - 12:4 as from 165 BCE.

[59] On the dating, cf. Jonathan Goldstein, *II Maccabees* (AB 41 A; Garden City, NY: Doubleday, 1983) 48 (between 159-132 BCE); Daniel Schwarz, *2 Maccabees* (CEJL; Berlin: de Gruyter, 2008) 3, 11 and 14; on p. 15 he even maintains that 2 Maccabees preceded 1 Maccabees; and George Nickelsburg, *Jewish Literature* 106-10.

The theme of resurrection dominates in chapter 7, the account of the martyrdom of seven brothers, and finally their mother. In 7:9 the second brother is represented as saying to Antiochus IV Epiphanes: "the King of the universe will 'raise us up' [ἡμᾶς ἀναστήσει] to an everlasting renewal of life because we have died for His laws." This motif is emphasized by repetition in vv. 11 (hope), 14 (hope and resurrection), 20 (hope in the Lord), 23 (God will again give back life and spirit / breath), 29 (the mother's getting her sons back again), and 40 (when dying, putting one's trust in the Lord). It is later supplemented in 14:46, where the author recounts that Razis, an elder of Jerusalem (v. 37), at his violent death was "calling upon the Lord of life and spirit to give them [his entrails, which he had just hurled at the crowd] back to him again."

The theme of resurrection also plays a major role in chapter 12.[60] Judas Maccabeus and his army waged a battle against Georgias, the governor of Idumea, and his forces (vv. 32-33), at which "a few of the Jews fell" (v. 34). After Georgias escaped, they put his troops to flight (v. 37). At this point Judas moved his army to the city of Adullam, where they "'purified themselves' according to the custom" before keeping the Sabbath there (v. 38). This verb is the Greek middle ἁγνίζεσθαι, not simply to wash,[61] but to purify oneself,[62] here after killing a person or touching a corpse.[63]

---

[60] "2Mcc 12,43s" is correctly found in the margin at 1 Cor 15:29 in Nestle-Aland's *Novum Testamentum Graece*[28]. Although the passage is adduced in numerous commentaries, this is the first extensive analysis of it in regard to the NT verse. The very competent historian of religion, Dieter Zeller, calls 2 Macc 12:43-45 a "distant analogy" (*Der erste Brief an die Korinther* 500). In "Gibt es religionsgeschichtliche Parallelen zur Taufe für die Toten (1 Kor 15,29)?" in *ZNW* 98 (2007) 69, he labels it instead a "noteworthy analogy." He also dealt with it in "Die Taufe für die Toten (1 Kor 15,29) - ein Fall von 'Volksfrömmigkeit'?" in *Volksglaube im antiken Christentum*, Theofried Baumeister Festschrift, ed. Heike Griese and Andreas Merkt (Darmstadt: Wissenschaftliche Buchgesellschaft, 2009) 393-406. Here he maintains that the rite of vicarious baptism belonged not to a minority, but to "a large number," thus "Volksfrömmigkeit" (395). This view is incorrect, as the results of the present study show. See also Ethelbert Stauffer, *Die Theologie des Neuen Testaments* (Stuttgart: Kohlhammer, 1947[3]) 28, n. 544: "Paulus bespricht die korinthische Totentaufe ganz im Geiste, ja in der Argumentationsform von 2 Makk 12. Er versteht demnach das korinthische *baptismum pro defunctis* in Analogie zur jüd. *oblatio pro defunctis* : als Fürbitteakt...."

[61] Against Daniel Schwarz, *2 Maccabees* 439.

[62] Cf. LSJ 11.

[63] Cf. Num 19:11-13 with ἁγνίζεσθαι ; it deals with being sprinkled with the water for cleansing (in the Red Heifer rite). See the troops which had gone to battle and

After the Sabbath was past, Judas and his men returned to the battlefield to take up the bodies of the fallen Jewish soldiers and to bury them properly. They are said to have discovered the reason these men had fallen: "under the tunic of each one of the dead they found sacred tokens of the idols of Jamnia" (v. 40).[64] After blessing the Lord for revealing this to them, "they turned to supplication, praying that the sin that had been committed might be wholly blotted out" (v. 42). Judas then also

> 43) took up a collection, man by man, to the amount of two thousand drachmas of silver, and sent it to Jerusalem to provide for a sin offering. In doing this he acted very well and honorably, taking account of the resurrection. 44) For if he were not expecting that those who had fallen would rise again, it would have been superfluous and foolish to pray for the dead. 45) But if he was looking to the splendid reward that is laid up for those who fall asleep in godliness, it was a holy and pious thought. Therefore he made atonement for the dead, so that they might be delivered from their sin.

Judas and his soldiers did two major things here. First, they turned to "supplication" (ἱκετεία),[65] "praying" (ἀξιόω)[66] (to God) that the sin of idolatry[67] which had been committed "might be wholly blotted out" (v. 42). This was intercessory prayer.

---

returned as needing purification in Num 31:13-24, especially if they had killed someone or touched a corpse (v. 19). The seven-day purification process would not have been possible under conditions of war. Immersing for purification (טָבַל [*ṭabal*] : Jastrow 517) is apparently not meant here.

[64] According to Daniel Schwarz, *2 Maccabees* 440, these were Heracles and Hauran. The author does not explicitly say that these idols were booty from the fallen enemy soldiers, yet this is of course possible. Cf. 1 Chron 14:12, as well as Judas's behavior towards captured carved images of the Philistine gods in 1 Macc 5:68. Jonathan Goldstein in *II Maccabees* 448 thinks that the few soldiers' bearing idolatrous objects caused pious people to think Dan 12:1-2 was fulfilled "in that the righteous in the time of troubles survived, and only the sinners perished."

[65] Cf. LSJ 826.

[66] Cf. LSJ 171-72, II. 2: esp. *pray*.

[67] Cf. Deut 7:25-26, where keeping an image of such a god causes one to be "set apart for destruction." The general prohibition of idolatry is found in Exod 20:3-5, with 22:20 (Heb. 19) stating that sacrificing to a god other than the Lord also causes one to be "devoted to destruction."

Secondly, Judas's collection of 2000 drachmas of silver came from all the members of his army (v. 43). That is, they *all* affirmed the project.[68] He sent the money to (the Temple of) Jerusalem to provide for a "sin offering" (ἁμαρτίας θυσίαν).[69] The author praises him for this action since he was thereby "taking account of 'the resurrection' (ἀνάστασις - v. 43)." In v. 45 he appears to equate this with "to pray for the dead" (ὑπὲρ νεκρῶν εὔχεσθαι).[70] His argument here strongly recalls that of Paul in 1 Cor 15:29. The author states: "For if he [Judas] were not expecting that those [soldiers] who had fallen would rise again, it would have been superfluous and foolish to pray for the dead." In addition, the preposition ὑπέρ, here in the genitive with "the dead," means "on behalf of,"[71] just as there.

---

[68] Cf. Robert Doran in 2 *Maccabees* (Hermeneia; Minneapolis, MN: Fortress Press, 2012) 246 on the expression κατ' ἄνδρα : " a collection from all the members ...."

[69] Daniel Schwarz in 2 *Maccabees* 442 notes that this phrase in the LXX corresponds to the Hebrew חַטָּאת (*ḥaṭṭa't* ; cf. BDB 309 for the various sin-offerings). Apparently atonement through one's own death was not yet known at this time. See for example *m. Sanh.* 6:2 (Albeck 4.186; Danby 390; Neusner 594) for a criminal being encouraged to confess his sins before his execution in order to share in the World to Come: "May my death be an atonement for all my sins." It is based on the case of Achan, who sinned by taking pieces of "things devoted to destruction" at the capture of Jericho under Joshua (Josh 7:19-21; see 6:18-19 and 7:1). In *Pseudo-Philo* 25:7 (*SC* 229.196, 198; *OTP* 2.335) Kenaz cites Achan as exemplary in this respect, for if transgressors declare their wicked deeds and schemes, they will now die, but "God will have mercy on you when He will resurrect the dead." This writing, originally from Palestine and in Hebrew, stems either from the time of Jesus (Daniel Harrington in *OTP* 2.298-99) or from around 70 CE (George Nickelsburg in *Jewish Literature* 269). *Sifre* Beha'alotekhah 112 on Num 15:31 states that with the exception of the idolater, of whom the text is interpreted, "All those who die attain atonement through their death" (Horovitz 121; Eng. Neusner 2.170). See also *t. Yoma* 4:9 (Zuckermandel / Liebermann 190; Eng. Neusner 2.208).

[70] Cf. LSJ 739 on εὔχομαι as to pray, pray for. Salomon Reinach in "De l'origine des prières pour les morts" in *REJ* 41 (1900) 161-73 deals with 2 Macc 12:38-43 on pp. 166-68. He maintains the author wanted to prove that Judas professed belief in the resurrection and in the efficacy of prayer for the dead, which for Reinach was an "induction absurde" (p. 167). For relevant talmudic sources he points to other studies.

[71] Cf. LSJ 1857, A. II., and the *Greek-English Lexicon of the Septuagint,* Revised Edition, 628-29.

Judas's action is praised by the author because "he was looking to the splendid reward that is laid up for those who fall asleep in godliness" (v. 45). As in the NT, "falling asleep" (κοιμάομαι)[72] here means "to die." Judas is represented as looking forward to the resurrection even for his dead, idolatrous soldiers. This is because "he made atonement for the dead [περὶ τῶν τεθνηκότων] so that they might be delivered from their sin" (ibid.). The "atonement" (ἐξιλασμός)[73] here thus includes not only the sin offering presented on the altar of the Jerusalem Temple, but also the intercessory prayers offered by Judas and his soldiers "on behalf of" / "for" their dead comrades who had strayed and committed idolatry.[74] Only some decades after the composition of Daniel 12, both themes are closely related here to a firm belief in the resurrection of the dead. The final author of 2 Maccabees was a Greek-speaking diaspora Jew who himself had no immediate access to the Jerusalem Temple in order to make an atoning sin-offering. However, for him intercessory prayer was nevertheless possible. Also for him, it was just as effective in atoning for a lapsed fellow Jew who was now dead.

Finally, it is noteworthy that the lapsed dead soldiers were only "a few" (v. 34) on whose behalf intercessory prayer was now made in regard to their future resurrection. This corresponds to the number of those Corinthian dead on whose behalf vicarious baptism took place in the hope that they too would participate in the resurrection (1 Cor 15:29). They were also only a minority ("some") within the Corinthian congregation. This rite was certainly also accompanied by intercessory prayer. If they were Jewish Christians, as I will suggest in the Summary and Conclusion, it would also have been difficult for them to bring a sin-offering for such people in the far-off Jerusalem Temple. Yet they could easily offer intercessory prayer for them.

For the above reasons 2 Maccabees, at the latest from 124 BCE, is analogous to the belief of some few Corinthian Christians that by having themselves baptized again "on behalf of the dead" (ὑπὲρ τῶν νεκρῶν), the latter could also participate in the resurrection of the dead.

---

[72] Cf. LSJ 967, 3., and BAGD 437.

[73] Cf. LSJ 594: propitiation, atonement; see also ἱλασμός (828, 2.) as atonement, sin-offering; and the *Greek-English Lexicon of the Septuagint*, Revised Edition, 215.

[74] Daniel Schwarz in *2 Maccabees* 444 aptly states that the general topic here is "the freeing of dead sinners from sin so as to allow them sinless life in the next."

3. *The Testament of Abraham*

The "Testament of Abraham" is a Jewish work originally written in Semitizing Greek, from Egypt, perhaps Alexandria. It appears to have originated in the first century CE, definitely before 117 CE, and some scholars even place it in the first century BCE.[75] It has been transmitted in two recensions, of which A is much longer. Even though the latter now has some terminology added by Christian copyists, its contents and order argue for its better preserving the original narrative. Its Greek is reminiscent of that found in 2-4 Maccabees,[76] which thus shows affinity with 2 Maccabees and the text in 12:38-45 analyzed in section 2. above.

Although called a testament, this writing does not describe Abraham's final advice to his son and heir Isaac. Instead, God commissions the archangel Michael to inform Abraham he should now "arrange for the disposition of his possessions" (1:4; 8:11; 15:1) because of his imminent death. Like Moses in Judaic tradition,[77] Abraham resists numerous attempts to convince him to give up his life. He prolongs the procedure by requesting to see the entire inhabited world. When God grants this wish, in a chariot drawn by cherubim Abraham then views from above three different forms of judgment.[78] Finally, the angel Death deceives Abraham, and the archangel Michael and other angels first bury his body, then carry his soul to heaven, where God instructs them to take His friend Abraham into Paradise (20:9-14).

---

[75] Cf. Dale Allison, Jr., *Testament of Abraham* 16, 32-38; George Nickelsburg, *Jewish Literature* 326-27; E. P. Sanders in *OTP* 1.873-76; and Mathias Delcor, *Le Testament d'Abraham* 33-34 and 73-77. I employ the Greek edition of Francis Schmidt, *Le Testament grec d'Abraham*. Sanders employed the earlier Greek edition of M. R. James, *The Testament of Abraham,* for his English translation. I cite Sanders' translation, yet have compared it with the Greek of Schmidt's more recent critical edition.

[76] Cf. N. Turner, cited by E. P. Sanders in *OTP* 1.873, n. 16. See also Mathias Delcor, *Le Testament* 34.

[77] I analyze this theme extensively in *The Death, Burial, and Resurrection of Jesus, and the Death, Burial, and Translation of Moses in Judaic Tradition* (Studies in Judaism; Lanham, MD: University Press of America, 2008) 52-84.

[78] They may ultimately be related to the triple judgment found in the Egyptian "Book of the Dead." Cf. Mathias Delcor, *Le Testament* 67; Dale Allison, Jr., *Testament of Abraham* 266-67 (see also 256-57, 262, 272, 279); and George Nickelsburg, *Jewish Literature* 326.

The following passages from this writing are relevant to the theme of intercessory prayer for the dead, connected to being raised up / resurrection.

When Abraham sees evil persons "who want to murder and rob and burn and destroy" (10:3), he asks Michael to "command that wild beasts come out of the thicket and devour them" (v. 6). This then occurs. The same happens to a man and a woman "engaging in sexual immorality with each other" (v. 8). The earth then splits in two and swallows them up. When thieves begin carrying off possessions from within a house, Abraham asks that heavenly fire consume them, which then happens. At this point God intervenes and makes sinless but merciless Abraham stop this behavior so that the sinner may have time before his death to repent and to live.[79]

When Abraham encounters the situation of a dead person whose righteous deeds and sins hang in the balance, Michael informs him that the (temporary) judge sentenced him neither to judgment nor to be saved "until the Judge of all should come" (14:2). Abraham then asks how this soul could be saved, and the archangel (called Commander-in-chief here) answers that one more righteous deed would suffice. Thus the patriarch tells Michael: "let us offer a prayer on behalf of this soul and see if God will heed us" (v. 5).[80] When Michael agrees, "they offered supplication and prayer to God on behalf of the soul, and God heeded them.[81] And when they arose from prayer, they did not see the soul standing there" (v. 6). Asked by Abraham where the soul now is, Michael answers: "It was saved through your righteous prayer, and behold, a light-bearing angel took it and carried it up to Paradise" (v. 8).[82]

When Abraham realizes how effective his and Michael's intercessory prayer is on behalf of someone who is already dead, he suggests to Michael that they do the same "on behalf of the souls of the sinners" he had earlier cursed and caused to be destroyed (v. 11). They thus "offer supplication before God" (v. 13) for a long time. God then informs

---

[79] Cf. 10:5-15 in *OTP* 1.887-88, and the Greek in Francis Schmidt, *Le Testament grec d'Abraham* 126 and 128.

[80] This and the other passages here on intercessory prayer for the dead are not the first ones to attest such a belief, as E. P. Sanders maintains in *OTP* 1.891, n. "b." Cf. the analysis of 2 Macc 12:38-45 above.

[81] The shorter recension, B, has here: "Abraham prayed to the Lord, and He raised [ἀνέστησεν] them" (Schmidt 80).

[82] Cf. Schmidt 140; *OTP* 1.890-91.

Abraham that He has heeded his supplication, calls them back, and leads them into life through His great goodness (v. 14).[83]

The Greek of "let us offer a prayer on behalf of this soul" in 14:5 is ποιήσωμεν εὐχὴν ὑπὲρ τῆς ψυχῆς. For "they offered supplication and prayer to God on behalf of the soul" in v. 6, the Greek is ἐποίησαν δέησιν καὶ εὐχὴν πρὸς τὸν Θεὸν ὑπὲρ τῆς ψυχῆς. For "It was saved through your [sing.] righteous prayer" in v. 8, the Greek reads σέσωσται διὰ τῆς εὐχῆς σου τῆς δικαίας. For praying (δέομαι) "on behalf of the souls of the sinners" in v. 11 the Greek is ὑπὲρ τῶν ψυχῶν τῶν ἁμαρτωλῶν. "Supplication" in v. 13 is δέησις. God in v. 14 then says, "I have led them into eternal life": εἰς ζωὴν αἰώνιον αὐτοὺς ἤγαγον.[84]

It is significant that while Michael is also mentioned, it is the supplication (δέησις) and prayer (εὐχή) of Abraham "on behalf of" (ὑπέρ) a dead person whose righteous deeds and sins hang in the balance, and on behalf of dead sinners, which causes God to "save" (σώζω) them, and for them to be carried to "Paradise," or for God to lead them to "life." This intercessory prayer is analogous to the belief of some Corinthian Christians that by undergoing baptism a second time, also "on behalf of" (ὑπέρ) the dead, these too would participate in the resurrection of the dead.[85]

Since the archangel Michael's efforts to take the soul of Abraham fail, God finally sends Death to him. First, however, the latter kills all of Abraham's male and female servants (17:18; 18:3). Death informs him that he himself should actually have died at the same time (18:7). Concerned about the fate of his dead servants, Abraham says to Death in v. 9: "since the servants died untimely, come, let us plead to the Lord our God that He should heed us and raise those who died untimely through your ferocity. 10) And Death said, 'Amen, let it be so.' Then Abraham arose and fell upon the face of the earth and prayed, and Death with him.

---

[83] Cf. Schmidt 142; *OTP* 1.891.

[84] Cf. Schmidt 142.

[85] In the "Testament of Abraham" such persons go to "Paradise" or God "leads them to life," whereas in Paul no concrete details are given in regard to the whereabouts of those deceased for whom one had oneself baptized again. Presumably they are thought of as being in a place with all the other deceased baptized Christians where they await the resurrection of the dead, which Paul expected during his own lifetime.

11) And God sent a spirit of life into the dead, and they were made alive again."[86]

The Greek of "to plead" in v. 9 is the verb δέομαι, of "to pray" in v. 10 προσεύχομαι. Very strangely, Death joins Abraham in pleading to God that He should now "raise" (ἀνίστημι)[87] Abraham's dead servants. God thereupon heeds their plea by sending into them a "spirit of life" (πνεῦμα ζωῆς). This causes them to be "made alive again" (ἀναζωοποιέω).[88] It is significant that it is Abraham's "pleading" and "praying" which causes God to "raise" dead individuals, to "give [them] life again."[89] This is a form of resurrection of the dead, even if the place to which the servants go, and for how long (until the general resurrection of the dead?), are not stated. Again, intercessory prayer on behalf of the dead (in this case not designated as sinners) is connected to the theme of resurrection. As stated above, this is analogous to the situation of some Corinthian Christians who underwent a second baptism on behalf of the dead.

The "Testament of Moses" is thus a second attestation after the early, second century BCE writing 2 Maccabees of belief in intercessory prayer for the dead in connection with the resurrection.[90] In addition to these

---

86 Cf. Schmidt 158-59; *OTP* 1.894.

87 Cf. LSJ 144: make to stand up, raise up; BAGD 70, 1. a. : "esp. of the dead *raise up, bring to life*." The cognate noun, ἀνάστασις, means "*resurrection* from the dead" (BAGD 60, 2.).

88 The only close Greek verb which LSJ (p. 104) can cite is ἀναζωόω, "recall to life." The term ἀναζωοποιέω, as Dale Allison, Jr., in discussion with E. P. Sanders points out in *Testament of Abraham* 366, appears to be Egyptian Jewish Greek. It is elsewhere found only in "Joseph and Aseneth" at 8:11(9), 15:4(5), and 27:10, as well as in some later patristic texts.

89 Cf. again recension B of 14:5 in n. 81.

90 The "Apocalypse of Zephaniah" is now found in Coptic, but originally was written by a Jew in Greek, probably in Alexandria, Egypt. It has variously been dated from 100 BCE to 175 CE (cf. O. Wintermute in *OTP* 1.500-01). In 11:2 (cf. v. 4) Abraham, Isaac and Jacob pray to God regarding the dead being tormented: "We pray to You 'on account of' those who are in all these torments so that You might have mercy on all of them." Together with other righteous figures (Enoch, Elijah and David - 9:4), the three patriarchs "pray to the Lord Almighty daily 'on behalf of' these who are in all these torments" (v. 6; *OTP* 1.515; see also Zephaniah in 2:8-9 [1.510]). Here Abraham, Isaac and Jacob, themselves dead, are clearly represented as offering intercessory prayer "on behalf of" dead Jews who are being tormented (in Hades). In light of the descriptions in chapter ten, it appears that these sinners are later than the patriarchs, not as having lived before

diaspora writings in Greek, Palestinian Judaic sources also bear witness to this belief.

4. *Korah*

The narrative of Korah's revolt against the authority of Moses is found primarily in Num 16:1-35.[91] It is one of the most colorful in the Hebrew Bible. Because it is paradigmatic for the next sections, I shall treat it more extensively here.

Although Korah and his fellow Levites served in the Lord's tabernacle, they wanted more - the priesthood of Aaron. Accused of the charge of nepotism, Moses proposed that on the following day they be present with their 250 censers, as well as Aaron with his. He tells the congregation: "If the Lord creates something new and the ground opens its mouth and swallows them [Korah and the other rebels], with all that belongs to them, and they go down alive into Sheol, then you shall know that these men have despised the Lord" (Num 16:30). Exactly this then happened (vv. 31-34). In addition, "fire came out from the Lord and consumed the 250 men offering the incense" (v. 35). This vivid account was interpreted extensively at an early date.[92]

4.1 *Sirach 45:18-19*

Ben Sira composed this writing in Hebrew, probably in Jerusalem at the beginning of the second century BCE. His grandson then translated it into Greek at the end of that century.[93] In 45:18-19 the author writes:

---

them. Nevertheless, the "Apocalypse of Zephaniah" is another attestation of the theme of intercessory prayer on behalf of the tormented in Hades.

[91] Cf. also 17:5 (Eng. 16:40); 17:14 (Eng. 16:49); 26:9-11; and 27:3. In chapter 16 it is merged with the revolt of Dathan and Abiram.

[92] Cf. the many sources cited on it by Louis Ginzberg in *The Legends of the Jews* 3.286-303 and the relevant notes in 6.99-105, as well as the art. "Korah" by Jacob Liver, S. David Sperling and Aaron Rothkoff in *EJ* (2007) 12.298-99. While Ps 106:16-18 only mentions Dathan and Abiram, Korah and his company are most probably also meant by implication. See already Sir 45:18-19, now to be analyzed.

[93] Cf. n. 44.

Outsiders conspired against him [Aaron],
and envied him in the wilderness,
Dathan and Abiram and their followers,
and the company of Korah, in wrath and anger.
19) The Lord saw it and was not pleased,
and in the heat of His anger they were destroyed;
He performed wonders against them
to consume them in flaming fire.

Here one of the "wonders" (LXX τέρατα) the Lord is said to have performed on this occasion (in addition to the earth's opening its mouth and swallowing up all who belonged to Korah together with all their goods) was that He consumed Dathan, Abiram and Korah with all their adherents in flaming fire. This increases the fiery punishment of Num 16:35 from the 250 men of Korah who offered incense on their censers to a much larger number of people. It shows Palestinian haggadic development of this narrative already in the early second century BCE.

4.2 *Philo*

This Jewish native of Alexandria, roughly a contemporary of Jesus,[94] wrote in Greek concerning the Korah narrative at three points of his works. In *Fug.* 145 the philosopher notes that the men of Korah's company failed to achieve (the priesthood and to remain in their service as Levites).[95] In *Praem.* 74-78 Philo briefly retells the narrative without specifically mentioning Korah. These "Temple attendants, servitors of the Sanctuary, appointed to the office of gate-keepers" (thus Levites), made their senior the leader of the sedition. They believed in respect to Moses "that in appointing his brother high priest and committing the priesthood to his nephews, he had given way to family affection." Thus they worked against "divine instructions" (78),[96] which for Philo led to chaos and anarchy (76).

---

[94] Cf. Erwin Goodenough, *An Introduction to Philo Judaeus* (Oxford: Basil Blackwell, 1962²) 1-2: ca. 25 BCE to 45-50 CE. See also F. Colson and G. Whitaker in the Loeb Classical Library edition of Philo's works, I. ix.

[95] The lacuna in the text is plausibly filled in by Colson and Whitaker.

[96] The text unfortunately breaks off at this point. See F. Colson's extensive note on this in VIII. 455.

One early haggadic detail found here is that Moses is accused of making his brother not "priest," but already "high priest" (ἀρχιερεύς).[97] This anachronistic detail is encountered again and again in Judaic sources.

Philo's major treatment of Korah's rebellion is found in *Mos.* 2.275-87. He himself greatly objects to the Temple attendants' attacking their rulers and causing a lack of "order" (τάξις - 277). Philo then creates a speech for Moses, who was inspired and transformed into a prophet, in 280-81. Moses says: "I see the earth opened and vast chasms yawning wide. I see great bands of kinfolk perishing, houses dragged down and swallowed up with their inmates, and living men descending into Hades" (281). This then occurs directly. "Shortly thereafter, thunderbolts[98] fell suddenly on the 250 men who had led the sedition and destroyed them in a mass, leaving no part of their bodies to receive the tribute of burial" (283). Earth and heaven had combined forces in this punishment, resulting in the victims never being seen again (287).

The Alexandrian philosopher is certainly in part creative himself (Moses' speech). Yet he also mentions other haggadic details such as the thunderbolts, which most probably were part of the narrative tradition known to him from Hellenistic (Alexandrian) Judaism.

4.3 *Pseudo-Philo*

Now only found in a Latin translation of the Greek, "Pseudo-Philo" was originally written in Hebrew in Palestine, either at about the time of Jesus or around 70 CE.[99] Chapter 16 deals with the rebellion of Korah,[100] making major haggadic changes in the biblical narrative. Already in the beginning sentence it changes the 250 men who supported Korah (Num 16:2) into 200.[101] Angered at their rebellion, God is represented in 16:2-3 as giving a long explanation of how He will now react for the first time since the earth swallowed up Abel's blood. Verse 3 reads:

---

[97] On this term, cf. also *Mos.* 2.176 and 178.

[98] Cf. LSJ 942 on κεραυνός : thunderbolt.

[99] For the first, cf. Daniel Harrington in *OTP* 2.298-99, for the second George Nickelsburg, *Jewish Literature* 269.

[100] It is also referred to later on by Samuel in 57:2 (*SC* 229.358, 360; *OTP* 2.371).

[101] Cf. 16:1 in *SC* 229.144; *OTP* 2.323. A scribal error, however, cannot be completely excluded here.

> Behold, I command the earth, and it will swallow up body and soul together. And their dwelling place will be in darkness and the place of destruction; and they will not die but melt away until I remember the world and renew the earth. And then they will die and not live, and their life will be taken away from the number of all men. And hell will no longer spit them back, and their destruction will not be remembered, and their passing will be like that of those tribes of nations of whom I said, "I will not remember them," that is, the camp of the Egyptians and the race that I destroyed with the water of the flood. And the earth will swallow them up, and I will do no more.[102]

Here Korah and his band first do not die when swallowed up by the earth, but descend to Sheol, both "body and soul." Only when God renews the earth will they die - finally and definitely. God will not "remember" them (positively) after their stay in Sheol. It is not a kind of "purgatory." Instead, they will remain there permanently, along with the Egyptian forces which died in the Re(e)d Sea (Exod 14:28) and the generation of the flood at the time of Noah (Gen 7:23). For this author there is definitely no later hope for Korah and his company after their first entering hell - Sheol alive.

While Num 16:32 notes that "everyone who belonged to Korah and all their goods" were swallowed up by the earth, 26:11 states that "the sons of Korah did not die." In this regard, *Pseudo-Philo* 16:4 says Korah had seven sons, a typical haggadic addition.[103] In v. 5 they give a speech reprimanding him for not obeying Moses and God's Torah. They even deny being begotten by him; instead God is their father, and in His ways they wish to walk. Verse 6 continues: When the earth opens before them all, the sons say to Korah that if his madness is still upon him, no one can help him now. Not heeding this warning, he and his adherents are swallowed up, for which Num 16:32 is explicitly quoted. Then the haggadic detail of a repeated earthquake is added: "And four times the foundation of the earth was shaken so as to swallow up the men as it had been commanded. And after this, Korah and his group cried out until the earth became solid again."[104]

Pseudo-Philo 16 thus shows how the narrative of Korah and his rebellion received major haggadic embellishment in Hebrew in the first half of the first century CE in Palestine. In addition, it emphasized that

---

[102] Cf. *SC* 229.144; *OTP* 2.324.

[103] Exod 6:24 only names Korah's three sons.

[104] Cf. *SC* 229.144, 146; *OTP* 2.324.

while Korah and his company first descended alive into hell - Sheol, "crying out," at the time God renews the earth they will all definitely die. Like other evil-doers, there is no hope for them, in contrast to the fate of Korah's sons based on their positive behavior towards Moses and the Torah of God.

4.4 *Josephus*

This native of Jerusalem was himself of priestly descent and had Aramaic as his native language.[105] In his *Antiquities*, finished in Greek when he was fifty-six years old in the year 93/94 CE (20.267), Josephus retells the rebellion or sedition (στάσις) of Korah in 4.11-58.

At the very outset Josephus betrays knowledge of the haggadic motif that Korah differed from other Hebrews by being especially rich (4.14). He repeats this in 19 and 25, and in 26 he notes that Korah even surpassed Moses and Aaron together in his abundance of possessions.

Based on Num 16:3, Josephus has Korah give a speech to the people in 4.18-19 contesting Moses' conferring the priesthood upon Aaron and his sons. In addition, Moses speaks to Korah, "shouting with all his might" (4.25), expanding Num 16:5-11 and 16-17 into the extensive discourse of 4.25-34. Moses' short prayer to the Lord in Num 16:15 is also expanded greatly by the Jewish historian in 4.40-50, where Moses delivers it before the multitude by "shouting out very loudly" (4.40). He "wept" while delivering the prayer (4.51).

Josephus then relates in broad brush strokes how a sudden earthquake, with the earth opening and engulfing them, obliterated Dathan and Abiram and their adherents together with their belongings (4.51-52). Their "perishing" (ἀπώλοντο) was an exhibition of God's might (4.52). Their relatives did not even grieve for them (4.53). In Num 16:31-34 the preceding is related only of Korah and his company.[106]

Then Aaron and Korah compete as to whose incense would be accepted by God at the Tabernacle. A stupendous fire arose and consumed Korah and his 250 censer-bearers (4.54-56). It had now become

---

105 Cf. *Vita* 1 and 7; *Bell.* 1.3.

106 As remarked above, the Dathan and Abiram narrative is interwoven with that of Korah in Numbers 16, and interpreters such as Josephus sought in part to unravel it.

clear that Aaron owed the high-priesthood (ἡ ἀρχιερωσύνη) to the judgment of God (4.58).

While some of the material Josephus includes in the Korah narrative is certainly from the historian himself, he much more probably borrowed most of it not only from Scripture, but also from contemporary Judaic tradition.

4.5 *Jude*

The very short (only twenty-five verses) pseudonymous letter of Jude purports to be written by Jude, "a servant of Jesus Christ and brother of James" (v. 1), also a brother of Jesus (Mark 6:3 - "Judas"). It is difficult to date precisely, yet the author probably belonged to the second or third generation of Christian writers.[107] It contains the only mention of Korah in the NT. In v. 5 he notes that the Lord "destroyed" (ἀπώλεσεν) the Israelites (in the forty-year wilderness wandering after the exodus from Egypt) "who did not believe."[108] In addition, "the angels who did not keep their own position, but left their proper dwelling [Gen 6:1-4], He has kept in eternal chains in deepest darkness for the judgment of the great day" (v. 6). Sodom and Gomorrah and the cities around them (Gen 19:1-29) "serve as an example by undergoing a punishment of eternal fire" (v. 7).

"Intruders" who have stolen into the (anonymous) Christian community which is addressed (v. 4) are "dreamers" who "reject authority" and slander the angels ("glorious ones" - v. 8). Verse 11 states regarding these ungodly persons: "Woe to them! For they go the way of Cain [the first murderer in Gen 4:1-16[109]] and abandon themselves to Balaam's error [the sexual sin of Numbers 25; 31:16] for the sake of gain,

---

[107] Cf. Hubert Frankemölle, *1. Petrusbrief, 2. Petrusbrief, Judasbrief* (Neue Echter Bibel 20; Würzburg: Echter Verlag, 1987) 129. Most commentators date it at the end of the first or beginning of the second century CE.

[108] Cf. Num 14:22-23 and 26:63-65.

[109] Cain was one "thoroughly depraved" who "had an eye only to gain"; he "indulged in every bodily pleasure" and in "rapine and violence," living "a life of craftiness." Cf. Josephus, *Ant.* 1.53, 60-61. Philo in *Conf.* 122 cites him as *the* example of depravity. *Pirq. R. El.* 22 notes that "all the generations of the wicked, who rebel and sin," descended from Cain. The angels (of Gen 6:2) cohabited with their daughters (Eshkol 71-72; Eng. Friedlander 159).

'and perish in Korah's rebellion.'" The verbs of the latter sentence are all in the past, the first two stating: "for they have gone" and "they have abandoned themselves." The third, ἀπώλοντο, literally "they have been destroyed / have perished," is meant as "they will be destroyed / perish" as in the rebellion of Korah. This is because the opponents are still alive, and it is the reason why the NRSV translates here in the present tense. For such immoral, anti-authoritarian intruders "the deepest darkness has been reserved 'forever'" (v. 13). The latter phrase, εἰς αἰῶνα, adds a note of finality to their punishment (in hell / Hades /Sheol). Their fate will be that of Korah, without any hope at the future judgment (v. 15).[110]

4.6 *Rabbinic Sources*

The narrative of Korah's rebellion also fascinated the rabbis, who commented on it extensively. Of the three references to it in the Mishnah, two are relevant here. In *m. ʾAvot* 5:17 it is noted that a dispute such as one between Hillel and Shammai is for the sake of Heaven and will finally yield results, but one such as that of Korah and all his company is not for the sake of Heaven.[111] In 5:6 "the mouth of the earth" (Num 16:32, as the opening of Gehennah / Gehinnom) is listed as the first of ten things created on the eve of the (first) Sabbath at twilight.[112] The Tannaitic *Sifre* Korah § 117 on Num 18:8 states that Korah came and laid claim against (Aaron) in regard to the priesthood. He belonged both to those who were swallowed up (by the earth - Num 16:32), and to those who were destroyed by fire (v. 35).[113] *Num. Rab.* Korah 18/1-20 deals with the entire Korah episode in Numbers 16. There the third generation

---

110 This may be alluded to in the "fire" of v. 23.

111 Cf. Albeck 4.379; Danby 458; Neusner 688.

112 Cf. Albeck 4.376 with notes; Danby 456; Neusner 686. For one of the three gates of Gehenna as found in the wilderness (Num 16:33), see *b. ʿErub.* 19a (Soncino 130). The mouth (of Gehenna) as found in the wilderness is explicitly stated in regard to Korah and his company in *Num. Rab.* Korah 18/20 on Num 16:25, referring to v. 30 (Mirkin 10.206; Soncino 6.733). See also *b. Sanh.* 110a (Soncino 757).

113 Cf. Horovitz 135; German in Kuhn 373. See also the baraitha in *b. Sanh.* 110a (Soncino 756).

Tannaim R. Judah (b. Ilai) and R. Nehemiah are cited,[114] as well as the fourth generation Tanna, R. Nathan.[115] The motifs of Korah's great wealth[116] and his desire to become the high priest[117] are also emphasized.

The early Tannaitic tradition in *m. Sanh.* 10 which begins in v. 1 by stating that "*all* Israelites have a share in the world to come," based on Isa 60:21, is most important in the development of the tradition that Korah was saved from Gehenna through intercessory prayer. In addition, one person mentioned here who has no share in the world to come is he who maintains there is no resurrection of the dead (as derived from the Torah), relevant to 1 Corinthians 15.[118] In 10:2 the argument continues by stating that three kings and four commoners also have no share in the world to come, and 10:3 also mentions the generation of the flood (of Noah's time), the generation of the dispersion, the men of Sodom, the spies, and the generation of the wilderness. The next example is that of Korah:

> The party of Korah is not destined to rise up, for it is written, "And the earth closed over them" (Num 16:33) - in this world. "And they perished from the midst of the assembly" (ibid.) - in the world to come. Words of R. Aqiba. R. Eliezer says, Concerning them Scripture says, "The Lord kills and resurrects, brings down to Sheol and brings up again" (1 Sam 2:6).[119]

---

[114] Cf. *Introduction* 84 and 85, respectively, and 18/13 on Num 16:32 (Mirkin 10.202; Soncino 6.724). They describe how the earth opened and swallowed the rebels.

[115] Cf. *Introduction* 88, and Korah 18/4 on Num 16:1 (Mirkin 10.194; Soncino 6.712). There it is also stated that "babies a day old were burned and swallowed up in the bottomless abyss" (p. 713).

[116] Cf. *Num. Rab.* Korah 18/15 on Num 16:33 (Mirkin 10.203; Soncino 6.726), where Korah is stated to have been "controller in Pharaoh's palace and was in charge of the keys of his treasuries." See also *b. Sanh.* 110a (Soncino 756) and *b. Pes.* 119a (Soncino 615).

[117] Cf. the mention of the high priest(hood) in *Num. Rab.* Korah 18/4 on Num 16:1 (Mirkin 10.193; Soncino 6.711-12); 18/8 on Num 16:6 (Mirkin 10.196; Soncino 6.716); 18/10 on Num 16:16 (Mirkin 10.199; Soncino 6.721); and 18/20, also on Num 16:1 (Mirkin 10.206; Soncino 6.731).

[118] Cf. Albeck 4.202; Danby 397; Neusner 604. See also Mark 12:26-27.

[119] Cf. Albeck 4.203-04; Danby 398; Neusner 605.

R. Aqiba was a second generation Tanna of the younger group, R. Eliezer (b. Hyrcanus) of the older group.[120] R. Eliezer, a disciple of R. Yoḥanan b. Zakkai, was known for attaching great importance to inherited tradition and himself once maintained: "nor have I ever in my life said a thing which I did not hear from my teachers."[121] It thus seems probable that his opinion of Korah's future was based on even earlier tradition.

One of the older students of R. Aqiba associated with R. Eliezer was the second generation Tanna R. Judah b. Bathyra / Betera.[122] He disagreed with Aqiba in regard to the future fate of Korah and his company, siding with R. Eliezer, but arguing differently. In *t. Sanh.* 13:9 he says: "They will come to the world to come, for concerning them it is written, 'I have gone astray like a perishing [אובד - *ʾwbhd*] sheep; seek Your servant, [for I do not forget Your commandments]' (Ps 119:176). 'Perishing' [אבידה - *ʾbhydh*] is said here, and in the matter of Korah and his company 'perishing' [אבידה - *ʾbhydh*] is also said (Num 16:33). Just as 'perishing' spoken of later on refers to that which is being sought, so 'perishing' here refers to that which is being sought."[123] The divine passive is employed here: it is God Himself who will seek the "perishing / lost" ones, Korah and his company, and will cause them to enter the world to come.

The tradition espoused by R. Eliezer, however, is most important for our purposes. It employs 1 Sam 2:6 as a proof text. This is also found at the end of R. Judah b. Bathyra's comment in *y. Sanh.* 10:4, 29c. The question is asked there, "Who will pray for them / on their behalf [Korah and his company]"? This is the Hebrew מי נתפלל עליהן (*my ntpll ʿlyhn*). First R. Samuel b. Naḥman states that Moses "will pray for them," based on Deut 33:6, "Let Reuben live and not die, [nor let his men be few]."[124] Then R. Joshua b. Levi says in the name of R. Yose (b. Ḥalafta), a

---

[120] Cf. *Introduction* 79 and 77, respectively.

[121] Cf. *b. Sukk.* 28a (Soncino 122, and 123 for him as a disciple of R. Yoḥanan b. Zakkai). On this, see the extensive discussion in Wilhelm Bacher, *Die Agada der Tannaiten* (Straβburg: J. Trűbner, 1903²) 1.96-101.

[122] Cf. *Introduction* 83.

[123] Cf. Zuckermandel / Liebermann 435; Eng. Neusner 4.240-41. See also *b. Sanh.* 109b (Soncino 753 with n. 1).

[124] Cf. Reuben's sin of lying with his father Israel's concubine Bilhah in Gen 35:22, alluded to in Gen 49:4.

third generation Tanna[125] : Hannah "will pray for them," for "thus did the party of Korah sink ever downward until Hannah arose and 'prayed for them' and said: 1 Sam 2:6."[126] In *Gen. Rab.* Vayeḥi 98/4 on Gen 49:4 with Reuben's "going up," after the quotation of Deut 33:6, "the Rabbis said" the latter statement about Korah and his company.[127]

The following shows how important and widespread 1 Sam 2:6, cited above, was in Judaic tradition in regard to intercessory prayer for someone already deceased, here Korah and his company. In 1 Sam 1:10 the childless Hannah prayed in Shiloh for a male child, praying silently with only her lips moving (v. 13).[128] Her prayer is then found in 2:1-10.[129] Verse 6 reads: "The Lord kills and brings to life; He brings down to Sheol and raises up."[130] The LXX substitutes "Hades" here for "Sheol." *Targum Jonathan* paraphrases the final verb as: "and He is also ready to bring up in eternal life."[131] The popularity of this scriptural verse as a proof text for the resurrection, including Korah and his company's attaining it through the intercessory prayer of Hannah, is shown in its being quoted twenty-three times in the relevant rabbinic sources.[132]

---

[125] Cf. *Introduction* 84.

[126] Cf. Neusner 31.357. Samuel b. Naḥman was a third generation Palestinian Amora (*Introduction* 97), and Joshua b. Levi a first generation Palestinian Amora (*Introduction* 92).

[127] Cf. Theodor and Albeck 1255; Soncino 2.952 with n. 2.

[128] This verse is cited to maintain that one may not raise one's voice when saying the daily Tefillah / Eighteen Prayer. Cf. *t. Ber.* 3:6 (Zuckermandel / Liebermann 6; Eng. Neusner / Zahavy 1.13); *b. Ber.* 31a (Soncino 190); and *y. Ber.* 4:1, 7a (Neusner / Zahavy 1.149).

[129] It became the model for Mary's "Magnificat" in Luke 1:46-53. See the study of Ulrike Mittmann-Richert, *Magnifikat und Benediktus*: die ältesten Zeugnisse der judenchristlichen Tradition von der Geburt des Messias (WUNT 2.90; Tűbingen: Mohr, 1996).

[130] It is noteworthy that this verse forms part of the background to the second benediction in the Tefillah / Eighteen Prayer, which deals with resurrection.

[131] Cf. Sperber 2.97; Eng. Harrington and Saldarini 106.

[132] This tendency later went so far as to have R. Berekhyah, a fifth generation Palestinian Amora (*Introduction* 105), say that the King Messiah "asked that even Korah and his companions, men who went down alive into Sheol, be raised up again, for it is said: 1 Sam 2:6" (*Midr. Pss.* 21/4 on Ps 21:5 [Buber 179; Eng. Braude 1.295, with n. 9 in 2.455]). In *Midr. Pss.* 45/4 on Ps 45:2 on Korah and his company, although they could not confess with their mouths, "their hearts overflowed with repentance" when they saw "the pit that was beneath them and

One example of the latter in regard to temporary suffering in Gehenna is found in the Tannaitic *t. Sanh.* 13:3. There the House of Shammai say:

> There are three groups [of humans when they die], one for eternal life, one "for shame and everlasting contempt" (Dan 12:2) - these are those who are completely evil. An intermediate group go down to Gehenna and scream and come up again, as it is said: "I will bring the third part through fire and will refine them as silver is refined and will test them as gold is tested, and [after this kind of purgatory] they shall call on My name, and I will be their God" (Zech 13:9). And concerning them Hannah said: 1 Sam 2:6.[133]

Here Hannah's prayer in 1 Sam 2:6 makes intercession for those Israelites and later Jewish deceased who are neither completely good nor completely evil, in other words, for almost everyone. As indicated in the numerous sources cited above, this included the deceased Korah and his company. Hannah prayed "on their behalf" / "for them." This intercessory prayer connected to the resurrection is thus in part also analogous to Corinthian Christians letting themselves be baptized again "on behalf of / for" (ὑπέρ) the dead, who thereby are also thought to be enabled to participate in the resurrection.

---

a fire burned around them." In addition, Hannah referred to them in 1 Sam 2:6 (Buber 270; Eng. Braude 1.451-52).

[133] Cf. Zuckermandel / Liebermann 434; Eng. Neusner 4.238-39. In 13:5 the text continues by noting that for those who deny the resurrection of the dead, "Gehenna is locked behind them, and they are judged for all generations," as Isa 66:24 is interpreted. Sheol will waste away, but they will not (ibid.). On the Beth Shammai tradition, see also *b. Rosh ha-Shanah* 16b-17a (Soncino 64, with notes). In *y. Sanh.* 10:3, 29b-c (Eng. Neusner 31.353), God judges the wicked in Gehenna for twelve months. The quotation of Ps 40:3 appears to give even these people hope for a portion in the World to Come. On R. Aqiba's stating that the judgment of the wicked in Gehenna will last twelve months, based on Isa 66:23, see already *m. 'Edu.* 2:10 (Albeck 4.292; Danby 426; Neusner 626). This is repeated in *Lam. Rab.* 1:12 § 40 (Vilna 31; Soncino 7.117). An early tradition may possibly also still be found in the late work *Pesiqta Rabbati* 20/2. It states: "Perhaps you will say that once man is plunged into Gehenna, there is no coming up for him. When mercy is besought 'on his behalf' [עליו - *'lyw*], however, he is shot up from Gehenna like an arrow from the bow" (Friedmann 95b; Eng. Braude 1.401).

5. *Deut 21:8 in Judaic Tradition*

Deut 21:1-9 deals with the case of someone murdered in open country by an unknown assailant. A heifer which had never been yoked was selected and its neck broken to atone for the innocent blood which had been shed. Judaic tradition relates that such blood even atones for persons who have long been dead.

Verse 8 states: "Forgive, O Lord, Your people Israel, whom You redeemed; do not let the guilt of innocent blood remain in the midst of Your people Israel. Then the guilt of blood will be forgiven them." Interpretation of this verse is attested very early, as indicated by the addition of "from the land of Egypt" in the LXX to "whom You redeemed." The first form of the verb "forgive" is the piel of כפר (*kphr*) : to cover over, atone for sin,[134] forgive, procure forgiveness.[135] The second form of the same verb is the rare nithpael.[136] The Mishnah at *Soṭah* 9:6 states that the priests say the first part of Deut 21:8, and the Holy Spirit the last part.[137]

The Tannaitic *Sifre* Shofeṭim 210 on Deut 21:8 also has the priests say "'Forgive, O Lord, Your people Israel, [whom You redeemed].' When Scripture says, 'whom You redeemed,' it teaches that this atonement [כפרה - *kprh*] atones for those who had left [the land of] Egypt. 'Forgive [כפר - *kpr*] Your people' - these are those alive now. 'Whom You redeemed' - these are the dead [המתים - *hmtym*]. This indicates that the dead [המתים - *hmtym*] also need forgiveness / atonement [כפרה - *kprh*]. We thus learn that the shedder of blood is a sinner even as far back as those who left Egypt."[138]

This is a rare Tannaitic text which maintains that atonement / forgiveness can also be obtained for the dead, even going back to the

---

[134] Cf. BDB 495.

[135] Cf. Jastrow 661.

[136] Cf. BDB 498; the form only occurs here.

[137] Cf. Albeck 3.258; Danby 304; Neusner 463. This is preceded by the elders' reciting Deut 21:7. The Tosefta repeats this at 9:2 (Zuckermandel / Liebermann 312; Eng. Neusner 3.289).

[138] Cf. Finkelstein 244; I modify the English of Hammer 223. See also Finkelstein's notes, and Hammer's on p. 465.

generation of the Israelites who left Egypt.[139] Other Judaic comment corroborates this basic motif. In *y. Soṭah* 9:5, 23d regarding Deut 21:8, it is stated that "in the case of the heifer it is as if part of the beast is offered on the altar."[140] In 9:6, 24a the breaking of a heifer's neck is a manner of atonement "suitable to make atonement [even] for those who went out of Egypt."[141]

Finally, the late midrash *Tanḥuma* Ha'azinu 1 deals in part with Deut 21:8. It notes that "They are accustomed to recall the dead on the Sabbath so that they do not return to Gehinnom. Thus it is written, "Atone for / forgive Your people Israel' - these are the living. 'Whom You redeemed' - these are the dead. Thus we are accustomed to recall the dead on the Day of Atonement and to provide alms / righteousness[142] 'for them' [עֲלֵיהֶם - *'ălēhem*]." The latter phrase is then also expressed by בִּשְׁבִילָם (*bishbhîlam*), "on their behalf," the almsgiving "leading and raising them [the dead] up like an arrow from a bow."[143]

This midrash cannot be dated, yet it attests the fact that at least in some Palestinian circles the earlier, definitely Tannaitic belief that the living can redeem the dead persisted. In addition, practicing almsgiving / charity is done "on their behalf" - on behalf of the dead. Judaic interpretation of a key text in Scripture, Deut 21:8, is thus another partial analogy to some Corinthian Christians' undergoing an additional baptism "on behalf of the dead" in 1 Cor 15:29.

---

139 Solomon Schechter in *Aspects of Rabbinic Theology* 196 notes that murder in such a case "is supposed to have a damaging effect upon the ancestors of the murderer." Thus they need atonement.

140 Cf. Neusner 27.242.

141 Cf. Neusner 27.248. On this assertion, see also *b. Hor.* 6a (Soncino 37; this also states that "since [the heifer] atones for the living, it may also atone for the dead"), and *b. Ker.* 26a (Soncino 196).

142 The term צדקה (*ṣdqh*) means both: Jastrow 1263.

143 Cf. Eshkol 934, and Jastrow 1514 on שְׁבִיל (*shebhîl*) with בִּ (*bi*): "on account of, for the sake of." See also the expression תַּחַת *(taḥat)* meant as "in place of, instead of" (Jastrow 1662) in *y. Hor.* 1:8, 46b (Neusner 34.39). There the question is asked: "A congregation, a member of which died - What is the law as to bringing a sin offering 'on his behalf'?" On the imagery of bow and arrow, see *Pesiq. R.* 20/2 in n. 133.

6. *David and His Son Absalom*

The third son of David was Absalom, with a heavy shock of hair considered to be the most handsome man in all Israel (2 Sam 14:25-26).[144] Because he gloried in his hair, according to Judaic tradition he was later hanged by it.[145] He dared to claim the kingship while his father was still alive, causing David to flee Jerusalem (2 Samuel 15; Psalm 3). He then even went in to his father's concubines (2 Sam 16:20-23). For these reasons a baraitha has R. Meir, a third generation Tanna,[146] say: "Absalom has no portion in the world to come, for it is written, 'And they smote Absalom, and slew him' (2 Sam 18:15). 'They smote him' - in this world. 'And slew him' - in the next."[147]

In spite of Absalom's usurping the throne, David urged the commander of his army: "Deal gently for my sake with the young man Absalom" (2 Sam 18:5).[148] Fleeing from defeat in battle later on, Absalom on his mule rode "under the thick branches of a great oak. His head caught fast in the oak, and he was put between heaven and earth, while the mule that was under him went on" (v. 9). He was then killed by Joab and his armor-bearers (vv. 14-15).[149] Again, because he exalted himself with his hair, according to the dictum "measure for measure" God punished him by having his head caught in a tree (and his being killed there).[150]

This incident is painted in broad brush strokes in the haggadah. *Num. Rab.* Naso 9/24 on Num 5:11-31, for example, has Abba Saul, a third generation Tanna,[151] say: "I was a grave-digger. Once a cave opened

---

[144] On him, cf. the art. "Absalom" in *EJ* (2007) 1.330-31, including the section by Louis Rabinowitz on Absalom in the haggadah (331). See also the art. "David," "In the Aggadah," by Israel Ta-Shma in *EJ* (2007) 5.451-53; and Louis Ginzberg, *The Legends of the Jews* 4.104-07, and notes 97-108 in 6.266-68.

[145] Cf. *m. Soṭah* 1:8 (Albeck 3.236; Danby 294; Neusner 449).

[146] Cf. *Introduction* 84; he was a student of both R. Ishmael and R. Aqiba.

[147] Cf. *b. Sanh.* 103b (Soncino 702). The first part is also found in *ʾAvot R. Nat.* A 36 (Schechter 108; Becker 260-61; Eng. Goldin 151).

[148] Cf. already 13:37, where David "mourned for his son day after day" when Absalom fled to Geshur and stayed there three years. David then "yearned" for him (v. 39).

[149] Cf. again *m. Soṭah* 1:8 on this.

[150] Cf. *Mek. R. Ish.* Shirata 2 on Exod 15:1 (Lauterbach 2.16-17).

[151] Cf. *Introduction* 86.

under me, and I stood up to my nose in the socket of a dead man's eye! When I got out, they said to me it was Absalom's."[152] The midrash continues with a tradition taught in the School of R. Ishmael[153] : "When Absalom was suspended from the oak, he seized his sword and attempted to cut off his hair. At that instant the netherworld [Sheol] opened up beneath him."[154] *Pirq. R. El.* 53 states here that Absalom "saw that Gehinnom was opened beneath him, and he said, 'It is better for me to hang by my hair and not to descend into the fire.' Therefore he was hanging in the oak," as in 2 Sam 18:10. R. Yose (b. Ḥalafta, a third generation Tanna,[155]) then stated: "There are seven doors to Gehinnom. Absalom entered as far as the fifth door. David heard [of this] and began to weep, to lament, and to mourn," stating 2 Sam 19:1 (Eng. 18:33). "And they [David's words of intercession] brought him back from the five doors of Gehinnom."[156] Here David is comforted by dead Absalom's escaping Gehinnom through his own intercession. This is also emphasized in the following passage.

In *b. Soṭah* 10b the above tradition from the School of R. Ishmael is first cited. This is followed by 2 Sam 19:1 (Eng. 18:33). "The king was deeply moved [at hearing of Absalom's death], and went up to the chamber over the gate, and wept. And as he went, he said, 'O my son Absalom, my son, my son Absalom! Would that I had died instead of you, O Absalom, my son, my son Absalom!" The midrash asks, "Why is 'my son' repeated eight times?[157] Seven to raise him from the seven divisions of Gehinnom. As for the last, some say to unite his [severed] head to his body, and others say to bring him into the World to Come."[158]

Interpretation of this passage is very old, as shown by the LXX's repetition of the phrase "instead of you" (ἀντὶ σοῦ). Josephus in *Ant.*

---

[152] Cf. Mirkin 9.198; Soncino 5.288. It adds: "And Abba Saul was the tallest man of his generation." A parallel is found in *b. Nidd.* 24b (Soncino 168).

[153] Ishmael was a second generation Tanna of the younger group: *Introduction* 79.

[154] Cf. Mirkin 9.198-99; Soncino 5.289. A parallel is found in *b. Soṭah* 10b (Soncino 51).

[155] Cf. *Introduction* 84. Although the attribution of definite sayings to specific rabbis can justifiably be questioned in *Pirqe de-Rabbi Eliezer*, I consider this example and this section to be basically trustworthy since they are found elsewhere in the same form.

[156] Cf. the edition translated by Gerald Friedlander in 432-33, with notes; Eshkol 214-15 differs slightly.

[157] This number includes five here and three in 19:5 (Eng. 4).

[158] Cf. Soncino 51.

7.252 also exhibits early Judaic tradition on the verse when he says David in his mourning beat his breast, tore his hair, and maltreated himself in various ways. He then said, "O my son, would that death had come to me and that I had died 'with you' [ἅμα σοι]!" The MT has for the last phrase "'instead of' you," with תַּחַת *(tahat)*.[159] *Targum Jonathan* has the similar חלוף *(hlwph)*.[160] David expressly states here that he would gladly have offered his own life in order that his dead son could remain alive - so great was his love for Absalom in spite of his treasonous behavior.

David's wish is expressed as a prayer not only in *Pirq. R. El.* 53 above, but also in *b. Soṭah* 10b. Altogether, he repeats "my son" eight times, seven of which are intended to "raise" dead Absalom from the seven divisions of Gehinnom. This verb is the *afēl* of נסק *(nsq)*: to cause to rise, bring up, raise.[161] In addition, some interpreters maintained that the eighth mention of "my son" (Absalom) by David meant he did so "to 'bring' him into the World to Come." This verb is the *afēl* of אתא (*ʾtʾ*), to bring, to cause to come.[162] In other words, David is represented here as being able through his intercessory prayer to raise a dead person from (the torments of) Gehinnom / Gehenna. He could even cause Absalom to enter the World to Come, in which he originally was supposed to have no portion because of his treacherous, double-dealing behavior. Such intercessory prayer can also be viewed as an analogy to some Corinthian Christians' undergoing an additional baptism in order for the dead person to participate in the resurrection with the World to Come, for the ends of the ages had already come (1 Cor 10:11; cf. 1:7; 7:26, 29, 31; and 15:51).

7. *R. Meir and Elisha b. Abuya (Aḥer).*

Elisha b. Abuya was a second generation Tanna of the younger group.[163] His father was an important person in Jerusalem and on the occasion of

---

[159] Cf. BDB 1065 II. 2. b., and Jastrow in n. 143.

[160] Cf. Sperber 2.194; Eng. Harrington and Saldarini 194. On the preposition, see Jastrow 472 as חולף *(hwlph)*: in place of, instead.

[161] Cf. Jastrow 918.

[162] Cf. Jastrow 132.

[163] Cf. *Introduction* 82. On him, see Wilhelm Bacher, *Die Agada der Tannaiten* 1.430-34, as well as the art. "Elisha ben Avuyah" by Stephen Wald in *EJ* (2007) 6.352-53.

Elisha's circumcision gave a banquet for all the eminent men of the city, including R. Eliezer and R. Joshua. On the basis of their learned conversation, Elisha's father dedicated him to the study of the Torah. In spite of this he later became an apostate, probably because of the issue of theodicy in connection with the gruesome Hadrianic persecution of 132-35 CE. The terrible deaths of innocent people led him to doubt a future reward for the righteous and the resurrection of the dead. For this reason he was called "Aḥer" (the Other).[164] The Tannaitic Tosefta already notes in *Ḥag.* 2:3 that he was one of the four scholars who entered the "Garden."[165] He "gazed and cut down sprouts. Concerning him Scripture says, 'Let not your mouth lead you into sin' (Eccl 5:5)."[166]

R. Meir was a third generation Tanna and for a while a disciple of Elisha b. Abuya; he remained faithful to him up until his death. When one of his own disciples informed R. Meir that Elisha was (deathly) ill, he went to him and asked him:

> "Will you not repent?" He said, "If sinners repent, are they accepted?" [R. Meir] replied, "Is it not written thus: 'You [God] cause a man to repent up to the point when he becomes dust' (Ps 90:3)? Up to the time when life is crushed, repentant sinners are received." At that point Elisha wept. Then he departed [this life] and died. R. Meir rejoiced in his heart, thinking: "My master died in repentance." When they buried him, fire came down from heaven and consumed his grave. They came and told R. Meir, "Behold, your master's grave has been set on fire." He went, intending to visit it, and found it burning. What did he do? He took his long prayer cloak and spread it over the corpse, saying: "'Pass

---

164 This is indicated in the highly embellished accounts found in the very similar passages *Ruth Rab.* 6/4 on Ruth 3:13 (Vilna 21; Soncino 8.76-80) and *Eccl. Rab.* 7:8 § 1 (Vilna 37-38; Soncino 8.183-87). It is highly doubtful that he then betrayed fellow Jews to the Romans. This is against the tendentious account in *y. Ḥag.* 2:1, 77b (Neusner 20.45).

165 This can mean either "Paradise" (Heaven) or deep theosophical discussion. See Jastrow 1216 on פַּרְדֵּס *(pardēs)* with park, pleasure garden, here "esoteric philosophy."

166 Cf. Zuckermandel / Liebermann 234; Eng. Neusner 2.313.This is interpreted in legendary fashion in *y. Ḥag.* 2:1, 77b (Neusner 20.45) to mean that he encouraged ongoing scholars to instead become tradesmen. Fear of his possibly heretical teaching is found in the general saying: If one sees Elisha b. Abuya in a dream, one should fear calamity. See *ʾAvot R. Nat.* A 40 (Schechter 128; Becker 282-83; Eng. Goldin 167) and B 46 (Schechter 129; Becker 404; Eng. Saldarini 290), as well as *b. Ḥag.* 15a (Soncino 93, with "Aḥer mutilated the shoots").

> the night' (Ruth 3:13). Stay in this world, which is like the night. 'And it shall be in the morning' (ibid.). This is the world to come, which is all morning. 'If He will redeem you, well and good; let Him redeem you' (ibid.). This is the Holy One, blessed be He, of whom it is written: 'The Lord is good to all, and His compassion is over all that He has made' (Ps 145:9). 'And if it does not please Him to redeem you, then, as the Lord lives, I will redeem you' (Ruth 3:13)." Then the fire was extinguished.[167]

In this haggadic account R. Meir is represented as interpreting the words of Boaz to Ruth in Ruth 3:13 to mean that if God is not willing to "redeem" his beloved teacher, Elisha b. Abuya, who wept (as a sign of repentance) just before he died, then he, R. Meir, would himself do so. Finding Elisha's grave on fire, Meir considered this to be a form of divine punishment, not just of purgatorial fire. Therefore he took his own prayer shawl (טַלִּית [*ṭallît*])[168] and spread it over the corpse, bargaining with God: If in spite of Elisha's repentance You refuse to redeem him, I will now do so myself. Because the fire then went out, R. Meir knew that his action was successful. God had accepted it. The rabbi's intercession for a dead person led to the latter's being "redeemed," that is, his (later) entering the World to Come.

R. Meir's covering the body of a deceased person with his own prayer shawl in order to "redeem" him is thus a variant of the rabbinic examples cited above of intercessory prayer for the dead. Here, however, it involves a concrete object, a *prayer* shawl.[169]

8. *The Intercession of Children for Their Dead Fathers*

Several rabbinical passages maintain that both infant and grown sons can make atonement, i.e. intercede, for their deceased father who is in Sheol. The following three narratives illustrate this.

---

167 Cf. *y. Ḥag.* 2:1, 77c (Neusner 20.49, slightly modified). The versions in *Ruth Rabbah* and *Ecclesiastes Rabbah* (see n. 164) are similar.

168 Cf. Jastrow 537.

169 Another version of the narrative has smoke rise from Elisha's grave *after* R. Meir himself dies (and prays for him). Cf. *b. Ḥag.* 15b (Soncino 96, with notes). This later variant contradicts the straightforward ductus of the earlier account.

8.1 *Eccl. Rab.* 4:1 § 1

In this passage R. Judah (b. Ilai) and R. Nehemiah, two third generation Tannaim,[170] comment on Eccl 4:1, "But I returned and considered all the oppressions that are done under the sun." R. Judah begins by stating:[171]

> It refers to the children who are buried early in life through the sins of their fathers in this world. In the World to Come they will range themselves with the band of the righteous, while their fathers will be ranged with the band of the wicked. They will speak before Him: "Lord of the universe, did we not die early only because of the sins of our fathers? Let our fathers come over to us through our merits!"[172] He replies to them, "Your fathers sinned also after your death, and their wrongdoings accuse them." R. Joshua b. Levi[173] said in the name of R. Judah: At that time Elijah (may he be remembered for good) will be there to suggest a defence. He will say to the children: "Speak before Him, Lord of the universe, which of Your attributes predominates, that of grace or punishment? Surely the attribute of grace is great and that of punishment is small, yet we died through the sins of our fathers. If then the attribute of grace exceeds the other, how much more should our fathers come over to us!" Therefore He says to them: "You have pleaded well. Let them come over to you," as it is written, "And they shall live with their children, and shall return" (Zech 10:9). This means that they returned from the descent to Gehinnom and were rescued through the merit of their children. Therefore every man is under obligation to teach his son Torah so that he may rescue him from Gehinnom.

Here not living, but children who died early in life because of the sins of their fathers are represented as being together with the righteous in the Hereafter. They plead with God that through their own merits, "for

---

[170] Cf. *Introduction* 84-85.

[171] Cf. Vilna 12b or 24; Soncino 8.110.

[172] The English translator, A. Cohen, comments in 8.110, n. 1: "Let our death be an atonement for their sins." He also calls attention to *b. Soṭah* 48b-49a (Soncino 262) dealing with the children of wicked Israelites who, by appealing to God, change the negative verdict against their fathers in the World to Come.

[173] He was a first generation Palestinian Amora (*Introduction* 92). The text mistakenly reverses the attribution. Cf. also Soncino 8.110, n. 2, for R. Nehemiah being correct for "R. Ḥanina" in the next paragraph.

their own sake,"[174] their fathers who are now with the wicked (in Sheol) may join them. Through the mediation of Elijah, God then lets His attribute of mercy dominate and allows the fathers to join their children, who are with the righteous. This is said to fulfill Scripture (Zech 10:9). The moral of the story is given at the end: Every man (even someone wicked) is obligated to teach his son the Torah, for then he can "rescue" his father from Gehinnom.[175]

8.2 *B. Qidd.* 31b

The Mishnah at *Qidd.* 1:7 deals with "every commandment concerning the father to which the son is subject."[176] The *gemara* says on this at *b. Qidd.* 31b:

> Our Rabbis taught: He [the son] must honor him [the father] in life and must honor him in death. "In life," e.g. one who is heeded in a place on account of his father should not say, "Let me go, for my own sake," "Speed me, for my own sake," but "for my father's sake." "In death," e.g. if one is reporting something heard from his mouth, he should not say, "Thus did my father say," but "Thus said my father, my teacher, for whose resting place may I be an atonement." But that is only within twelve months [of his death]. Thereafter he must say, "His memory be for a blessing, for the life of the World to Come."[177]

This Tannaitic tradition notes that a man honors his father, (a rabbi who has at least in part been his teacher), when the latter has died by repeating a tradition in the father's name. Yet this should be prefaced with the words: "Thus says my father, my teacher, for whose resting place may I be an atonement."[178] Rashi explains the latter to mean: "May I make atonement for all the punishment in the Hereafter that may have

---

174 Cf. Jastrow on זְכוּת *(zekhut)* in 398, 3): the protecting influence of good conduct, merit. The phrase בז׳ (*bz* ´) means "for the sake of."

175 Cf. also *Eliyyahu Zuṭa* 12 (Friedmann 194; Eng. Braude and Kapstein 453-54), where a father unlettered in the Torah had his son read and write Torah: "Such a son can deliver even a [simple] father from the punishment of Gehenna."

176 Cf. Albeck 3.315; Danby 322; Neusner 488.

177 Cf. Soncino 154.

178 Cf. Jastrow 662 on כַּפָּרָה *(kaparah)* in this passage: "may I be an expiation for his rest."

to come upon him."[179] The son should say this, however, only for twelve months after the father's death. This is because punishment in the Hereafter for one who was not completely righteous, but belonged to the vast majority of human beings, was considered to last twelve months.[180]

A son's presently making atonement within a period of twelve months for his recently deceased father,[181] thus reducing his punishment in Gehenna / Sheol,[182] is somewhat analogous to the Corinthian Christians' attempt to achieve redemption for the dead by having themselves baptized again on their behalf. This is true even if the Corinthian baptism was performed only once and was meant to have immediate and permanent consequences, whereas a son's making atonement for his deceased father could be done more than once.

8.3 *Eliyyahu Zuṭa* 17

The following narrative in *Eliyyahu Zuṭa* 17 relates a tradition concerning R. Yoḥanan b. Zakkai, a first generation Tanna.[183] In the same section R. Eliezer (b. Hyrcanus), R. Simeon (b. Yoḥai), Yoḥanan Ben Bag-Bag, Ben He-He, and Eleazar b. Azaryah speaking in the name of Ḥanina are cited, all pre-Tannaitic rabbis or those of the first and second generation.[184] *Eliyyahu Zuṭa* , now part of *Eliyyahu Rabbah,* is variously dated in its final form from the third to the ninth century CE.[185] The author appears to

---

179 This is noted by the translator, H. Freedman, in the Soncino edition, p. 154, n. 2.

180 On this time limit, cf. section "4. Korah," n. 133, as well as H. Freedman, Soncino 154, n. 3.

181 This could be thought of as personal suffering, but for Sages also to "toil" in the Torah. Cf. the saying of R. Simeon b. Yoḥai in *Gen. Rab*. Vayyera 49/4 on Gen 18:19 (Theodor and Albeck 503; Soncino 1.424): "He who leaves his son 'toiling' in the Torah is as though he had not died."

182 The phrase may have deteriorated into "A respectful way of mentioning one's deceased parent or teacher." Cf. Resh Laqish in regard to R. Ḥiyya and his sons in *b. Sukk*. 20a (Soncino 86-87, and Israel Slotki's n. 1 on p. 87). However, the original intention of making atonement certainly still remained in the background.

183 Cf. *Introduction* 74-75.

184 On these, cf. Appendix III in Danby, *The Mishnah* 799.

185 Cf. Braude and Kapstein 6-9; its provenance unfortunately cannot be determined (p. 10).

have attributed a later tradition here to R. Yoḥanan b. Zakkai.[186] It has him relate:

> Once, as I was walking along a road, I came upon a man who was gathering pieces of wood. When I spoke to him, he did not reply. Afterwards he came over to me and said to me: "I am dead, not alive." When I asked, "If you are dead, what need do you have of wood?", he replied: "Rabbi, listen to me while I tell you something. When I was alive, my friend and <I> engaged in sodomy. So when we were sentenced to come here [to Gehenna], a penalty of punishment by burning was handed down against both of us. Now when I gather pieces of wood, they are used to burn my friend. And when he gathers pieces of wood, they are used to burn me." I asked, "How long is your [pl.] sentence to last?" He replied: "When I came here, I left my wife pregnant, and I know that the child she bears will be a male. And so I beg you, please watch over him from the time of his birth until he reaches the age of five. Then take him to the house of a teacher to learn Scripture. For when he learns how to say, 'Bless the Lord, Who is to be blessed,' I shall be brought up from the punishment of Gehenna."[187]

It is important to note here that the two men who gather pieces of wood have committed sodomy.[188] According to *m. Sanh.* 10:3, sodomites have no share in the World to Come.[189] Thus the two are now being punished in Gehenna and are constantly burned without being consumed. They need to gather the wood from the world above to use as fuel for their own punishment. One left his wife pregnant when he died, and he supernaturally knows that the child still to be born will be male. He requests Yoḥanan b. Zakkai, a famous rabbi, to make sure the boy learns how to read Scripture with a proper teacher when he turns

---

186 In this respect it resembles *Pirqe de-Rabbi Eliezer*, where the attributions of traditions to specific early rabbis may often be questioned.

187 Cf. Friedmann, Supplement 22-23, and Eng. Braude and Kapstein 488-89, which I somewhat modify.

188 On the origin of this foreign word in the Hebrew, *plṭri*, cf. Braude and Kapstein 488, n. 20. Their translation of "woods" as "fagots" is a pun on the (negative) English term "faggot" for a male homosexual, something not found in the Hebrew text.

189 Cf. Albeck 4.203; Danby 397; Neusner 605. R. Nehemiah says they will not even stand in judgment.

five. His learning to recite "Bless the Lord, Who is to be blessed,"[190] will then cause his father to rise from the punishment of Gehenna.[191]

Here God not only changes the verdict on an evil person, a sodomist, because he now wants Him to be praised later on by a blessing through his as yet unborn child. The main reason is that God is represented as granting the (implied) request of an innocent child for his wicked father to be released from the agony of Gehenna. This is when the child is five years old, can consider the fate of his wicked father, and has learned what redeeming words to say on his father's behalf. This is thus another Judaic example, although probably quite late, of a child's atoning for its dead parent - in the patriarchal world of the rabbis the child always being male. Such an action is also somewhat analogous to the Corinthian Christians' having themselves baptized again on behalf of the dead in 1 Cor 15:29.

9. *The Circumcision of Deceased Infant Boys*

Circumcision of boys[192] was a major tenet of Judaism, traced back to the Lord's making a covenant with Abraham through circumcision in Genesis 17. Therefore it is often simply called "the covenant" because the term is mentioned there thirteen times.[193] Unless mitigating circumstances obtain, it should always take place on the eighth day after birth, even if this is a Sabbath. This is indicated in the Lord's command to Abraham in Gen 17:12,[194] as well as in Lev 12:3. In the Mishnah, *Shab.* 19:5 states: "The rule is that it should be done on the eighth day."[195] This is why John the Baptist was circumcised then (Luke 1:59), as well as Jesus

---

[190] Cf. Braude and Kapstein 489, n. 22, on this in liturgical usage.

[191] Cf. also the somewhat similar story with R. Aqiba's meeting a ghost in a cemetery in *Kallah Rabbathi* 2:9, 52a (*The Minor Tractates of the Talmud* 434-35).

[192] Cf. the articles on it by J. Hyatt in *IDB* (1962) 1.629-31, and Leonard Snowman, Jonathan Seidel and Judith Baskin in *EJ* (2007) 4.730-34.

[193] Cf. *m. Ned.* 3:1 in the name of R. Ishmael (b. Elisha), a second generation Tanna (*Introduction* 79). See Albeck 3.157; Danby 268; Neusner 412. There "Great is circumcision, for..." is explained by five Tannaim.

[194] Cf. also Stephen's words in respect to Abraham's circumcising Isaac on the eighth day in Acts 7:8.

[195] Cf. Albeck 2.62; Danby 117; Neusner 203. The entire chapter deals with circumcision.

(2:21). Paul notes that if he wanted to show confidence in the flesh, he could maintain that he was circumcised on the eighth day (Phil 3:5), and that he was a Pharisee (v. 5), the Jewish party known for belief in the resurrection in contrast to the Sadducees.[196] Acts 16:3 relates that Paul circumcised Timothy, whose father was a Greek, but whose mother was Jewish (v. 1). In addition, without being circumcised one could not participate in the annual Passover festival (Exod 12:48).

Circumcision was especially emphasized during times of persecution, such as that under Antiochus IV Epiphanes (reigned 174-164 BCE). He ordered under the threat of death that Jews should leave their sons uncircumcised (1 Macc 1:48, 50; cf. 2 Macc 6:10). The author of *Jubilees,* written in Hebrew in Palestine ca. 150 BCE,[197] thus took a very strong position in regard to the necessity of having Jewish sons circumcised. In 15:26 the author states in drastic language:

> And anyone who is born whose own flesh is not circumcised on the eighth day is not from the sons of the covenant which the Lord made with Abraham since [he is] from the children of destruction. And there is therefore no sign upon him so that he might belong to the Lord because [he is destined] to be destroyed and annihilated from the earth and to be uprooted from the earth because he has broken the covenant of the Lord our God.[198]

The Roman emperor Hadrian's prohibiting circumcision was also one of the reasons for Jewish resistance to the Roman occupation of their land, including the Bar Kokhba War of 132-35 CE. Circumcision on the eighth day after a male child's birth as a major tenet of Judaism was thus still firmly established at this time. Willful neglect of it meant that one simply did not belong to the people of God through this sign of the covenant He had made with Abraham.

Two examples from rabbinic literature suffice to illustrate how being circumcised was thought to deliver one from Gehenna. The first is *Gen. Rab.* Vayyera 48/8 on Gen 18:1. There R. Levi, a third generation

---

196 Cf. Acts 23:6-8. On the Pharisees' belief in resurrection, see the "Hellenized" accounts in Josephus, *Bell.* 2.163 (also 3.374) and *Ant.* 18.14.

197 Cf. O. Wintermute in *OTP* 2.43-45, and 46 on Antiochus IV.

198 Cf. *OTP* 2.87. Verse 34 continues regarding Jews who do not circumcise their sons: "And there is therefore no forgiveness or pardon so that they might be pardoned and forgiven from all the sins of this eternal error."

Palestinian Amora,[199] states: "In the time to come Abraham will sit at the entrance to Gehenna and permit no circumcised Israelite to descend therein." In regard to those evil Jews who sinned very much, however, "he will remove the foreskin from infants who died before circumcision and set it upon them [the sinners], and then let them descend into Gehenna," as Ps 55:21 (Eng. 20) is interpreted.[200]

The second example is *Exod. Rab.* Bo 19/4, dealing with Exod 12:43, "This is the ordinance of Passover," whereby v. 48 states that "no uncircumcised person shall eat of it." It flatly states: "No Israelite who is circumcised will go down to Gehinnom." R. Berekhya, a fifth generation Palestinian Amora,[201] then explains how God treats Jewish heretics and wicked people who maintain they will not descend to Gehinnom because they are circumcised. He sends an angel, who stretches their foreskin, (making them look uncircumcised), also based on Ps 55:21 (Eng. 20). "When Gehinnom sees their hanging foreskins, it opens its mouth and devours them."[202]

While acknowledging that God must later requite some evil Jews with punishment, such sources attest in the Amoraic period that (almost) no Israelite who was circumcised was expected to go down to Gehenna / Gehinnom. This is because he bore the sign of the Lord's covenant with His people.

Yet the problem arose of how to view infant Jewish males who died before the eighth day, when they should have been circumcised. The tractate "Mourning" (*ʾEbel Rabbathi*) in the *Minor Tractates of the Talmud* states in 3:1, 44b: "A boy who lived only one day counts to his father and mother as a fully-grown man [lit., 'complete bridegroom': חָתָן שָׁלֵם - *ḥatan shalēm*]."[203] This is taken from *m. Nidd.* 5:3.[204] In *b. Nidd.* 44b the Mishnah's statement is appropriately described as referring to the law of mourning.[205]

---

[199] Cf. *Introduction* 98.

[200] Cf. Theodor and Albeck 483; Soncino 1.409-10. In *b. ʿErub.* 19a (Soncino 130) there is a very abbreviated version of Abraham's behavior in regard to the wicked.

[201] Cf. *Introduction* 105.

[202] Cf. Mirkin 5.224-25; Soncino 3.234-35.

[203] Cf. Zlotnick, Hebrew 5; Soncino 335.

[204] Cf. Albeck 6.390; Danby 750; Neusner 1084.

[205] Cf. Soncino 307. It is spoken by R. Papa (bar Ḥanan), a fifth generation Babylonian Amora who died in 375 CE (*Introduction* 106).

In *y. Shebi.* 4:10, 35c the question is raised of how old an Israelite child which died early must be for it to live again at the resurrection of the dead. R. Ḥiyya I b. Abba, a fifth generation Tanna,[206] and Simeon b. Rabbi[207] dispute this issue. One says as soon as it is born, the other when it learns to speak. The rabbis of the Land of Israel also are of the opinion "after he is born." This is not the opinion of Babylonian rabbis, however, who state: "after he is circumcised."[208]

The Babylonian Jewish belief that a boy who dies early may only participate in the resurrection of the dead if he is circumcised is later found in regard to a question directed to R. Naḥshon, the gaon or head of the rabbinical academy at Sura in Babylonia from 871-879 CE.[209] In connection with an inquiry regarding an infant who dies within eight days, he first states it is not necessary to circumcise him because God says "on the eighth day." However, he continues: "And if one circumcises him above his grave, as we are accustomed [to doing], it is not necessary to speak a blessing [over him]...."[210] According to Louis Ginzberg, this is the first mention of the custom, implying that it is also found later.[211]

Here the custom of circumcising an infant boy who has died before the prescribed time of the eighth day is clearly attested for the ninth century CE among Jews in Babylonia. The major reason for doing so will have been the fervent desire for the infant to belong to the people of God through His covenant of circumcision made with Abraham. The fear that otherwise the infant would be excluded from the people of God,

---

206 Cf. *Introduction* 90.

207 Str-B 6.239 says he was Palestinian, ca. 220 CE. I suspect this may be an error for R. Simeon b. Ḥalafta, another fifth generation Tanna, who was R. Ḥiyya the Elder's friend (*Introduction* 91).

208 Cf. Alan Avery-Peck in Neusner's English edition of the Jerusalem Talmud, 5.165. It is based on Ps 88:15.

209 Cf. the art. "Nahshon bar Zadok" by Meir Havazelet in *EJ* (2007) 14.757. He was known for writing responsa in "terse and difficult Aramaic."

210 Cf. Rav Naḥshon's work שערי צדק *(sh ʿry ṣdq)*, now found online under www.hebrewbooks.org/1265, on p. 58 of the PDF version, number 5 (book 50). I thank Rabbi Yisrael Meyerowitz of the Jewish Theological Seminary of America's library staff for forwarding this to me, and him and Dr. Niko Oswald for aid in analyzing it.

211 Cf. his *The Legends* 6.341, n. 118. This is after he refers to *y. Shebi.* 4, where 45c is a misprint for 35c.

including in the World to Come, will also have played a role.[212] To this extent the above ninth century CE Babylonian Jewish practice is also analogous to the situation in first century CE Corinth. Some Christians there had themselves baptized again "on behalf of the dead." They wanted to ensure that those who were so baptized vicariously could now also belong to the church, the new "Israel of God" (Gal 6:16), created through a "new covenant" (1 Cor 11:25; 2 Cor 3:6, see also v. 14). They too would then also be part of the body of Christ, the church (Rom 12:12-31).

10. *Summary and Conclusion*

As a Hellenistic Jew who knew the LXX almost by heart, Paul was very probably acquainted with the saying in Tobit 4:17, "Place your bread on the grave of the righteous," as well as Sir 7:33 and 30:18 (and possibly the Letter of Jeremiah 27). This also applies to 2 Macc 12:38-45, involving a sin offering in the Jerusalem Temple and intercessory prayer for the dead in the hope of their later resurrection. If the Testament of Abraham, written in Greek, is from Paul's time or even earlier, there is also the possibility that it too was known to him. These sources, primarily the first ones, help to explain why the Apostle did not castigate some of the Corinthian Christians for having themselves baptized again "on behalf of the dead." As a Jew who was very zealous for the traditions of his fathers (Gal 1:14), Paul was probably himself well-acquainted with the analogous phenomena noted in the scriptural passages above in the LXX, and possibly with those described in what are now only found in later sources in sections 3.-8. If those who practiced vicarious baptism in Corinth did so in the hope that the now baptized dead would thereby also be able to participate in the resurrection, why should he object to it? This is what the rhetorical question of 1 Cor 15:29 implies.

---

[212] My wife, the pediatrician Elsge Schmidt-Aus, calls my attention to the situation of Christian infants born prematurely in the hospital whose chances of survival were slim. Up until recent times it was common for a Christian nurse or even a doctor, thus a layperson, to perform an "emergency baptism" (German "Nottaufe") of such an infant, although in contrast to the situation in ninth century CE Babylonia the child (male or female) was still (barely) alive. The practice also reflected the parents' gratitude for its now belonging officially to the people of God, the Christian church.

Yet where did the practice of vicarious baptism in Corinth come from, for it appears to have been introduced there *after* Paul left the congregation? In light of the Judaic sources cited in 1.-8. above, I suggest that it derived from some Jewish members of the Christian community who were themselves acquainted with intercessory acts and prayer on behalf of the dead in early Judaism. As Johannes Weiβ already noted in 1910, such vicarious baptism was "certainly coupled with [intercessory] prayer."[213]

In 38 CE there was a major pogrom of Jews in Alexandria, Egypt. Two years later, in 40 CE, Agrippa I left Palestine for Rome to implore his patron, the Roman emperor Gaius Caligula, to rescind the order that a colossal statue of Zeus be erected in the Jerusalem Temple.[214] Philo notes in *Leg. Gai.* 281 that Agrippa wrote a letter to Gaius in which he maintained that Jerusalem is not only the mother city of Judea, but also of many Jewish colonies[215] in neighboring lands, one of which was Corinth. This notice testifies to the presence of a significant number of Jews (a colony), certainly enough to have a synagogue, long before the Alexandrian persecution of 38 CE. The emperor Claudius later expelled the Jews from Rome, probably in 49 CE.[216] Some may have gone to Corinth, definitely known of Aquila and Priscilla, with whom Paul stayed, working together with them (Acts 18:3).[217] Acts 18:7 mentions that there was definitely a synagogue in Corinth. Paul succeeded in converting Crispus, the leader (ἀρχισυνάγωγος)[218] of the synagogue,

---

213 Cf. his *Der erste Korintherbrief* 363. He adds it is not impossible that Paul also attributed some value to the faith expressed by such an act. Even today no Christian baptism takes place without prayer.

214 On the dating, cf. Emil Schürer, *The History of the Jewish People in the Age of Jesus Christ (175 B.C. - A.D. 135)* 1. 445.

215 Cf. ἀποικία in LSJ 200: colony. Michael Hull in *Baptism* 163 misunderstands this text, stating that all the Jewish colonies listed, including Corinth, resulted from the pogrom in Alexandria of 38 CE. Agrippa writes instead that they were sent out (from Jerusalem and Judea) "at diverse times" (ἐπὶ καιρῶν: 281). Interestingly, Cilicia is also mentioned as having a Jewish colony, the area from which Paul came (Tarsus).

216 Cf. Emil Schürer, *The History* 3.77-78; see also Acts 18:2.

217 In 1 Cor 16:19 they are also with Paul in Ephesus (v. 8); Acts 18:2 says Aquila was a native of Pontus. See Acts 18:18 for their accompanying Paul when he sailed in the direction of Syria.

218 Cf. BAGD 113: leader, president.

"together with all his household" (v. 8).[219] It is probable that numerous Jews followed the example of their leader. In addition, Paul converted Titius Justus, who lived next door to the synagogue. He was a "God-fearer" (σεβόμενος, v. 7),[220] certainly not the only one in Corinth. Such people observed Judaism's basic tenets without, however, a male having himself circumcised. Paul's new message of belief in the Jew Jesus as the Messiah, without the necessity of circumcision and keeping the entire Torah (Gal 5:2-3), would have especially appealed to such formerly pagan adherents of the synagogue. It is important to note that by now basically adhering to Jewish teachings they had already become monotheists and knew much about Judaism.

Most of the members of the Corinthian Christian congregation were apparently former pagans.[221] In light of the above, however, it appears that converted Jews (probably together with God-fearers and possibly some proselytes) formed a strong minority there.[222] It thus seems plausible that sometime shortly after the departure of Paul, some of these Jewish Christians became increasingly conscious of the impending end

---

219 In 1 Cor 1:14 Paul remarks that he baptized Crispus and Gaius, as well as the household of Stephanas (v. 16; cf. 16:17). The Corinthian Jews had to appoint a new synagogue leader, Sosthenes (Acts 18:17), which certainly angered them. In 1 Cor 7:18 Paul notes that some members of the congregation were already circumcised at the time of their call (to become Christians). That is, they were members of the Jewish congregation, or some were possibly proselytes.

220 Cf. BAGD on σέβω : 746, 2. a. On the various terms for, and expectations of, a "God-fearer" (in contrast to a proselyte), see Emil Schűrer, *The History* 3.162-76.

221 Cf. 1 Cor 5:1 (idolater; see also 6:9); 6:1 - taking a law suit to a worldly court; 6:9-11 : some of the Corinthians had been fornicators, idolaters, adulterers, male prostitutes, sodomites, thieves, greedy, drunkards, revelers and robbers; 7:19 - uncircumcised at the time of one's call (to become a Christian); 8:1-13 : eating food sacrificed to idols; 10:14 - flee from the worship of idols; 12:2 - when you were pagans; 12:13 - Jews or Greeks; and 15:12 - some say there is no resurrection of the dead.

222 The congregation will basically have consisted of "house churches," which on occasion may have assembled together (cf. 11:18; 14:26). In addition, the converted Alexandrian Jew Apollos was also active in Corinth (after Paul; see Acts 18:27-28, and on him vv. 24-26, including the fact that he first only knew the baptism of John). In 3:6 Paul states that after he planted, Apollos watered, i.e., continued the Apostle's missionary work. In 16:12 he appears to be in Ephesus with Paul. Cephas (Peter) also appears to have passed through Corinth at one time (1 Cor 1:12; 3:22; see also 9:5), perhaps on his way to Rome or elsewhere.

of the world, which the Apostle had so greatly emphasized.[223] They therefore developed the fervent desire that their own relatives and friends, who had already passed on, should share in the good news of Christ's victory over death through his crucifixion and resurrection from the dead. They wanted them not only to belong to the people of God, Israel, which they already were through His covenant with Abraham, circumcision. They also wanted them to belong to the Lord's new people, the "Israel of God" (Gal 6:16).

These Jewish Christians were acquainted with baptism as a rite of initiation into the new people of God, the church, for Paul himself practiced it (1 Cor 1:14-16) and assumed it for all Christians (12:12-13; Rom 6:3-4; Gal 3:27). On the basis of their knowledge of Jewish atonement sacrifice in the Temple, food and drink placed on the grave, and intercessory prayer for the dead in connection with the resurrection, as I have described these in sections 1.-8. above, some of them came upon the idea of baptizing themselves again "on behalf of" (ὑπέρ) their dead Jewish relatives and friends. Paul as a well-educated and zealous Jew, who had even sat as a student at the feet of the leading authority Gamaliel I in Jerusalem (Acts 22:3), was himself cognizant of such Judaic practices on behalf of the dead. Thus in 1 Cor 15:29 he did not object to some people holding such a view, but simply tolerated them. "After all," he probably reasoned, "they have expressed a firm belief in the resurrection.[224] The time is very short. Why object to such a practice of vicarious baptism, especially since it is analogous to other Jewish customs I know of, and is only carried out by a minority ('some')?"

In all probability some Gentile Christians in Corinth then followed the example of their Jewish fellow believers. In contrast to those of the Jewish Christians, their deceased pagan relatives and friends had not already belonged to the people of God, Israel.[225] It was thus even more

---

[223] He also emphasizes it in 1 Cor 1:7; 3:13; 4:5; 5:5; 7:1-11 : remaining in one's marital or non-marital state; 7:26, 29-31; 10:11; and 15:51-52. See already 1 Thess 1:10.

[224] Cf. also the later belief that Christ after his crucifixion and resurrection "went and made a proclamation to the spirits in prison, who in former times did not obey" (at the time of the flood) in 1 Pet 3:19. In 4:6 it is stated that "the gospel was proclaimed even to the dead" so that "they might live in the spirit...." See also Hermas, *Sim.* 93 (IX. 16:4-7).

[225] 1 Cor 6:9-10 at first sight appears to be a standard listing of various vices, yet it actually refers to some of the Gentile Corinthian Christians, as Paul specifically says in v. 11. Therefore they could now also have had themselves baptized on

reassuring to these Gentile Christians that by having themselves baptized again on their behalf, their relatives and friends would now also belong to the new people of God, the Christian church.[226] A deep human yearning on their part was thus now fulfilled.[227]

Interestingly, this was a custom which prevailed in a few Christian circles until it was officially forbidden, along with giving the Eucharist to the dead, in canon six of the Third Council of Carthage in 397 CE. This shows that the practice had retained its attraction and vitality at least up until then.[228]

---

behalf of their deceased relatives and friends who were also such immoral persons. Cf. the above examples of intercessory prayer for evil persons such as Korah, Absalom, and wicked fathers, which led to their ascending from Sheol / Gehenna and being united with the righteous, partaking with them in the resurrection and the World to Come.

226 Cf. the words of Ambrosiaster, active in Rome at the time of Pope Damasus I (366-84 CE), in his "Commentary on Paul's Epistles" (CSEL 81.3: 175, cited in *1-2 Corinthians*, ed. Gerald Bray [Ancient Christian Commentary on Scripture, New Testament VII] 162-63): "It seems that some people were at that time being baptized for the dead because they were afraid that someone who was not baptized would either not rise at all or else rise merely in order to be condemned."

227 I thus disagree with scholars who define the dead of 1 Cor 15:29 more precisely as deceased catechumens, apostles, or even some of the 500 Paul mentions in v. 6 who have already "fallen asleep" / died. Cf. the commentaries. "Relatives and friends" is a broad enough, inclusive term.

228 I have purposely restricted myself in this study to an analysis of 1 Cor 15:29 in its original setting. Topics such as additional masses, prayers for the dead, and the dogma of purgatory in contemporary Roman Catholicism, as well as the Mormon Church's still active practice of baptism on behalf of the dead, must be pursued elsewhere.

SOURCES AND REFERENCE WORKS

I. The Bible

Kittel, *Biblia Hebraica,* ed. Rudolf Kittel et al. (Stuttgart: Privilegierte Württembergische Bibelanstalt, 1951[7]).

Rahlfs, *Septuaginta,* ed. Alfred Rahlfs (Stuttgart: Württembergische Bibelanstalt, 1962[7]), 2 vols.

Pietersma and Wright, *A New English Translation of the Septuagint* [*NETS*], ed. Albert Pietersma and Benjamin Wright (Oxford, New York: Oxford University Press, 2007).

Hatch and Redpath, *A Concordance to the Septuagint,* ed. Edwin Hatch and Henry Redpath (Oxford: Clarendon, 1897; corrected reprint Grand Rapids, MI: Baker Book House, 1983).

Nestle / Aland, *Novum Testamentum Graece,* ed. Eberhard and Erwin Nestle, Barbara and Kurt Aland, et al. (Stuttgart: Deutsche Bibelgesellschaft, 2012[28]).

Hebrew New Testament, by Franz Delitzsch (Berlin: Trowitzsch and Son, 1885).

Hebrew New Testament (Jerusalem: The United Bible Societies, 1979).

II. The Targums

Sperber, *The Bible in Aramaic,* ed. Alexander Sperber (Leiden: Brill, 1959), 4 vols.

Clarke, *Targum Pseudo-Jonathan of the Pentateuch*: Text and Concordance, ed. Ernest Clarke (Hoboken, NJ: Ktav Publishing House, 1984).

Díez Macho, *Neophyti 1,* ed. Alejandro Díez Macho (Madrid - Barcelona: Consejo Superior de Investigaciones Científicas, 1968-78), 5 vols.

Klein, *The Fragment-Targums of the Pentateuch,* ed. and trans. Michael Klein (AnBib 76; Rome: Biblical Institute, 1980), 2 vols.

Grossfeld, *The Targum Onqelos to Exodus,* trans. Bernard Grossfeld (The Aramaic Bible 7; Edinburgh: T & T Clark, 1988).

Maher, *Targum Pseudo-Jonathan: Exodus,* trans. Michael Maher (The Aramaic Bible 2; Edinburgh: T & T Clark, 1994).

McNamara, *Targum Neofiti 1: Exodus,* trans. Martin McNamara (The Aramaic Bible 2; Edinburgh: T & T Clark, 1994).

Grossfeld, *The Targum Onqelos to Numbers,* trans. Bernard Grossfeld (The Aramaic Bible 8; Edinburgh: T & T Clark, 1988).

Clarke, *Targum Pseudo-Jonathan: Numbers,* trans. Ernest Clarke (The Aramaic Bible 4; Edinburgh: T & T Clark, 1995).

McNamara, *Targum Neofiti 1: Numbers,* trans. Martin McNamara (The Aramaic Bible 4; Edinburgh: T & T Clark, 1995).

Grossfeld, *The Targum Onqelos to Deuteronomy,* trans. Bernard Grossfeld (The Aramaic Bible 9; Edinburgh: T & T Clark, 1988).

Clarke, *Targum Pseudo-Jonathan: Deuteronomy,* trans. Ernest Clarke (The Aramaic Bible 5B; Edinburgh: T & T Clark, 1998).

McNamara, *Targum Neofiti 1: Deuteronomy,* trans. Martin McNamara (The Aramaic Bible 5A; Edinburgh: T & T Clark, 1997).

Harrington and Saldarini, *Targum Jonathan of the Former Prophets,* trans. Daniel Harrington and Anthony Saldarini (The Aramaic Bible 10; Edinburgh: T & T Clark, 1987).

Stenning, *The Targum of Isaiah,* ed. and trans. J. Stenning (Oxford: Clarendon, 1949).

Levey, *The Targum of Ezekiel,* trans. Samson Levey (The Aramaic Bible 13; Edinburgh: T. & T. Clark, 1987).

Merino, *Targum de Salmos,* ed. with a Latin translation by Luis Diez Merino (Madrid: Consejo Superior de Investigaciones Científicas, 1982).

Stec, *The Targum of Psalms,* trans. David Stec (The Aramaic Bible 16; Collegeville, MN: Liturgical Press, 2004).

Le Déaut / Robert, *Targum des Chroniques,* ed. R. Le Déault and J. Robert (AnBib 51; Rome: Biblical Institute Press, 1971).

McIvor, *The Targum of Chronicles,* trans. J. Stanley McIvor (The Aramaic Bible 19; Edinburgh: T & T Clark, 1994).

III. The Mishnah and Tosefta

Albeck, *Shisha Sidre Mishnah,* ed. Chanoch Albeck (Jerusalem and Tel Aviv: Bialik Institute and Dvir, 1975), 6 vols.

Danby, *The Mishnah,* trans. Herbert Danby (London: Oxford University Press, 1933).

Neusner, *The Mishnah,* trans. Jacob Neusner (New Haven: Yale University Press, 1988).

Zuckermandel, *Tosephta,* ed. Mosheh Zuckermandel, with a supplement by Saul Liebermann (Jerusalem: Wahrmann Books, 1970).

Lieberman, *The Tosefta,* ed. Saul Lieberman [sic] (New York: The Jewish Theological Seminary of America, 1955-92), 10 vols.

Neusner, *The Tosefta,* trans. Jacob Neusner et al. (Hoboken, NJ: KTAV, 1977-86), 6 vols.

IV. The Talmuds

Soncino, *The Babylonian Talmud,* ed. Isidore Epstein, various translators (London: Soncino, 1952), 18 vols. and index.

Soncino, *The Minor Tractates of the Talmud,* ed. Abraham Cohen, various translators (London: Soncino, 1965), 2 vols.

Zlotnick, *The Tractate 'Mourning' (Semaḥot),* ed. and trans. Dov Slotnick (New Haven: Yale University Press, 1966).

Goldschmidt, *Der Babylonische Talmud,* ed. with a German translation by Lazarus Goldschmidt (Haag: Nijoff, 1933), 9 vols.

Krotoshin, *Talmud Yerushalmi,* Krotoshin edition (Jerusalem: Shiloh, 1969).

Neusner, *The Talmud of the Land of Israel,* trans. Jacob Neusner et al. (Chicago: University of Chicago Press, 1982-95), 34 vols.

V. Halakhic Midrashim

Lauterbach, *Mekilta de-Rabbi Ishmael,* ed. and trans. Jacob Lauterbach (Philadelphia: The Jewish Publication Society of America, 1976), 3 vols.

Nelson, *Mekhilta de-Rabbi Shimon bar Yoḥai,* ed. and trans. W. David Nelson (Philadelphia: The Jewish Publication Society, 2006).

Horovitz, *Siphre ad Numeros adjecto Siphre zutta,* ed. Haim Horovitz (Jerusalem: Wahrmann Books, 1976).

Neusner, *Sifré to Numbers,* trans. Jacob Neusner (BJS 118-19; Atlanta: Scholars Press, 1986), 2 vols.

Kuhn, *Der tannaitische Midrasch Sifre zu Numeri,* German by Karl Kuhn (Stuttgart: Kohlhammer, 1959).

Börner-Klein, *Der Midrasch Sifre zu Numeri,* German by Dagmar Börner-Klein (Stuttgart: Kohlhammer, 1997).

Börner-Klein, *Der Midrasch Sifre Zuta,* German on Numbers by Dagmar Börner-Klein (Stuttgart: Kohlhammer, 2002).

Neusner, *Sifré Zutta to Numbers,* trans. Jacob Neusner (Studies in Judaism; University Press of America, 2009).

Finkelstein, *Sifre on Deuteronomy,* ed. Louis Finkelstein (New York: The Jewish Theological Seminary of America, 1969).

Hammer, *Sifre.* A Tannaitic Commentary on the Book of Deuteronomy, trans. Reuven Hammer (YJS 24; New Haven: Yale University Press, 1986).

Neusner, *Sifre to Deuteronomy.* An Analytical Translation, trans. Jacob Neusner (BJS 98 and 101; Atlanta: Scholars Press, 1987), 2 vols.

VI. Haggadic Midrashim and Midrashic Collections

Midrash Rabbah, with the five Megilloth at the end of volume 2 (Vilna: Romm, 1887), 2 volumes.

Mirkin, *Midrash Rabbah,* Pentateuch. Ed. and vocalized by Mosheh Mirkin (Tel Aviv: Yavneh, 1981), 11 vols.

Soncino, *Midrash Rabbah*, ed. H. Freedman and Maurice Simon, various translators (London: Soncino, 1939), 9 vols. and index.

Theodor and Albeck, *Midrash Bereshit Rabba*, ed. Judah Theodor and Chanoch Albeck (Jerusalem: Wahrmann Books, 1965), 3 vols.

Hoffmann, *Midrasch Tannaim zum Deuteronomium*, ed. David Hoffmann (Berlin: Itzkowski, 1908-09; reprint Jerusalem, 1984).

Liebermann, *Midrash Debarim Rabbah*, ed. Saul Liebermann (Jerusalem: Wahrmann 1964).

Dunsqi, *Midrash Rabbah. Shir ha-Shirim*, ed. Shim'on Dunsqi (Jerusalem: Dvir, 1980).

Grünhut, *Midrasch Schir ha-Schirim*, ed. L. Grünhut (Jerusalem: Wilhelm Gross, 1897).

Midrash Tanḥuma, Eshkol edition (Jerusalem: Eshkol, no date), 2 vols.

Berman, *Midrash Tanhuma-Yelammedenu*. An English translation of Genesis and Exodus ... by Samuel Berman (Hoboken, NJ: KTAV Publishing House, 1996).

Buber, *Midrasch Tanḥuma*: Ein agadischer Commentar zum Pentateuch, ed. Salomon Buber (Vilna: Romm, 1885), 2 vols.

Townsend, *Midrash Tanḥuma (S. Buber Recension)*, Vol. I, Genesis, trans. John Townsend (Hoboken, NJ: KTAV Publishing House, 1989). Vol. II, Exodus and Leviticus, 1997. Vol. III, Numbers and Deuteronomy, 2003.

Bietenhard, *Midrasch Tanḥuma B*, German by Hans Bietenhard (Judaica et Christiana 5-6; Bern: Peter Lang, 1980-82), 2 vols.

Becker, *Avot de-Rabbi Natan*. Synoptische Edition beider Versionen, ed. Hans-Jürgen Becker with Christoph Berner (Tübingen: Mohr Siebeck, 2006).

Schechter, *Aboth de Rabbi Nathan* (A and B), ed. Solomon Schechter (Vienna, 1887; reprinted New York: Feldheim, 1945).

Goldin, *The Fathers According to Rabbi Nathan (A)*, trans. Judah Goldin (YJS 10; New Haven: Yale University Press, 1955).

Neusner, *The Fathers According to Rabbi Nathan*. An Analytical Translation and Explanation, trans. Jacob Neusner (BJS 114; Atlanta: Scholars Press, 1986).

Saldarini, *The Fathers According to Rabbi Nathan (B)*, trans. Anthony Saldarini (SJLA 11; Leiden: Brill, 1975).

Friedmann, *Pesikta Rabbati*, ed. Meir Friedmann (Vienna, 1880; reprint Tel Aviv, 1962-63).

Braude, *Pesikta Rabbati*, trans. William Braude (YJS 18; New Haven: Yale University Press, 1968), 2 vols.

Mandelbaum, *Pesikta de Rav Kahana*, ed. Bernard Mandelbaum (New York: The Jewish Theological Seminary of America, 1962), 2 vols.

Braude and Kapstein, *Pesikta de-Rab Kahana*, trans. William Braude and Israel Kapstein (Philadelphia: The Jewish Publication Society of America, 1975).

Neusner, *Pesiqta de Rab Kahana*. An Analytical Translation, trans. Jacob Neusner (BJS 122-23; Atlanta: Scholars Press, 1987), 2 vols.

Friedmann, *Seder Eliahu rabba und Seder Eliahu zuta*, ed. Meir Friedmann (Vienna, 1902-04; reprint Jerusalem, 1969).

Braude and Kapstein, *Tanna debe Eliyyahu*, trans. William Braude and Israel Kapstein (Philadelphia: The Jewish Publication Society of America, 1981).

Buber, *Midrasch Tehillim*, ed. Salomon Buber (Vilna: Romm, 1891).

Braude, *The Midrash on Psalms*, trans. William Braude (YJS 13,1-2; New Haven: Yale University Press, 1959), 2 vols.

Visotzky, *Midrash Mishle*, ed. Burton Visotzky (New York: The Jewish Theological Seminary of America, 1990).

Visotzky, *The Midrash on Proverbs*, trans. Burton Visotzky (YJS 27; New Haven: Yale University Press, 1992).

Eshkol, *Pirqe Rabbi Eliezer*, Eshkol edition (Jerusalem: Eshkol, 1973).

Friedlander, *Pirke de Rabbi Eliezer*, trans. Gerald Friedlander (London, 1916; reprint New York: Hermon Press, 1970).

Guggenheimer, *Seder Olam*. The Rabbinic View of Biblical Chronology, ed. and trans. Heinrich Guggenheimer (Northvale, NJ, and Jerusalem: Jason Aronson, 1998).

Milikowsky, *Seder Olam: A Rabbinic Chronography*, by Chaim Milikowsky (1981 Yale dissertation).

VII. Apocrypha, Pseudepigrapha, Philo, Josephus, and the Dead Sea Scrolls

Apocrypha: see Rahlfs, *Septuaginta*.

Beentjes, *The Book of Ben Sira in Hebrew*, ed. Pancratius Beentjes (VTSup 68; Leiden: Brill, 1997).

OTP. *The Old Testament Pseudepigrapha*, ed. James Charlesworth (Garden City, NY: Doubleday, 1983-85), 2 vols.

Delamarter, *A Scripture Index to Charlesworth's The Old Testament Pseudepigrapha*, by Steve Delamarter (Sheffield: Sheffield Academic Press, 2002).

APOT. *The Apocrypha and Pseudepigrapha of the Old Testament*, II. *Pseudepigrapha*, ed. Robert Henry Charles (Oxford: Clarendon, 1913).

Charles, *The Greek Versions of the Testaments of the Twelve Patriarchs*, ed. Robert Charles (Oxford: The Clarendon Press, 1908).

Allison, *Testament of Abraham*, ed. Dale Allison, Jr. (CEJL; Berlin: de Gruyter, 2003).

Delcor, *Le Testament d'Abraham*, ed. Mathias Delcor (SVTP 2; Leiden: Brill, 1973).

Schmidt, *Le Testament grec d'Abraham*, ed. Francis Schmidt (TSAJ 11; Tűbingen: Mohr Siebeck, 1986).

Harrington, *Les Antiquités Bibliques*, ed. Daniel Harrington, French by Jacques Cazeaux (*SC* 229-230; Paris: du Cerf, 1976), 2 vols.

LCL, *Philo*, Greek and English translation by F. H. Colson, G. H. Whitaker and Ralph Marcus (Loeb Classical Library; Cambridge, MA: Harvard University

Press, 1971), 10 vols. with 2 Supplements: *Questions and Answers on Genesis*, and *Questions and Answers on Exodus.*

The Philo Index, ed. Peder Borgen, Kåre Fuglseth, and Roald Skarsten (Grand Rapids, MI: Eerdmans, 2000).

LCL, *Josephus*, Greek and English translation by H. St. John Thackeray, Ralph Marcus and Allen Wikgren (Loeb Classical Library; Cambridge, MA: Harvard University Press, 1969), 9 vols.

The Complete Concordance to Flavius Josephus, Study Edition, ed. Karl Rengstorf (Leiden: Brill, 2002), 2 vols., including the *Namenwörterbuch zu Flavius Josephus* by Abraham Schalit.

Martínez and Tigchelaar, *The Dead Sea Scrolls Study Edition*, ed. and trans. Florentino García Martínez and Eibert Tigchelaar (Leiden: Brill, 2000), 2 vols.

Washburn, *A Catalog of Biblical Passages in the Dead Sea Scrolls*, by David Washburn (Text-Critical Studies 2; Atlanta: Society of Biblical Literature, 2002).

Fitzmyer, *A Guide to the Dead Sea Scrolls and Related Literature, Revised and Expanded Edition*, by Joseph Fitzmyer (Grand Rapids: Eerdmans, 2008).

VIII. The Early Church

Ehrman, *The Apostolic Fathers*, ed. and trans. Bart Ehrman (Loeb Classical Library; Cambridge, MA; Harvard University Press, 2003), 2 vols.

Marcovich, *Iustini Martyris, Dialogus cum Tryphone*, ed. Miroslav Marcovich (Berlin: de Gruyter, 1997).

Bobichon, *Justin Martyr. Dialogue avec Tryphon*, ed. and French by Phillippe Bobichon (Paradosis 47/1; Fribourg: Academic Press, 2003).

The Ante-Nicene Fathers, Vol. I: The Apostolic Fathers - Justin Martyr - Irenaeus, trans. Alexander Roberts and James Donaldson (Grand Rapids, MI: Eerdmans, 1979).

Jerome, *De Viris Illustribus*, ed. and trans. Claudia Barthold (Műlheim / Mosel: Carthusianus-Verlag, 2011[2]).

Ambrose, "The Mysteries," in *1-2 Corinthians*, ed. Gerald Bray (Ancient Christian Commentary on Scripture, New Testament VII: Downers Grove, IL: InterVarsity Press, 2006). This includes Cyril of Jerusalem, "Mystagogical Lectures I 1.3," and Ambrosiaster, "Commentary on Paul's Epistles," 81.3:175.

IX. Dictionaries and Reference Works

BDB, *A Hebrew and English Lexicon of the Old Testament*, by Francis Brown, S. R. Driver and Charles Briggs (Oxford: Clarendon: 1962).

Jastrow, *A Dictionary of the Targumim, the Talmud Babli and Yerushalmi, and the Midrashic Literature*, by Marcus Jastrow (Peabody, MA: Hendrickson Publishers, 2005; original 1903).

Levy, *Neuhebräisches und chaldäisches Wörterbuch über die Talmudim und Midraschim*, by Jacob Levy (Berlin and Vienna, 1924²), 4 vols.

Sokoloff, *A Dictionary of Jewish Palestinian Aramaic in the Byzantine Period*, ed. Michael Sokoloff (Dictionaries of Talmud, Midrash and Targum, 2; Ramat-Gan: Bar Ilan Press, 2002²).

A Dictionary of Jewish Babylonian Aramaic of the Talmudic and Geonic Periods (Dictionaries of Talmud, Midrash and Targum, 3; Ramat-Gan: Bar Ilan Press, 2002).

A Dictionary of Judean Aramaic (Ramat-Gan: Bar Ilan Press, 2003).

Alcalay, *The Complete Hebrew-English Dictionary*, by Reuben Alcalay (Tel Aviv / Jerusalem: Massadah, 1965).

Krauss, *Griechische und Lateinische Lehnwörter in Talmud, Midrasch und Targum*, by Samuel Krauss (Berlin: Calvary, 1898-99), 2 vols.

Hyman, *Torah Hakethubah Vehamessurah*. A Reference Book of the Scriptural Passages Quoted in Talmudic, Midrashic and Early Rabbinic Literature, by Aaron Hyman, second edition by Arthur Hyman (Tel Aviv: Dvir, 1979), 3 vols.

IDB. *The Interpreter's Dictionary of the Bible*, ed. George Buttrick et al. (New York and Nashville: Abingdon Press, 1962), 4 vols. *Supplementary Volume*, ed. Keith Crim, 1976.

Schürer, *The history of the Jewish people in the age of Jesus Christ (175 B.C. - A.D. 135)*, by Emil Schürer, ed. Geza Vermes, Fergus Millar and Matthew Black (Edinburgh: T. and T. Clark, 1973-86), 3 vols. and index.

Goodenough, *Jewish Symbols in the Greco-Roman Period*, by Erwin Goodenough, Abridged Edition, ed. Jacob Neusner (Princeton: Princeton University Press, 1988).

Strack and Stemberger, *Introduction to the Talmud and Midrash*, by Hermann Strack and Günter Stemberger (Minneapolis: Fortress, 1992).

Ginzberg, *The Legends of the Jews*, by Louis Ginzberg (Philadelphia: The Jewish Publication Society of America, 1968), 6 vols. and index.

Str-B, *Kommentar zum Neuen Testament aus Talmud und Midrasch*, by (Hermann Strack and) Paul Billerbeck (Munich: Beck, 1924-61), 6 vols.

Nickelsburg, *Jewish Literature Between the Bible and the Mishnah*, by George Nickelsburg (Minneapolis: Fortress Press, 2005²).

JE. *The Jewish Encyclopedia* (New York: Funk and Wagnalls, 1905), 12 vols.

EJ. *Encyclopaedia Judaica* (Jerusalem: Keter, 1971), 16 vols. New edition 2007².

LSJ. *A Greek-English Lexicon*, by Henry Liddell, Robert Scott and Henry Jones (Oxford: Clarendon, 1966⁹).

Greek-English Lexicon of the Septuagint, Revised Edition, ed. Johan Lust, Erik Eynikel and Katrin Hauspie (Stuttgart: Deutsche Bibelgesellschaft, 2003).

BAGD. *A Greek-English Lexicon of the New Testament and Other Early Christian Literature*, by Walter Bauer, William Arndt, F. Wilbur Gingrich and Frederick Danker (Chicago: University of Chicago Press, 1979^{2}).

TDNT. *Theological Dictionary of the New Testament*, ed. Gerhard Kittel and Gerhard Friedrich (Grand Rapids, MI: Eerdmans, 1964-76), 9 vols. and index.

Chambers Murray, *latin-english Dictionary*, ed. William Smith and John Lockwood (Edinburgh: Chambers; London: Murray, 1986).

Blass, Debrunner, Funk, *A Greek Grammar of the New Testament and Other Early Christian Literature*, ed. F. Blass, A. Debrunner and Robert Funk (Chicago: The University of Chicago Press, 1961).

AUTHOR INDEX

Alexander, P. xiii
Allen, L. 57
Allison, D. 43, 90, 93
Arzt-Grabner, P. 26
Aus, R. .... xiv, 66, 72, 77
Avemarie, F. xi
Avery-Peck, A. .... viii, 6, 119

Bacher, W. 102, 109
Bachmann, P. 2
Bandstra, A. 64
Barnard, L. 38
Barrett, C. K. 15
Barth, G. .... xi, 15
Baskin, J. 116
Berger, K. 70, 72
Bienaimé, G. 3, 29, 40
Bieringer, R. .... xii, 3
Billerbeck, P. (Str-B) .... xii, 3, 6,
.... 15, 22, 23,
.... 38, 46, 68, 119
Block, D. 57–58
Boyarin, D. 85
Braude, W. 103, 114–16
Bruce, F. F. 2

Christensen, D. 81
Ciampa, R. 74–75, 77
Cohen, A. 112
Collier, G. 69, 71
Collins, R. 69, 72, 75, 77
Colson, F. 8, 95
Conzelmann, H. 3, 75, 77
Cross, A. xi
Cullmann, O. 3

Dahl, N. 69
De Maris, R. 75, 78
Di Lella, A. 85
Doran, R. 88
Driver, S. R. 81

Ehrensperger, K. 54
Eissfeldt, O. 27
Ellis, E. 2, 28
Enns, P. 2

Fee, G. 77–78
Ferguson, E. .... xi, 15
Finkelstein, L. 105
Fitzmyer, J. .... xiv, 30, 80
Ford, J. 79
Foschini, B. 76
Fotopoulos, J. 54
Frankemölle, H. 99
Freedman, H. 114

Gielen, M. 77
Gieschen, C. 65
Ginzberg, L. 3, 94, 107, 119
Godet, F. 2, 76
Goldstein, J. 85, 87
Goodenough, E. 40, 95
Greenberg, M. 57, 85

Hammer, R. 105
Hannah, D. 65, 68
Harrington, D. 13, 88, 96
Hartman, Lars xi
Hartman, Louis 85
Havazelet, M. 119
Hays, R. 2, 75
Hellholm, D. xi
Héring, J. 69
Herr, M. 70
Holtz, G. xiv
Horbury, W. .... xiii–xiv
Hull, M. 75-77, 121
Hyatt, J. 116

Jacobs, J. 16, 46
Jacobs, L. 14
Jaffee, M. .... xii, 3
Jeremias, J, ... 37
Jeske, R, ... 67
Jewett, R. 43

Kapstein, I. 114–16
Keesmat, S. 1
Keitzer, L. 8
Klaiber, W. 71

Lehrman, S. 14, 28, 50
Levey, S. 59–61
Lightfoot, J. 37, 79
Lincoln, A. 64
Lindemann, A. .... vii, 2
Lindenberger, J. 81
Liver, J. 94

Marcus, R. 87
Marmorstein, A. 78
Martínez, F. 80
McEwen, A. 70
Meeks, W. 70
Merklein, H. 2–3, 77
Meyer, H. 21, 38, 63
Meyerowitz, Y. 119
Minto, A. 32
Mittmann-Richert, U. 103
Moore, C. 82
Morris, L. 54
Murphy-O'Conner, J. 76

Neusner, J. .... iii, vii, 6,
.... 39–40, 72, 111
Nickelsburg, G. 13, 43, 80, 82,
.... 85, 88, 90, 96

Őhler, M. .... xi, 78
Oepke, A. 37
Orr, W. 78
Ostermeyer, K.-H. 15
Oswald, N. .... viii, 119

Patrick, J. 75, 77
Plummer, A. 8, 76
Pokorný, P. 64
Porter, S. xi

Rabinowitz, L. 107
Reichert, A. .... xi, 15, 76
Reinach, S. 88
Rissi, M. 75–76
Robertson, A. 8, 76
Rosner, B. 74–75, 77
Rothkoff, A. 94

Sanders, E. 43, 90–91, 93
Schechter, S. 79, 106
Schmidt-Aus, E. 120
Schottroff, L. 72
Schrage, W. 2, 72
Schwarz, D. 85–89
Seidel, J. 116
Senft, C. 70, 75
Siegel, S. 85
Smit, J. 71
Snowman, L. 116
Sperling, S. D. 94
Staab, K. 76–77
Stauffer, E. 86

Ta-Shma, I. 107
Thackeray, H. 9, 33
Thiessen, M. 2, 68
Thiselton, A. 2–3, 77
Tigchelaar, E. 80
Turner, N. 90

Urbach, E. 79

Vermes, G. .... xiii–xiv
von der Osten-Sacken, P. .... iii, vii,
.... 3, 71

Wald, S. 109
Walther, J. 78
Wedderburn, A. 1, 70, 76
Weiss, J. 32, 69
Whitaker, G. 8, 95
White, J. 76–77
Willis, W. 54
Wintermute, O. 93, 117
Witherington III, B. 76

INDEX OF SOURCES CITED

The Hebrew Bible (MT)

Genesis

1:2 12
1:4 68
1:9 14
4:1–16 99
6:1–4 99
6:2 99
7:23 97
15 59
17 116
17:5 7
17:12 116
18:1–15 41
18:4 .... 41–43, 47, 63
18:5 41–42
18:6 49
18:7 42
18:8 42
19:1–29 99
19:30–38 61
21:9 56
22:17 46
29:1–14 66
35:22 102
49:4 102
49:10 102

Exodus

1:1ff. 45
1:12 46
1:14 46
1:22 .... 32, 46, 59
4:20 38
6:24 97
7:14–24 27
12:1–28, 43–51 7
12:35–36 51
12:37–38 26
12:38 9
12:48 117–18
13:1–20 16
13:2–10 7
13:8 5–6
13:17 44
13:21 .... 16–17, 19, 21–24, 34, 41–42, 44, 59
13:21–22 .... 16, 18, 22, 44, 63, 66
13:22 .... 10, 45
14 11–12
14:15–16 13
14:16, 21–22, 29–31 12
14:16, 29 14
14:19 .... 19, 22
14:19–20 .... 20, 23
14:21 11
14:22, 29 13
14:28 97
14:30 51
14:31 66
15:1–21 .... 12, 24
15:2 .... 15, 22, 46–47, 51–52, 63, 65
15:19 12
15:21 31
15:21ff. 16
15:22–26 27
16 12–13
16:1 9
16:3 9
16:4 .... 23–25, 34–35, 38, 42, 44
16:4–24 16
16:25ff. 16
17 .... 13, 24
17:1–7 .... 12, 16, 31, 33–34
17:3–4, 6 27
17:6 .... 8, 17, 27–28, 32, 40, 43, 49
17:12 116
19:4 44
19:7 11
19:10 37
20:3–5 87
20:8 24

22:19 (Eng. 20) 87
23:20–21 20
23:20, 23 19
24:5 37
24:8 37
32:2–4, 24 57
32:6 .... 54, 56, 60, 70
32:34 19
33:20 51
40:9 50
40:36-38 18

Leviticus

8:3 35
12:3 116

Numbers

1:46–47 26–27
9:11–12, 15, 20 17
9:19 18
11:4–5 9
11:8 41
11:31 42
14:14 18
14:14–16 17
14:22–23 99
14:29–33 53
15:14 37
15:37–41 14
16:1–35 94
16:2 96
16:3 .... 96, 98
16:5–11, 16–17 98
16:15 98
16:30–35 94
16:31–34 98
16:32 .... 97, 100
16:33 100–2
16:35 95
17:5 (Eng. 16:40) 94
17:14 (Eng. 16:49) 94
20:2–13 .... 28, 31
20:4, 11 9
20:5 .... 9, 34
20:10 35
20:11 17
20:16 19
20:19 10
21:5–6 .... 29, 65, 67, 70
21:6 10
21:8 41
21:9 29
21:16–17 29
21:16–18 34
21:17 .... 42, 44–45
21:18 30
21:18–20 .... 29, 34
21:19 .... 29, 34
21:20 39
21:23 10
25 99
25:1–9 .... 60, 70
25:2, 9 54
25:5 54
25:9 54
26:9–11 94
26:11 97
26:51 27
26:62 54
26:63–65 99
27:3 94
31:13–24 87
31:16 99
32:1 9

Deuteronomy

1:35–39 53
2:7 .... 25, 34
6:4–9 14
7:25–26 87
8:4 45
8:15 .... 8, 10, 49
8:15–16 49
11:13–21 14
16:3 14

21:1–9 ... 105
21:7 ... 105
21:8 ... 105–6
26:3 ... 7
26:14 ... 80–81, 84
26:15 ... 7
32:10 ... 8, 10
32:10, 13 ... 49, 57
32:13 ... 47–48, 52
32:16, 21 ... 55
32:17 ... 55
32:18 ... 53
32:21 ... 50
32:24 ... 10
33:6 ... 102–3
34:1 ... 29

Joshua

5:12 ... 24
6:18–19 ... 88
7:1 ... 88
7:19–21 ... 88

Judges

13:22 ... 51
17:1–6 ... 55
19 ... 61

Ruth

3:13 ... 111

1 Samuel

1:10, 13 ... 103
2:1–10 ... 103
2:6 ... 101–4

2 Samuel

13 ... 61
13:37, 39 ... 107
14:25–26 ... 107
15 ... 107
16:20–23 ... 61, 107
18:5, 9, 14–15 ... 107
18:10 ... 108
19:1 (Eng. 18:33) ... 108
19:5 (Eng. 4) ... 108

1 Chronicles

3:24 ... 22
14:12 ... 87

Nehemiah

9:9–11 ... 12
9:11–12, 15–20 ... 24
9:12 ... 12, 17, 31
9:15 ... 9–10, 12, 17, 25, 31
9:19 ... 17
9:19–20 ... 12, 17
9:20 ... 17, 31

Job

9:30 ... 63

Psalms

3 ... 107
6:7 ... 63
8:3 (Eng. 2) ... 52
23:2 ... 34, 45
40:3 ... 104
55:21 (Eng. 20) ... 118
67:24 ... 63
68:14 (Eng. 13) ... 46
68:26 ... 52
72:16 ... 38
72:17 ... 68
78:11–16 ... 12–13
78:12–16, 20 ... 17
78:13–16, 20 ... 13, 24
78:13–16 ... 31

78:16 36
78:20 34
78:24 25
78:24–25 .... 13, 17
78:25 25
88:15 119
89:21 (Eng. 20) 50
89:39 (Eng. 38) 50
89:52 (Eng. 51) 50
90:3 110
105:37, 39, 41 13
105:38–42 17
105:39 35
105:39–41 .... 24, 31–32
105:40 25
105:41 34
106:16–18 94
113–18 5
114:8 .... 5, 32, 49
119:176 102
129:3 47
145:9 111

Proverbs

5:15 36
8:22 69

Ecclesiastes

1:9 38
4:1 112
5:5 110

Canticles

4:2 64
4:15 36
6:6 64
8:5 47

Isaiah

6:5 51
11:1–5 30
11:2 68
11:4–5 23
25:6 48
33:21 34
40:4 18
48:21 31
49:10 11
60:21 101
65:1 28
66:23 104
66:24 104

Jeremiah

7:31 58
19:5 58
23:6 23
32:35 58

Ezekiel

1:26 27
16:1ff. 46, 57
16:3 48
16:4 .... 47–48, 52
16:4, 9 .... 15, 45, 63, 65
16:5 52
16:6 .... 37, 59
16:7 .... 47–48, 50–51, 59
16:8 59
16:9 .... 42, 44, 47, 50–51, 64
16:10 .... 44–45, 51
16:11 50
16:13, 17, 19–21 57
16:13, 19 49
16:19 .... 49, 56
16:20–21 57
16:22, 43, 60 58
16:26 58
16:32 56
16:36 60
20:7 56

Daniel

7:13 22
12:1–2 87
12:2 104
12:2–3 85

Hosea

3:1 56
9:10 57

Joel

4:18 38

Habakkuk

3:14 14

Zechariah

9:9 38
10:9 113
13:9 104

Septuagint

Genesis

12:3 4
17:5 4
18:10, 14 43
18:16 21
18:18 4
22:18 4

Exodus

13:21 .... 16, 23
13:22 16
17:6 27
23:20–21 21

Numbers

14:16 17–18
19:11–13 86
20:8 28
20:11 28
21:16–17 29

Deuteronomy

8:15 49
21:8 105
26:14 80
32:13 .... 33, 50
32:17, 21 50

1 Kingdoms

2:6 103

2 Kingdoms

19:1 108

2 Esdras

19:15 31

Psalms

77(78):16, 20 31
77(78):24 25
104(105):41 32

Proverbs

8:22 69

Canticles

4:2 64
6:6 64

Isaiah

48:21 31

Ezekiel

16:4 63
16:9 50

Apocrypha

Tobit

1:21–22 81
2:10 81
4:16–17 .... 80, 82, 84, 120
11:18 81
14:10 81

Sirach

7:33 .... 82, 120
24:9 69
30:18 .... 82, 120
45:18–19 94–95

Wisdom of Solomon

10:18 13
10:21 52
11:4 .... 13, 32
11:7 32
16:20 25
16:20–21 24
18:3 10
19:7 11

Letter of Jeremiah

1 83
26–27 .... 82–83, 120

1 Maccabees

1:48–50 117
5:68 87

2 Maccabees

1:10 85
2:20 85
2:23 85
6:10 117
7:9, 11, 14, 20, 23, 29, 40 86
12:32–34, 37–38 86
12:38–45 .... 85–89, 120
12:40, 42–45 87–88
14:37, 46 86

Targums

Targum Pseudo-Jonathan

Exod 13:21 19–20
Exod 15:2 52
Exod 17:6 27
Exod 40:9 50
Num 14:14 11
Num 20:16 19
Deut 26:14 81

Targum Neofiti 1

Exod 13:21 20
Exod 15:2 53
Exod 17:6 28
Deut 26:14 81
Deut 32:10, 13 49

Fragment Targum, MS "P"

Exod 13:21 20
Deut 32:13 49

Fragment Targum, MS "V"

Exod 15:2 52–53
Deut 26:14 81
Deut 32:13 49

Targum 1 Samuel

2:6 103

Targum 2 Samuel

19:1 109

Targum Chronicles

1 Chron 3:24 22

Targum Psalms

89:21 (Eng. 20) 50

Targum Isaiah

11:1–2 69
16:1 38

Targum Ezekiel

16:1–13 58–59
16:3 .... 48, 60
16:4 .... 47–48, 63–64
16:5 46
16:6–8 60
16:9 63
16:12 19
16:13 49
16:15–17, 19–20, 22,
25–26, 29, 33–34, 36 60
16:45 60
16:61 61

Pseudepigrapha

Ahiqar

2:10 81

Apocalypse of Zephaniah

9:4 93
11:2–4 93
11:6 93

Joseph and Aseneth

8:11(9) 93
15:4(5) 93
27:10 93

Jubilees

15:26 117
15:34 117

Pseudo-Philo

10:5–6 13
10:7 .... 18, 24, 33
11:15 35
16 96
16:1 96
16:3 97
16:4–6 97
20:8 30
25:7 88
57:2 96

Sibylline Oracles

4.165 36

Testament of Abraham A

1:4 90
3:7–9 43

6:6 43
8:11 90
10:5–15 91
14:2, 5–6, 8 91
14:11, 13–14 91–92
15:1 90
17:18 92
18:3, 7, 9–11 92–93
20:9–14 90

Testament of Reuben

4:6 56

Dead Sea Scrolls

Damascus Document (CD-A)

6:2–11 30
6:11–12 30
6:19 30

4Q Patriarchal Blessings (4Q252)

5:3–4 30

Philo

Legum Allegoricae

2.86 32
3.162–76 24

Quod Deterius

115 32–33

De Agricultura

51 20

De Confusione Linguarum

122 99

De Migratione Abrahami

174 21

De Fuga

145 95

De Somniis

2.221–22 49

De Vita Mosis

1.147 27
1.164 8
1.165–66 20
1.167 8
1.170–80 13
1.177 13
1.178 20
1.179 13
1.180 13
1.181 10
1.183 10
1.191 9
1.192 10
1.194 8
1.197 9
1.200–08 24
1.210 .... 10, 32
1.211 32
1.215 10
1.216 9
1.238 8
1.255–56 32
1.320 9
1.331 9
1.333 9
2.176, 178 96

2.247 8
2.254 20
2. 258 8–9
2.275–87 96

De Praemiis

74–78 95

De Legatione ad Gaium

281 121

Quaestiones ... in Exodum

2.13 20

Josephus

Bellum

1.3 98
2.163 117
3.374 117

Antiquitates

1.53, 60–61 99
2.316 9
2.317 27
2.338–39 13
2.338–46 13
3.1 9–10
3.26 24
3.30 24–25
3.33 .... 10, 33
3.33–38 33
3.46 9
3.290 .... 13, 19
3.310 .... 13, 19
3.314 9
4.1 9
4:11–58 98
4.18–19 98
4.19, 25–26 98
4.25–34 98
4.40–51 98
4.45 9
4.51–53 98
4.54–56, 58 98–99
4.76 10
4.86 .... 10, 33
4.239 9
7.252 109
18.14 117
20.267 .... 9, 98

Vita

1, 7 98

Mishnah

Maʿaser Sheni

5:13 7

Bikkurim

1:4 7

Shabbath

19:5 116

Pesaḥim

10:5 4–5
10:5–6 .... 7, 60
10:6 5

Megillah

4:10 58

Nedarim

3:1 116

Soṭah

1:7–9 41
1:8 107
9:6 105

Qiddushin

1:7 113

Sanhedrin

6:2 88
10:1–3 101
10:3 .... 101, 115

ʿEduyoth

2:10 104

ʾAvot

5:6 .... 24, 34, 40, 100
5:17 100

Miqvaot

1:8 36
5:5 36

Niddah

5:3 118

Tosefta

Berakoth

3:6 103

Shabbath

8:25 48

Yoma

4:9 88

Sukkah

3:11 .... 34, 39–40, 61
3:11–13 34

Megillah

3:31 61
3:32–34 61
3:34 .... 58, 61

Ḥagigah

2:3 110

Soṭah

4:1 41
4:2 .... 10, 19, 34
4:4 43
6:4 51–52
6:6 56
9:2 105

Sanhedrin

13:3 104
13:9 102

Babylonian Talmud

Berakoth

31a 103
50b 84

Shabbath

35a 36, 39
129b 61

ʿErubin

19a 100, 118

Pesaḥim

119a 101

Yoma

37a 41
75a 46

Sukkah

20a 114
28a 102

Rosh ha-Shanah

16b–17a 104

Megillah

25b 58

Ḥagigah

15a 110
15b 111

Yebamoth

46a–b 37

Soṭah

10b 108–9
11b 46, 48, 57
48b–49a 112

Qiddushin

31b 113

Baba Meṣia

86a 41
86b 42

Baba Bathra

75b 23

Sanhedrin

44b 48
103b 107
109b 102
110a 100–1

Horayoth

6a 106

Kerithot

9a 37
26a 106

Niddah

24b 108
44b 118

The Minor Tractates

ʾEbel Rabbathi

3:1, 44b 118
8:2, 47a 84
8:3, 47a 84

8:4, 47a ... 84
10:2, 48b ... 83

Kallah Rabbathi

2:9, 52a ... 116

Derek ʾEreṣ Rabbah

4:2 ... 41

Palestinian Talmud

Berakoth

4:1, 7a ... 103

Sheviʿith

4:10, 35c ... 119

Bikkurim

1:4, 64a ... 7

Ḥagigah

2:1, 77b ... 110
2:1, 77c ... 110–11

Soṭah

9:5, 23d ... 106
9:6, 24a ... 106

Sanhedrin

10:3, 29b–c ... 104
10:4, 29c ... 102

Horayoth

1:8, 46b ... 106

ʾAvot de-Rabbi Nathan A

33 ... 14
34 ... 56
36 ... 107
40 ... 110

ʾAvot de-Rabbi Nathan B

37 ... 51
38 ... 14
46 ... 110

Mekilta de-Rabbi Ishmael

Pisḥa 5 on Exod 12:6 ... 55–56, 59
Pisḥa 13 on Exod 12:36 ... 51
Beshallaḥ 1 on Exod 13:21 ... 10, 18, ... 42
Beshallaḥ 3 on Exod 14:12 ... 11
Beshallaḥ 4 on Exod 14:15 ... 14
Beshallaḥ 5 on Exod 14:16 ... 14
Beshallaḥ 5 on Exod 14:19 ... 35
Shirata 2 on Exod 15:1 ... 107
Shirata 3 on Exod 15:2 ... 19, 51
Shirata 7 on Exod 15:9 ... 73
Vayassa 1 on Exod 15:22 ... 56
Vayassa 2 on Exod 16:3 ... 9
Vayassa 3 on Exod 16:5 ... 24
Vayassa 4 on Exod 16:14 ... 24
Vayassa 5 on Exod 16:23 ... 24
Vayassa 6 on Exod 16:32 ... 24
Vayassa 7 on Exod 17:6 ... 27
Baḥodesh 3 on Exod 19:10 ... 37
Baḥodesh 8 on Exod 20:12–14 ... 56

Mekilta de-Rabbi Shimʿon bar Yoḥai

Beshallaḥ on Exod 13:21 ... 11, 18, 43
Beshallaḥ on Exod 14:19 ... 36

Shirata on Exod 15:2 51
Vayassa on Exod 17:6 27
Baḥodesh on Exod 19:4 19

Sifre Numbers

Beha'alothekha 67 on 9:5 55
Beha'alothekha 83 on 10:34 .... 10, 19
Beha'alothekha 84 on 10:35–36 55
Beha'alothekha 87 on 11:5-6 24
Beha'alothekha 88 on 11:6 25
Beha'alothekha 89 on 11:8 25
Beha'alothekha 95 on 11:22 35
Beha'alothekha 112 on 15:31 88
Korah 117 on 18:8 100
Balak 131 on 25:1 56

Sifre Deuteronomy

Shofeṭim 210 on 21:8 105
Ki Tabo' 303 on 26:14 81
Ha'azinu 313 on 32:10 18
Ha'azinu 318 on 32:17 55
Vezot ha-Berakah 343 on 33:2 51

Midrash Rabbah

Genesis Rabbah

Bereshith 1/4 on 1:1 68
Bereshith 2/4 on 1:2 68
Vayyera 48/8 on 18:1 117
Vayyera 48/10 on 18:1–15 42
Vayyera 49/4 on 18:19 114
Vayyera 51/2 on 19:24 19
Vayeḥi 97 on 49:8 68
Vayeḥi 98/4 on 49:4 103

Exodus Rabbah

Shemoth 1/8 on 1:8 55
Shemoth 1/12 on 1:14 .... 46–47, 65
Shemoth 3/2 on 3:7 52
Shemoth 5/9 on 4:27 49
Va'era 12/4 on 9:23 19
Bo 19/4 on 12:43 118
Bo 19/6 on 12:43 19
Beshallaḥ 20/11 on 13:17 .... 44, 65
Beshallaḥ 22/3 on 14:31 14
Beshallaḥ 23/8 on 15:1 .... 46, 48
Beshallaḥ 23/15 on 15:2 51
Beshallaḥ 25/4 on 16:4 .... 9, 28
Beshallaḥ 25/5 on 16:4 42
Beshallaḥ 25/6 on 16:4 44
Yethro 27/4 on 18:1 51
Ki Thissa 4/1 on 31:8 56

Leviticus Rabbah

Thazria 14/1 on 12:2 68
Aḥare Moth 22/3 on 17:3 39
Aḥare Moth 22/4 on 17:3 .... 31, 36
Aḥare Moth 22/8 on 17:3 55
Qedoshim 25/7 on 19:23 58
Behar 34/8 on 25:25 43

Numbers Rabbah

Bemidbar 1/2 on 1:1 .... 19, 31, 39
Naso 8/9 on 5:10 7
Naso 9/24 on 5:11–31 107
Naso 13/11 on 7:13 68
Naso 14/2 on 7:48 42
Korah 18/1–20 on 16 100
Korah 18/4 on 16:1 101
Korah 18/8 on 16:6 101
Korah 18/10 on 16:16 101
Korah 18/13 on 16:32 101
Korah 18/15 on 16:33 101
Korah 18/20 on 16:1 101
Korah 18/20 on 16:25 100
Korah 18/22 on 16:25 36
Ḥuqqat 19/19 on 20:10 35
Ḥuqqat 19/25 on 21:17 .... 30, 34
Ḥuqqat 19/26 on 21:20 39

Deuteronomy Rabbah

Ki Thabo 7/11 on 29:4 45

Deuteronomy Rabbah, ed. Liebermann

Chapter I, n. 207 48

Ruth Rabbah

6/4 on 3:13 110
7/2 on 3:15 69

Ecclesiastes Rabbah

1:9 § 1 38
1:12 § 1 73
4:1 § 1 112
5:8-9 § 5 36
7:8 § 1 110
11:1 § 1 42

Canticles Rabbah

1:7 § 2 17
2:15 § 2 59
4:11 § 2 45
4:12 § 3 35

Canticles Rabbah, ed. Grűnhut

1:7 48
2:6 51

Lamentations Rabbah

1:12 § 40 104
1:16 § 51 23

Midrash Tannaim

Vezot ha-Berakah on Deut 33:2 52

Midrash Psalms

5/1 on 5:1 34
21/2 on 21:2 23
21/4 on 21:5 103
23/4 on 23:2 .... 45, 66
45/4 on 45:2 103

Midrash Proverbs

19 23

Tanḥuma

Vayyera 4 on Gen 18:1 43
Toledoth 14 on Gen 27:33 22
Beshallaḥ 3 on Exod 13:21 18
Beshallaḥ 22 on Exod 17:6 27–28
Teṣaveh 1 on Exod 27:20 50
Ki Thissa 14 on Exod 31:18 56
Ki Thissa 35 on Exod 34:27 19
Ḥuqqat 21 on Num 21:18 40
Ha'azinu 1 on Deut 21:8 106

Tanḥuma Buber

Vayyera 5 on Gen 18:2–4 43
Toledoth 20 on Gen 27:28 22
Shemoth 22 on Exod 4:27 49
Beshallaḥ 10 on Exod 13:17 44
Bemidbar 2 on Num 1:1 39
Ḥuqqat 50 on Num 21:18 40

Pesiqta de-Rav Kahana

11/8 on Exod 13:17 44

Pesiqta Rabbati

14/3 on Num 19:2 43
20/2 .... 104, 106
33/6 on Isa 51:12 68
33/10 on Isa 51:12 50
36/1 on Isa 60:1–2 68

47/2 on Lev 16:1 .... 48, 51

Eliyyahu Rabbah

(12)13 43
(15)16 37

Eliyyahu Zuṭa

12 113
17 114–16

Pirqe de-Rabbi Eliezer

22 99
42 53
53 108–9

Seder ʿOlam

10 30

The Gaon of Sura (871-79 CE)

Shʿry ṣdq 119

New Testament

Matthew

28:19 xi

Mark

1:4 xi
1:9 xi
6:3 99
12:26 49
15:7 15

Luke

1:46–53 103
1:59 116
2:21 117

John

1:1 21
1:1-3, 10, 14 69
3:14–15 29
6:48–49, 55 26
7:38 38
11:39 84

Acts

2:38 xi
5:34 5
5:35–39 5
7:8 116
7:35–36 67
8:16 xi
9:18 xi
10:48 xi
16:1, 3 117
16:13, 15 37
18:2 .... 4, 121
18:3, 7–8 121
18:7 .... 4, 122
18:8 .... 4, 122
18:11 .... 4, 71
18:11–12 74
18:12–17 8
18:17 .... 8, 122
18:18 121
18:24–26 122
18:27–28 122
19:5 xi
22:2–3 49
22:3 .... 5, 21, 71, 123
22:16 .... xi, 64
23:6–8 117
23:16 6
26:4 71

Romans

1:3, 9 21
1:4 21
4:16–17 4
4:17 7
6:3 .... xi, 62, 123
6:4 .... xi, 123
8:3 68
8:3, 29, 32 21
8:29 21
9:9 43
11:1 4
12:12–31 120
11:1 4
16:16 4
16:23 4

1 Corinthians

1:7 .... 109, 123
1:7–8 31
1:9 21
1:12 .... xi, 122
1:13 .... 62, 77
1:13, 15 .... xi, 62
1:13–17 xi
1:14 .... 4, 122
1:14, 16–17 .... xi, 122–3
3:3 78
3:6 122
3:13 123
3:18 78
3:22 122
4:5 123
4:6 77
4:21 78
5 54
5:1 122
5:2 78
5:5 123
5:6 78
5:7 4
6:1 122
6:5, 8 78
6:9 54
6:9–11 122–3
6:11 64
6:12–20 54
6:16 20
7:1–11 123
7:18 4
7:19 122
7:26, 29–31 .... 31, 109, 123
8:1–13 122
8:6 67
8:12 78
9:5 122
9:20 4
10:1–5 .... passim in chapter I
10:6–8, 11, 14, 16–33 54
10:9 .... 10, 65, 67
10:11 .... 31, 72, 109, 123
10:12 54
10:14 .... 60, 71, 122
10:14–22 .... 54, 72
10:16 65
10:16–17, 21 25–26
10:19 60
10:20 .... 50, 55, 60
10:21 .... 26, 55, 60, 65
10:22 55
10:23–33 60
10:32–33 4
11:1 60
11:18 122
11:22 78
11:24 77
11:25 .... 4, 120
12:2 122
12:12–13 123
12:13 .... xi, 4, 26, 122
12:25 77
14:26 122
15:3 77
15:3–8 67
15:12 .... 74, 122
15:20–28 74

15:29 .... passim in chapter II
15:30–34 75
15:45 25
15:51 109
15:51–52 123
16:1 71
16:8 .... 74, 121
16:12 122
16:17 122
16:19 121
16:22 49

2 Corinthians

1:19 21
3:6, 14 .... 4, 120
3:17–18 25
4:4–5 68
8:9 67
10:10 20

Galatians

1:14 .... 5, 21, 71, 120
1:16 21
1:24 15
2:20 21
3:7–8 4
3:27 .... xi, 62, 123
3:28–29 4
4:4 68
4:4, 6 21
5:2–3 122
5:2–6 4
6:16 .... 4, 123

Ephesians

4:5 xi
4:13 21
5:25–26 64
6:4 72

Philippians

2:6–11 67–69
2:7 66
3:3 4
3:5 117
3:5–6 6

Colossians

1:15, 18 21
1:15–20 68
2:12 xi

1 Thessalonians

1:10 123
4:13–18 74
4:17 16

Titus

3:5 64
3:10 72

1 Peter

3:19 123
4:6 123

1 John

1:2 69

Jude

1 99
4–8 99
5 .... 68, 99
11 99
13, 15 100
23 100

Revelation

1:5 63

Apostolic Fathers

1 Clement

4:8 8
31:2 8
60:4 8

Didache

7:1 37
10:3 25

Hermas

Similitudes 93 (IX. 16:4–7) 123

Church Fathers

Ambrose

The Mysteries 8.48 26

Ambrosiaster

Commentary on Paul's Epistles
81.3: 175 124

Cyril of Jerusalem

Mystagogical Letters I 1.3 66

Jerome

De Viris Illustribus 5 6

Justin Martyr

Dialogue with Trypho 114 39

Dura Europos Synagogue

Wall painting 47 40

ABOUT THE AUTHOR

Roger David Aus, b. 1940, studied English and German at St. Olaf College, and theology at Harvard Divinity School, Luther Seminary, and Yale University, from which he received the Ph.D. in New Testament studies in 1971. He is an ordained clergyman of the Evangelical Lutheran Church in America, and pastor emeritus of the German-speaking Luther-Kirchengemeinde Alt-Reinickendorf in Berlin-Reinickendorf, Germany. His study of New Testament topics always reflects his great interest in, and deep appreciation of, the Jewish roots of the Christian faith.

OTHER VOLUMES BY ROGER DAVID AUS

Essays in the Judaic Background of Mark 11:12-14, 20-21; 15:23; Luke 1:37; John 19:28-30; and Acts 11: 28 (Studies in Judaism; Lanham, MD: University Press of America. 2015).

Simon Peter's Denial and Jesus' Commissioning Him as His Successor in John 21:15-19. Studies in Their Judaic Background (Studies in Judaism; Lanham, MD: University Press of America, 2013).

Feeding the Five Thousand. Studies in the Judaic Background of Mark 6:30-44 par. and John 6:1-15 (Studies in Judaism; Lanham, MD: University Press of America, 2010).

The Death, Burial, and Resurrection of Jesus, and the Death, Burial, and Translation of Moses in Judaic Tradition (Studies in Judaism; Lanham, MD: University Press of America, 2008).

Imagery of Triumph and Rebellion in 2 Corinthians 2:14-17 and Elsewhere in the Epistle. An Example of the Combination of Greco-Roman and Judaic Traditions in the Apostle Paul (Studies in Judaism; Lanham, MD: University Press of America, 2005).

Matthew 1-2 and the Virginal Conception in Light of Palestinian and Hellenistic Judaic Traditions on the Birth of Israel's First Redeemer, Moses (Studies in Judaism; Lanham, MD: University Press of America, 2004).

My Name Is "Legion." Palestinian Judaic Traditions in Mark 5:1-20 and Other Gospel Texts (Studies in Judaism; Lanham, MD: University Press of America, 2003). Essays on Mark 5:1-20; Luke 4:16-30; The Name "Iscariot" and Ahithophel in Judaic Tradition; Luke 19:41-44; John 8:56-58; Matt 24:28 // Luke 17:37b; and Luke 13:34b // Matt 23:37b.

The Stilling of the Storm. Studies in Early Palestinian Judaic Traditions (International Studies in Formative Christianity and Judaism; Binghamton, NY: Global Publications, Binghamton University, 2000). Essays on Mark 4:35-41; 1:16-20; and Luke 24:13-35.

"Caught in the Act," Walking on the Sea, and the Release of Barabbas Revisited (South Florida Studies in the History of Judaism, 157; Atlanta: Scholars Press, 1998). Essays on John 7:53 - 8:11; Mark 6:45-52 par.; and 15:6-15 par.

The Wicked Tenants and Gethsemane (International Studies in Formative Christianity and Judaism, University of South Florida, 4; Atlanta: Scholars Press, 1996). Essays on Mark 12:1-9 par.; 14:32-42 par.; 2 Cor 12:1-12; and Judas' handing Jesus over to certain death through a kiss.

Samuel, Saul and Jesus. Three Early Palestinian Jewish Christian Gospel Haggadoth (South Florida Studies in the History of Judaism, 105; Atlanta: Scholars Press, 1994). Essays on Luke 2:41-51a; Mark 6:1-6a par.; and the prodigia at Jesus' Crucifixion.

Barabbas and Esther and Other Studies in the Judaic Illumination of Earliest Christianity (South Florida Studies in the History of Judaism, 54; Atlanta: Scholars Press, 1992). Essays on Mark 15:6-15 par.; John 11:45-54; Luke 15:11-32; Matt 2:1-12; Gal 2:9; Isa 66:7, Revelation 12 and 2 Thessalonians 1; 2 Thess 2:6-7; Rom 11:25; and 2 Thess 1:3.

Weihnachtsgeschichte, Barmherziger Samariter, Verlorener Sohn. Studien zu ihrem jüdischen Hintergrund (ANTZ 2; Berlin: Institut Kirche und Judentum, 1988). Essays on Luke 2:1-20; 10:30-37; and 15:11-32.

Water into Wine and the Beheading of John the Baptist. Early Jewish-Christian Interpretation of Esther 1 in John 2:1-11 and Mark 6:17-29 (Brown Judaic Studies, 150; Atlanta: Scholars Press, 1988).

www.ingramcontent.com/pod-product-compliance
Lightning Source LLC
Chambersburg PA
CBHW020125240426
43673CB00038B/598
* 9 7 8 0 7 6 1 8 6 9 3 9 9 *